MYANMAR
State, Society and Ethnicity

MYANMAR
State, Society and Ethnicity

EDITED BY

N. Ganesan and Kyaw Yin Hlaing

ISEAS

INSTITUTE OF SOUTHEAST ASIAN STUDIES
Singapore

HPI

HIROSHIMA PEACE INSTITUTE
Japan

First published in Singapore in 2007 by ISEAS Publishing
Institute of Southeast Asian Studies
30 Heng Mui Keng Terrace
Pasir Panjang
Singapore 119614

E-mail: publish@iseas.edu.sg
Website: http://bookshop.iseas.edu.sg

jointly with
Hiroshima Peace Institute
Hiroshima City University
Ote-machi Heiwa Bldg. 9F
4-1-1 Ote-machi, Naka-ku,
Hiroshima, 730-0051 Japan

The responsibility for facts and opinions in this publication rests exclusively with the editors and contributors and their interpretations do not necessarily reflect the views or the policy of the publisher or its supporters.

ISEAS Library Cataloguing-in-Publication Data

Myanmar : state, society and ethnicity / edited by N. Ganesan and Kyaw Yin Hlaing.
1. Burma.
2. Burma—Politics and government.
3. Minorities—Burma—Politics and government.
4. Ethnicity—Burma.
5. Burma—Foreign relations.
6. Burma—Economic conditions.
7. Sanctions (International law).
I. Ganesan, N. (Narayanan), 1954–
II. Kyaw Yin Hlaing.
DS527.4 M992   2007

ISBN: 978-981-230-434-6 (hard cover)
ISBN: 978-981-230-433-9 (soft cover)
ISBN: 978-981-230-722-4 (PDF)

Typeset by Superskill Graphics Pte Ltd
Printed in Singapore by Utopia Press Pte Ltd

Contents

Acknowledgements

This edited volume is the outcome of two workshops convened at the Hiroshima Peace Institute in March and October 2005. Most of the chapter contributors were commissioned on the basis of their availability and expertise to contribute to the project. The workshops were in turn part of a larger project entitled the "Myanmar Peace Initiative" that was wholly funded by the institute through the Hiroshima City Government. We are extremely grateful to both the institute and the local government for the generous funding of the project. Additionally, partial funding for a closing dinner during the first workshop was generously provided by the Singapore-based Konrad Adenauer Stiftung. We are also deeply grateful to Dr Colin Duerkop for his assistance and interest in funding projects related to Myanmar.

Naturally, there are numerous individuals to whom we owe an immense debt of gratitude. Professors David Steinberg and Robert Taylor were the senior scholars anchoring the project. There were an equally able number of indigenous scholars who assisted us with the project. In this regard we are especially thankful to Alan Saw Oo, Ja Nan Lahtaw and Sai Kham Mong for their contributions, as we are to Tin Maung Maung Than as the senior native scholar. Vincent Boudreau, Rachel Safman and Khin Zaw Win attended to our request for participation in the project at rather short notice.

Finally, we are deeply indebted to the administrative and support staff at the Hiroshima Peace Institute for their patience and skill in attending to the needs of the conference participants. We are especially grateful to Miki Nomura and Michiko Yoshimoto who assisted with various aspects of administration. President Motofumi Asai and the research staff have also been supportive of the publication of this volume under the joint auspices of the Institute of Southeast Asian Studies and the Hiroshima Peace Institute. From ISEAS, we are equally grateful to Triena Ong who expressed an early interest in the publication of this volume.

N. Ganesan
Kyaw Yin Hlaing

Acknowledgements

The Contributors

N. Ganesan is Professor at the Hiroshima Peace Institute, Hiroshima City University, Japan.

Ja Nan Lahtaw is Assistant Director, Program and International Relation, Shalom (Nyein) Foundation, Yangon, Myanmar.

Khin Zaw Win is an Independent Researcher and Scholar, based in Myanmar.

Kyaw Yin Hlaing is Assistant Professor, Department of Political Science, National University of Singapore.

Kei Nemoto is Professor, Research Institute for Languages and Cultures of Asia and Africa, Tokyo University of Foreign Studies, Japan.

Rachel M. Safman is Assistant Professor, Department of Sociology, National University of Singapore.

Sai Kham Mong is Researcher on Sources and Development of Shan Thammahsat (Dhammathat), Myanmar.

Alan Saw U is Coordinator, Kayin Development Network (KDN) and Secretary, Christian Literature Society (CLS), Myanmar.

David I. Steinberg is Distinguished Professor, Director, Asian Studies Program, School of Foreign Service, Georgetown University, U.S.A.

Robert Taylor is Associate Senior Fellow, Institute of Southeast Asian Studies, Singapore. He was formerly Professor of Politics at the University of London, Pro-Director of the School of Oriental and African Studies, and Vice-Chancellor of the University of Buckingham, U.K.

Tin Maung Maung Than is Senior Fellow, Institute of Southeast Asian Studies, Singapore.

1

Introduction

N. Ganesan and Kyaw Yin Hlaing

This book is an attempt to cumulatively increase scholarly interest and research on Myanmar. We are mindful that the scholarly community on Myanmar is intensely polarized and there are scholars who would not even refer to the country by its new name, preferring the older Burma. Yet, the truth of the matter is that Myanmar had closed itself off from international interactions for a very long time after the installation of the Burma Socialist Party Programme (BSPP) government in 1962. The initial reason for this closure was fighting by external powers on its soil, a situation precipitated by the Chinese nationalist Kuomintang detachment trapped in the Shan states and the involvement of China and the United States in the ensuing conflict. Already wrecked by internal problems that included the failure of a civilian parliamentary government and ethnic insurgencies, Burma decided to pursue a policy of neutrality through self-imposed isolationism. The collapse of the BSPP government in 1988, the subsequent suppression of the democracy movement in the country and the holding of nationwide election in 1990 opened up the country to international scrutiny once again. External events that included the collapse of communist regimes in Eastern Europe and the fragility of the Soviet Union that eventually imploded in 1991 appeared to have provided external causes for optimism. Aung San Suu Kyi's presence in Myanmar in 1988 and her subsequent leadership of the National League for Democracy (NLD) also appeared to portend changes. However, it needs to be noted that Suu Kyi herself never stood in the elections despite serving as leader of the NLD.

With the hindsight of history, we now know that the pressures for internal change bore no fruit. Subsequent developments led to political violence, the displacement of a large number of pro-democracy activists and the periodic detention of Aung San Suu Kyi. The international pressure piled on by the United States and the European Union in particular must have left the Myanmar military junta bewildered. After all, it was responding to a series of seemingly domestic developments and had indicated its express desire to isolate itself from the world. Unfortunately, by the time of the collapse of the BSPP government, it was a very different world that was in the euphoria of celebrating the defeat of communism and the triumph of liberal democracy. Aung San Suu Kyi's lengthy stay in the West and her charismatic personality won her many admirers in the West as a courageous and convicted democrat, evidenced by the decision to award her the 1995 Nobel Prize for Peace. Yet, despite being the daughter of the Burmese independence leader Aung San, Suu Kyi had lived much of her life in the West and had returned only to look after her ailing mother when she became deeply involved in Myanmar politics. Given the government's deep suspicion of the West and Suu Kyi's own stay in the United Kingdom and marriage to a Briton, she was naturally viewed as a rank outsider for domestic political involvement. Since the perception of both the junta and Suu Kyi is one of the virtuous self and the stereotypical other, there has been little by way of compromise or reconciliation. At the time of writing in 2006, Suu Kyi remains under house arrest and the military government has periodically been convening meetings to draw up a new charter for the country. These Constitutional Conventions have been boycotted by the NLD in turn, many of whose leaders are under detention in any event.

Not all the developments that took place after 1988 have been negative for the country. One of the more positive developments has been the ceasefire agreements that the military government has arranged with some seventeen of the ethnic insurgent groups. Of the larger groups, only the arrangement with the Karen National Union (KNU) has yet to be ratified. Fighting still continues sporadically between the military and the Karenni National Progressive Party (KNPP) and the Shan Sate Army — South (SSA) and a number of smaller groups in Chin and Arakan states. In the areas where ceasefire arrangements have been observed, insurgent groups control a swathe of contiguous territory and retain the right to bear arms. It is hoped that at some point in the future they will be disarmed. Their representatives are part of the Constitutional Convention although privately many members of such groups complain about losing confidence in the process as well as morale among their adherents. Notwithstanding such difficulties, it would be fair to note that the ceasefire arrangements have brought a measure of calm to the highland areas since the 1990s.

The political developments that have taken place in Myanmar from the time of independence in 1948 until now are certainly unique and not replicated anywhere else in Southeast Asia. Self-imposed isolationism, while allowing the country to negotiate a way out of major power conflict, has also dealt a very harsh blow to economic development in the country. Traditionally, Myanmar was a rich country and used to be referred to as the "ricebowl of Asia". Internal political difficulties, an absence of external investments, the imposition of a broad-ranging economic sanctions regime by the international community in June 2003 after Suu Kyi's detention have all contributed to the steep decline of the economy. Within the immediate external environment, countries of the Association of Southeast Asian Nations (ASEAN) led by Thailand and Singapore sought to engage Myanmar rather than isolate it. The argument in favour of engagement was that an isolated country was less likely to heed friendly advice and institute political changes. Yet, engagement has brought very little by way of domestic political changes that the Association had sought to achieve. In fact, the converse has obtained and many members of ASEAN have quite publicly chided Myanmar for refusing to undertake political reforms. There is indeed a growing sense of frustration among countries that had previously championed the engagement policy, in particular Malaysia, Singapore and Thailand. ASEAN is acutely mindful of the fact that the stalemated situation in Myanmar is eroding its international credibility and goodwill. On a number of occasions, senior American and European representatives have abstained from attending ASEAN-hosted or sponsored meetings.

The irony of all these developments and pressures brought to bear on Myanmar is that it will have very little impact, if any at all, on domestic political developments. There is very little incentive for the military government to step down from power and hand it over to a person considered a rank outsider. In effect, the Myanmar Government constantly exhorts its citizens to be wary of Western machinations and projects the military as the saviour of the nation and its cultural and religious heritage. The large infrastructural projects, in particular roads, bridges and power plants are regularly held up as efforts by the government to uplift the welfare of its citizens. Patriotic posters and banners mark most major cities, rallying the people against the intervention of Western powers in domestic political developments. Self-sufficiency and solidarity with the government is regularly emphasized.

Fortunately for Myanmar, to counter the perceived Western hegemony of politics and development in general, its immediate neighbours, China and India, have offered the country investments and technical and financial assistance. Myanmar's strategic location between China and India and its long coastline along the Andaman Sea and the Bay of Bengal provides an opportunity for China and a constraint for India. Regardless of the motivations, both countries have been anxious to secure a positive bilateral relationship with Myanmar. There are also a number of cross-cutting issues of interest and areas of cooperation between Thailand and Myanmar, though the relationship is occasionally subjected to hiccups over illegal migration and refugees, ethnic insurgency and drug trafficking, to name a few difficult issues. Then, there are investments, especially in the tourism and hospitality sector from Malaysia and Singapore that help to cushion some of the shock of the sanctions regime. Similarly, an important foreign exchange earner for the Myanmar Government is the sale of oil and natural gas to Thailand, especially from the Yadana fields. Additionally, there are construction projects currently underway to tap hydroelectric power from the Salween River. Nonetheless, sanctions have exacted a heavy toll on Myanmar, in particular on its labour intensive garment manufacturing industry. The opposition NLD's support for the sanctions policy appears to have taken a greater toll on the average citizen in Myanmar rather than the government as Khin Zaw Win's chapter reveals. The writer, by no means an apologist of the government, makes it clear that economic sanctions are a collective punishment that weighs disproportionately on the civilian population.

More importantly though, the collection of chapters in this edited volume addresses questions that we regard as important for a serious social science survey of Myanmar. At the same time, there is an attempt to place developments in Myanmar within a broader historical and geographical frame. Accordingly, the book begins with two broad chapters that survey the Southeast Asian landscape before locating Myanmar within it. The aim of these two chapters is to alert readers to the similarities and differences between regional developments in general and those in Myanmar. The first chapter by N. Ganesan explores state-society relations in Southeast Asia before examining the situation in Myanmar. Within this broad conception of state-society relations, some attempt is made to address civil-military relations as well. The point of departure in this chapter is the argument that the conditions that precipitated the downfall of military authoritarian regimes in Thailand and Indonesia in the 1990s do not obtain in Myanmar. There truly appears to be a bifurcated existence between the military on the one hand, and the civilian population on the other. Consequently, some of the more recent and innovative approaches in the comparative politics literature like the "state in society" approach is particularly useful in examining the Myanmar case. In fact, it could be argued that the state and society are responsive towards each other, although the spillover effect is not the sort of positive interactive experience envisaged by social scientists. In all fairness though, the model did not rule out negative changes arising from such interactions. Consequently, responses are aimed at the self-preservation of the state rather than positive symbiotic influence.

Rachel Safman's chapter also locates Myanmar within the broader context of ethnic minorities and state-building in mainland Southeast Asia. By looking at how the dominant discourse of state-building has evolved. She also examines the historical dynamics of majority-minority relations and how these have been forged over the years. Safman details the nature of majority claims to preeminence, how such claims are in turn contested by the minorities and how sometimes such contestation deteriorates into violence. As a general rule of thumb, the majority-minority divide also coincides with the lowland-highland divide with all the attendant connotations. In the Myanmar case, Safman argues that there was little by way of an early and premeditated Bamar ethnic identity and part of the reason for this phenomenon was indirect rule from India that only ended prior to the outbreak of World War II in 1939. However, colonial British conceptions of "Burma Proper" and "Ministerial Burma" on the one hand and "excluded territories" or "frontier areas" on the other, helped in the formulation of such an identity. Nonetheless, the various ethnic groups were not so easily separated or indeed, separable on the basis of location. In fact, this observation is abundantly true of even the ethnic states that the British had identified like Kachin, Karen, Mon and Shan. Complicating this situation were the number of subgroups that were contained within each broad ethnic category.

The second part of the book contains a total of five chapters. These begin by detailing various aspects of foreign historical influences on Myanmar. Robert Taylor's chapter looks at the impact of the British colonization of Burma that was in turn determined by multiple accidents, historical contingencies and a set of human relationships. He looks at how these developments were brought together, leading to the creation of the "Burma problem" with implications well beyond their individual impact. Specifically, he argues that the present state of Myanmar was territorially created when imperial Britain was at the peak of its power and managed to obtain victory in three wars against Burma. Nevertheless, since the country was ruled from British India in any event, some of the traditional territories like Assam and Manipur were not included in the creation of the state. Similarly, the British utilized ethnicity as a yardstick for administration and presented themselves as protectors of minority groups and also disbanded the monarchy and displaced Buddhism as the central religion. The second chapter on historical influences by Kei Nemoto traces the origins of the "special relationship" between Japan and Burma that was embedded in the Japanese training of the "Thirty Comrades" who led the Burmese independence movement against the British. Nemoto argues that this special relationship sustained bilateral ties between the two countries, allowing Japan direct access to Ne Win even when the country was cocooned from the rest of the world. He also argues that it is this special relationship that has generated positive images of Myanmar in Japan. Nemoto then goes on to examine the Myanmar community in Japan, its characteristics and significance.

David Steinberg's chapter provides an assessment of the concept of political legitimacy in Myanmar and how it has traditionally been contested. He argues that external and in particular, Western, assessments of legitimacy are derived from the outcome of the 1990 national election when the NLD won some 80 per cent of the seats that it contested. Yet, internally, electoral victories have had a much more varied influence on perceptions of legitimacy. During times of parliamentary rule they have been pivotal in the past and yet after the BSPP government came into power, such legitimacy is hardly forthcoming. Additionally, Steinberg's observation that the traditional concept of legitimacy in Myanmar is conflated with power and influence also buttresses a more *de facto* conception of legitimacy as derivatives of the exercise of power and influence. The personalization of power, the flexibility of regulations and the disproportionate endowment in the coercive power of the state and conversely, the absence of it in other societal actors again favours the military in no uncertain terms. Finally, Steinberg also alerts the readers to a "mythification" of Burman nationalism and military nationalism and the military's continued obsession with rewriting history and portraying itself as the champion of internal cohesiveness, nationalism and state interests.

The subsequent chapter by Kyaw Yin Hlaing examines the state of associational life in Myanmar over all the major historical periods from the colonial times to the present drawing on first hand research and numerous interviews. There are some interesting observations, among them that associational life involving religious activities were generally freer during the parliamentary period than trade and business associations. Similarly, student groups are described as autonomous during that period, and professional, native and community organizations were totally independent from state power. During the socialist period, however, many forms of associational life were curtailed and generally support was restricted to activities that were condoned by the BSPP government. As a result of the restrictions, associational life tended to become more informal to escape state scrutiny. Similarly, there were attempts to disguise the true purpose of certain types of associations. So for example, political associational groups often converted themselves into literature and reading clubs or student organizations. More recently, the SLORC/SPDC governments have vigorously monitored political activities and outlawed many groups considered to be anti-junta and sympathetic to or supportive of the political opposition. It has also required the registration of associations and forbidden the public assembly of six or more persons. GONGOS and social welfare organizations have proliferated during the current period, though there are also attempts being made by trade and occupational groups to organize and lobby the relevant ministry for assistance. Kyaw also argues that the expansion of legal and associational space since the 1990s has led to several INGOs becoming active in the country and also led to the formation of indigenous NGOs that cater to the welfare of the sick, needy and poor. In sum, Kyaw notes that the general perception among scholars that associational life in Myanmar is either wholly absent or severely restricted, is untrue.

The final chapter in the second section details the human security situation in Myanmar. It examines the general welfare of Myanmar citizens on the basis of seven broad criteria — economic security, food security, health security, environmental security, personal security and community security. After evaluating these various categories of security on the basis of international benchmarks and practices, Tin examines some of the complications arising from ethno-communal organization in Myanmar. He then advocates the incorporation of a human security perspective in state-sponsored attempts to create security. Tin's chapter provides a wealth of meticulously compiled statistical information about the well being of the inhabitants of Myanmar and the problems that they encounter on a day-to-day basis.

The third and final section of the book comprises a total of four chapters. The first three of these are devoted to an examination of three major ethnic groups in the country and their attempts in coming to terms with the current situation. In the case of the Karen and the Kachin groups, such attempts involve managing life within the terms of the ceasefires negotiated with the government. Alan Saw Oo details the specific nature of the involvement of the Anglican and Baptist churches in negotiating the ceasefire agreement between the KNU and the government. He provides specific names and dates of mediators and areas of agreement and disagreement in the course of the dialogue. He then outlines the humanitarian and developmental efforts of church-based organizations in attending to the needs of the Karen community. Such efforts also involve capacity-building, especially in the areas of health and education as well as peace-making and peace-building as part of community-based social action. Ja Nan Lahtaw's chapter looks at the Kachin ethnic community and the various linguistic sub-divisions within it and how these groups have fared over time. She then identifies the various ceasefire groups and how the community appropriated the traditional Manau Harvest Festival as the focal point to bring the splintered community together. Subsequently she identifies how the Kachin Nyein (Shalom) Foundation utilizes a pyramidal approach to peace-building initiatives, both within the community as well as across ethnic groups in order to build trust in preparation for post-conflict reconstruction.

Sai Kham Mong's point of departure from the other two ethnic paper writers is his conceptualization of Shan in both ethnic and spatial terms. He begins by defining the territory referred to as the Shan states and then goes on to document their development from the mid-nineteenth century. He appraises the political fortunes and misfortunes of the Shan *sawbwas* and how the crisis created by the Chinese nationalist army in the Shan states led in turn to the territory reverting to central control. Sai also notes how the traditionally independent *sawbwas* have been deprived of their power and how some of the other minorities inhabiting the northern Shan states like the Wa and the Kokang have moved down south and come to occupy large swaths of territory. He also details the various insurgent movements located within the Shan states. Finally, Khin Zaw Win's chapter details the conceptual parameters and utility of economic sanctions as a policy instrument and then examines the impact of international economic sanctions on Myanmar. He identifies the various ways in which sanctions have been counter-productive in achieving the lofty goal of pressuring rogue regimes. He then argues that contrary to Western perceptions, much progress has been achieved within the country since the 1990 election and that much more can be achieved if the West relents on its sanctions policy. Finally, Khin draws the readers attention to the 700-year old Mongol attempts to lay siege to a Burmese town that eventually ended in failure. Drawing on this analogy, he makes the point that this historical development is deeply etched in the psyche of Myanmar citizens and that they will patiently await the lifting of the economic sanctions and eventually determine their own destiny.

As mentioned at the outset, it is hope that collectively these chapters will contribute to enhancing social science knowledge on Myanmar. Some of the details regarding the actual negotiations and the personalities involved in negotiating ceasefire arrangements are new. Nonetheless, the situation is indeed fluid and evolving. The final outcome of the Constitutional Convention and the structures and procedures obtained from it will have an enduring impact on state-society relations in Myanmar as it will on the structuration of power and legitimacy within the country. Despite being objective scholars, or perhaps because of it, we hope that the political and socio-economic situation in Myanmar will get better and that there will be the eventual filtration of these positive developments onto Myanmar society as a whole. After all, as Tin Maung Maung Than reminds us, human security should be the new and legitimate unit of measurement rather than the traditional conception of state security that privileges elites and structures.

2

State-society Relations
in Southeast Asia

N. Ganesan

The literature on state-society relations, despite maintaining a measure of thematic unity, has undergone some major transformations in recent times. Of these changes, the most significant in terms of influence has been the attempt to correlate the state with society rather than treat the two as separate entities. In other words, rather than treat the two units as separate but interactive, recent writings have tended to view the state as a microcosm of society or the state as embedded within society.[1] Such a conception of the state naturally has serious implications. These include the treatment of society as an organic and holistic concept as well as the state as a part of society. Hence, whereas the 1980s was concerned with bringing the state back in and treating it as a separate entity though interactive with society, the 1990s witnessed a major change in how the two units were conceived.[2] The literature of the 1980s can be characterized as state centric owing to its starting point, and attempting to resurrect the traditional way of envisioning and conceptualizing state-society relations. Subsequently, the literature in comparative politics, perhaps in response to the hegemony of the state, tended towards being society centric. Consequently, the state-in-society approach presented a more balanced and holistic approach. It would be fair to note that this state-in-society approach continues to hold sway in the social sciences.

There has also been renewed interest in political and regime transitions, although it might be added that this thrust is not entirely new and is in effect a continuation of the study of regime transitions and the factors contributing to them in the 1980s in Latin America. Equally important in the literature has been the attempt to examine changes initiated from the bottom up.[3] This bottom up approach has been dominated by the literature on social movements and associational life. Within this approach, one of the most influential strands of thought has been Robert Putnam's conception of social capital — norms of reciprocity and trustworthiness in society.[4] To the extent that the utility of society lies in providing a measure of soft and hard structural support to mediate relations between the individual and the state, social capital and its accumulation and/or dissipation are important and to some extent measurable concepts in the study of state-society relations.

As for the literature on civil-military relations, that is in turn a microcosm of state-society relations, Western political scientists generally concluded early on that newly independent developing states that were not structurally predisposed towards competitive party politics and democratic tendencies naturally gravitated towards military authoritarian regimes.[5] The weakness of political parties, administrative structures and civil society and conversely, the strength of the military and its seemingly legitimate use of force empowered it to the point where, as an institution, it could not be easily challenged. In any event, during the Cold War period, both the communist as well as the United States and Western countries in general supported and sustained military authoritarian regimes as long as their own national interests were maintained. In this regard, there was certainly a seeming schism between what was preached and what was practised. The academic literature in the field gravitated towards the identification of conditions that spawned military authoritarian regimes. Elaborate taxonomies were then created to categorize such conditions and their impact on the possible mutation of regimes.[6]

The literature in the 1980s tended to be less judgmental though comparative conceptualizations of such regimes persisted. The categories were often functionally defined in relation to role performance and interactions with the state and society at large. The conditions leading to the persistence and collapse of military authoritarian regimes were also studied. In fact, for most of the 1980s, much of the literature on this topic tended to draw from the Latin American experience.[7] And since democratic regime types were often viewed as the antithesis of authoritarianism, the study of regime types tended to encompass more than one type.[8] At the very least, inferences could be made *via negatio* regarding conditions suitable for democratic regimes by studying those that undermined authoritarianism and *vice-versa*. After all, the typical conceptualization of scholars regarding these two regime types was that they were polar opposites or at the very least at opposite ends of a continuum.

In the 1990s comparative conceptualizations especially those detailing conditions favourable for the collapse of authoritarian regimes persisted in the academic literature. These studies were aided and abetted in no small measure by developments in the international arena. Communism was collapsing in Eastern Europe in the late 1980s and the Soviet Union itself imploded in 1991. Given the strong prevailing view of failing authoritarian regimes as the precursor for the onset of democratization, regime studies received a tremendous boost with the failure of socialist systems. Consequently, studies on democratization also acquired increased significance. Specifically, the study of democratization as a field became significantly nuanced and the number of approaches in the field were magnified. This so-called "third wave of democratization", "a group of transitions from nondemocratic to democratic regimes that occurs within a specified period and that significantly outnumbers transitions in the opposite direction" was different from the second wave in the aftermath of colonization and World War II in that the elements that precipitated the change were primarily internal and indigenous.[9] However, Huntington adhered to the typology provided by Juan Linz in the 1980s to distinguish between different types of transitions. These include transformations when the transition is elite initiated, replacements when the political opposition is able to collapse a regime or orchestrate its overthrow and transplacements when change is brought about by both political elites and members of the opposition.

Traditional State-society Relations in Southeast Asia

With the exception of Thailand, all the states in Southeast Asia were colonized by Western powers, mostly in the nineteenth century, though the Portuguese were in the region much earlier establishing trading communities. Approximately a century of colonization was in turn followed by World War II and the trauma of the Japanese Occupation from 1942 to 1945. Most countries achieved their political independence shortly after the war. It is generally accepted that independence came in two waves — the first beginning just after the conclusion of the war and Philippine independence in 1946. This was swiftly followed by Burma in 1948 and Indonesia in 1949. Subsequently, the Indochinese countries of Laos and Cambodia achieved their independence under international supervision in 1953. The first wave then culminated with Vietnam being severed into two halves after the Geneva Accords in 1954. The second wave began with the

Malay peninsula in 1957. This federation was then extended to include the Borneo territories of Sabah and Sarawak and Singapore in 1963. Subsequently, Singapore separated from the Malaysian federation in 1965. In 1975, following the conclusion of the Second Indochina War, North and South Vietnam were reunited and renamed the Socialist Republic of Vietnam. This event brought an end to the major involvement of Western powers in the Southeast Asian theatre to contain communism during the Cold War. Unfortunately though, Sino-Soviet rivalry was played out in the Vietnamese invasion and occupation of Cambodia that did not end until 1989. Brunei was in effect the last country to gain its independence in 1984 after the United Kingdom removed its protectorate status.

So how did colonial history and its aftermath impact on state-society relations in Southeast Asia, assuming that it is superfluous to talk about civil-military relations during the pre-independence period? Arguably Western conceptions of statehood, territoriality and sovereignty were brought into the region. Traditional Southeast Asian societies were hardly constituted the way that they are now. Much more traditional patterns of power and authority befitting a "charismatic leader", to borrow a Weberian phrase, existed then. In the Southeast Asian context, such persons have been variously described as "Chief", "Big Man" or "man of prowess" as described by O.W. Wolters.[10] Persons exercising such power were typically skilled in warfare and trade, exercising jurisdiction over territories and people through extended kinship ties, followers and in some instances, even slaves. Nonetheless, the newly independent states were forced to adapt swiftly and naturally, some fared better than others. Apart from the countries in the Indochinese peninsula that were ravaged by war, the countries in maritime Southeast Asia generally fared better in terms of development and state-society relations. Countries where independence was achieved through negotiated settlement like Brunei, Malaysia, the Philippines and Singapore tended to generally fare better, at least in terms of overall development. In this regard, the settlement in Burma did not hold and we will return later in the chapter to identify the forces that made the Burmese case different. Conversely, it could be argued that countries that obtained their independence on the basis of revolutionary struggle, as in the case of Indonesia and Vietnam, there was lesser external legitimacy and despite the seeming summoning of a Rousseauite national will, bouts of violence continued, especially in Indonesia. In fact, in the Indonesian case, the state continued to expand outwards by occupying territories — West Papua in 1963 and East Timor in 1975.

However, it is equally important to note that in socialist states like Vietnam, Laos and Cambodia, communist ideology became intertwined with nationalism. In the Indonesian case, there is some evidence to suggest that Islam aided the nationalist cause.[11]

Traditionally, Southeast Asian societies had a number of mediating mechanisms in state-society relations. Apart from the family being the central unit and frame of reference beyond the individual level, agrarian societies were characterized by village elders and headmen who mediated between the state and its officials on the one hand, and their communities on the other. Through the headmen, traditional postcolonial societies were able to effect both participation and protection at the same time. Participation in national schemes led to a sense of sovereignty inherent in the state and utilizing headmen simultaneously provided a measure of protection against the state as well.[12] This pattern of interaction is pervasive till today in many parts of rural Southeast Asia. In this regard, it is arguable that to large numbers of rural residents, the state is a fairly abstract and distant entity. In more urban areas however, where traditional patterns of power and authority do not obtain and where the state and its bureaucracy and services are more visible, the situation is significantly different. As a rule of thumb, the demands of urban living and culture exert demands on the state. Similarly, in a reciprocal manner, the state is able to extract capital in a number of ways to service both its own needs and the needs of its citizens. It remains a truism in Southeast Asia as elsewhere that urban communities have a disproportionate influence on the political culture of the region. This political culture both determines and defines state-society and civil-military relations. Both sets of relations are malleable and indeed, have been subject to significant changes in the last two decades.

Monarchies have also performed an important political role in Southeast Asian societies. Although many of them have lost much of their former glory, they remain important institutions in many countries. Often they provide the inhabitants of a state with a linkage to the past and some conception of glory or greatness in a bygone era. In the past, deriving from Hindu, Buddhist and Islamic traditions, superior men of prowess were able to claim royal and noble status, thereby concentrating greater levels of power and influence in society. Similarly, they were equally capable of exacting and extracting more from their followers. Such claims to superior status had the added advantage of accumulated power trickling down to the descendants of such nobility. More typically however, they remain as important institutions that retain a measure of symbolic power. Sometimes, as in the case of absolute and constitutional monarchies, the state is able to capitalize on such symbolic power by fusing these early elements of power with newer structures of the state. Over time, such state crests and flags provided what Murray Edelman characterizes as condensation symbols that can be invoked in times of need.[13] This observation is certainly true in the case of Cambodia, Malaysia and Thailand. In the case of Brunei that is still an absolute monarchy, the patterns of traditional power and authority continue to obtain. In Thailand and Cambodia, the monarchy continues to play an important political role as well. It may be remembered that it was King Norodom Sihanouk who played a crucial role in brokering the disputes between factions in the Cambodian Government in 1997 when the situation deteriorated into a state of civil war. Similarly, it was King Bhumiphol Adunyadej of Thailand who brokered the dispute between social movement protest leaders and the military in 1991 and most recently between the People's Alliance for Democracy (PDA) and Thaksin Shinawatra in 2006. Consequently, it is arguable that some Southeast Asian kings have retained a measure of their traditional role as arbitrators of disputes.

State-society relations are naturally different between states that utilize a capitalist model for their economy than those that adopt a socialist model. In this regard, Vietnam, Laos and Cambodia have different models of state-society relations, and the state, despite being a leveller philosophically, is often portrayed as one concerned with the accumulation and protection of power. Economic transactionalism that often empowers individuals and groups are sometimes viewed with a measure of suspicion. Empowerment does after all presuppose a corresponding weakening or displacement of power on the part of the state. Since most socialist governments in Southeast Asia came to power on the basis of nationalist revolutionary struggles, power and its distribution is jealously guarded. And since such states typically controlled, aggregated and distributed resources as well, they truly held access to power. Membership in the relevant party was also materially rewarding and conferred status. Sometimes such status came into conflict with power and prestige derived from material wealth. The liberalization of the economy — a trend that has characterized even socialist states since the 1990s, has exaggerated this problem. The state now has to assist in the implementation of a capitalist system which was traditionally anathema to socialist countries. Complicating the situation is the existence of a dual economy that provides tremendous opportunities for corruption through the disposal of state or communal assets. Since ownership of assets was previously not assigned, detection of such corruption is often difficult and too late. This situation leads to a constant dialectic between socialism and its conception of the good on the one hand and its trade-off with the material gains of capitalism on the other. Additionally, the introduction of capitalism with its emphasis on consumption and accumulated wealth, dissipates much of the social capital that was accrued within the earlier exclusively socialist framework.

Ethnicity and religion are two other issues that significantly complicate state-society relations in Southeast Asia. For the most part, Southeast Asian states are multi-ethnic. However, how the percentages of the various groups are expressed and whether the state has been captured by a majority ethnic group has a significant bearing on state-society relations for minority groups. Minority groups that are often socio-politically and economically marginalized and exist on the fringes in Southeast Asia typically view the state as an overwhelming oppressor rather than a strong protector or benevolent provider of goods and services. For such groups, the state is simply an extra means of the majority group exercising hegemony over vulnerable minority groups. For such small dispossessed groups, states are involved in structural discrimination and violence. Alternatively, if some minority groups had in the past sought alignment with an external power to enhance its standing or fend better for itself like the Hmong in Laos and the Montagnards in Vietnam that were involved in covert operations against the states, such groups are regularly persecuted and often driven out of the country. To most such marginalized minority groups, Western conceptions of a rational-legal state embodying and protecting citizens' rights simply does not exist. Fortunately though, despite existing in the margins, such groups have often evolved important exchange and clientelist relationships with traditional elite and patrons. The latter are then able to intervene and negotiate on behalf of such communities.

Like ethnicity, religion also has a powerful impact on state-society relations. This observation is especially valid in states that have a clear religious identification like Brunei, Myanmar and Thailand. Alternatively, in a state whose inhabitants are overwhelmingly of a particular religion, there exist the possibility of discrimination both within the majority group in all its various manifestations or of minority religions that are viewed as heretical or at least less than equal. The extreme example is of course the socialist states like Vietnam that in the past used to persecute practitioners of organized religion since socialism regarded religion as "false consciousness". It would be fair to note that since ethnicity and religion are both important identity markers in Southeast Asia, they in turn have an impact on the structure of state-society relations. Where such identities are malleable or moderated by other considerations like class and locale, the accommodation of minority groups has typically been better.

As for civil-military relations, the situation is equally complicated and attention can be drawn to a number of developments that are common to the region.[14] It would be a fair comment to note that Southeast Asia, like Latin America, has had its fair share of military authoritarian regimes. Indonesia, Myanmar, the Philippines and Thailand immediately come to mind when discussing this issue. Indeed there are as many commonalities as there are differences between the various countries and the writer is free to choose which ones to play up.

For commonalities, most countries that hosted military authoritarian regimes tended to have weak and depoliticized mass organizations. The military would typically have acquired its legitimacy at the outset on the basis of its struggle for political independence. This was certainly the case with Indonesia, Myanmar and Vietnam though the case can be made that in communist countries the military is, to all intents and purposes, an arm of the state. For that matter even in democratic countries, it is difficult to conceive of the military as being functionally independent of the state. After all, the military is authorized by the state, together with other enforcement agencies, to legitimately utilize force. And although theorists often talk of the military as traditional protectors of sovereignty and territoriality in the classical sense, it is arguable that modern militaries are often called on to assist in everything from natural calamities to civil strife. The requirement of objective civilian control does, however, continue to obtain in democratic societies.

Other sources of political legitimacy that have been advanced include the suppression of insurgency and separatist movements. Since this falls well within the classic function of the military in that it involves the protection of state sovereignty and power, it is an argument that is often and readily advanced. All military authoritarian regimes in Southeast Asia have claimed such legitimacy in the past. For example, the legitimacy of the Indonesian military was tied to the prevention of insurgency and separatism in Aceh. West Papua and East Timor until it became independent in 2000. In the Philippines, Ferdinand Marcos justified the imposition of a state of emergency that subsequently deteriorated into a military authoritarian regime in 1972 on the basis of a deteriorated security situation in the Cordilleras and Mindanao. Similarly, when Ne Win seized power in Burma in 1962, ethnic insurgencies were as large a consideration as the seeming incompetence of a civilian government. And in fact, ethnic insurgencies continue to be a major justification for the *primus inter pares* position of the *tatmadaw* in Myanmar.[15] Although the government has signed a number of ceasefire agreements with many of the larger insurgent groups, fighting continues against groups from the Chin, Karen, Karenni and Shan ethnic groups.

Another major source of legitimacy among military authoritarian regimes was involvement in the developmental process. This claim typically became more important as traditional sources of legitimacy like internal and external threats to the state waned. The Thai military, for example, claimed just such a developmental role after the communist insurgency dissipated by the late 1980s and Vietnam no longer presented an external security threat. Similarly, in Indonesia, the territorially-based army was involved in administering the areas under its control and Suharto skillfully deployed military commanders into senior ranks of the bureaucracy. Similarly, Marcos surrounded himself with large numbers of men in uniforms to run the country. As for Myanmar, as it will become apparent later, there is essentially no distinction between the military and the state and the two terms might as well be used interchangeably. Nonetheless, it should be noted that the Myanmar military has always claimed legitimacy on the basis of preserving national unity and the renovation of religious and historical buildings. The latter aspect of legitimacy also draws on the military's role as defender of the faith since a significant majority of Myanmar nationals are devout Buddhists. And finally, it should be noted that successful military authoritarian regimes always have access to independent financing. Such access may be in the form of direct appropriations from the state or through state enterprises like in Suharto's Indonesia, Myanmar and Thailand. Occasionally, external training and developmental aid is also channelled to the military rather than utilized for the purpose it was designated for.

In examining factors that contribute to and sustain military authoritarian regimes, the importance of mass organizations and competing centres of power cannot be downplayed. It is in the very nature of authoritarian regimes to monoplize discourse within a state. Consequently, it is to be expected that such regimes will crush or outlaw mass organizations. Similarly, authoritarian regimes always seek to disband or dissipate alternative centres of power though such attempts are not always met with success. Where success in controlling such power does not obtain, there is often an attempt to strike a deal of sorts that will not threaten the regime in power. Such a deal may however become unstuck. For example, Ferdinand Marcos had an informal alliance with the all-powerful Catholic church in the Philippines and yet it was the same church that took side with rebel soldiers that staged the coup against the Marcos government in 1986. In a similar manner, although Sarit Thanarat empowered the monarchy in Thailand to provide him with symbolic legitimacy, it was the same monarch who took the side of student protestors against the military in 1973 and deflected coup attempts in 1981 and 1992.

Finally, most military authoritarian regimes in Southeast Asia had an external sponsor. With the exception of the communist states, this guarantor was invariably the United States. As part of its strategy of containing communism in the region, the United States endorsed and supported authoritarian regimes in Indonesia, Thailand and the Philippines. The Philippines and Thailand were important bases for preventing the spread of communism from China downward and into Southeast Asia during the Cold War. Their assistance was sought as early as 1954 when they were inducted as members of the Manila Pact that gave birth to the Southeast Asia Treaty Organization (SEATO). Similarly, the United States supported the developmentalist patrimonial regime of Suharto that took over from Sukarno who was dangerously leaning towards China and the Soviet Union in the 1960s.

Recent Developments in State-society Relations in Southeast Asia

Fortunately for Southeast Asia as a region, the military authoritarian regimes of the Cold War period have since been replaced by much more democratic ones. And just like how certain factors facilitated the emergence and entrenchment of military authoritarian regimes, there were a number of common factors that have in turn led to their collapse more recently. Such factors have included elite dissension within the ranks of the military, the emergence of political and social consciousness and groups representing them in the form of social movements, structural changes that undermine the privileged position of the military and the withdrawal of external political support. Dissension within the ranks of the military appears to be a crucial indicator of signalling ripeness for a change of regime. The Thai situation in 1973, 1981, 1986 and 1991 all pointed towards dissension within the ranks of the military that in turn resulted in a loss of support or a failed coup attempt. In 1986, important elements within the Philippine military including the Defence Minister Juan Ponce Enrile defected to the side of the rebels that was the harbinger of the downfall of Marcos. Similarly, leading military commanders withdrew support for Suharto in Indonesia after the outbreak of violence and food riots in 1998, signalling an imminent collapse of the government. Such dissension is, however, not to be confused with a purging of senior members of the military. These happen on a fairly regular basis in all authoritarian regimes and were a frequent feature in Indonesia under Suharto and more recently, Myanmar.

The widespread emergence of socio-political consciousness is not always easy to ascertain and can often be determined only on an *ex-post facto* basis. Structural changes in society and the economy that undermine the predominant role of the military like what happened in Indonesia and Thailand in the 1980s, including the emergence of an empowered middle class in the urban areas, was a significant development. However, sometimes the evidence is overwhelming, as happened in the case of Indonesia in the 1990s to the point that the government tried to co-opt this consciousness through a policy of accommodation. Similarly, there was widespread empowerment of social groups and movements under the Prem and Chatichai governments in the 1980s in Thailand before the 1991 coup by the military was deflected through widespread street protests. However, it should be noted that if there is no dissension within the ranks of the military and the regime is prepared to use overwhelming force as in the case of Myanmar in 1988, an authoritarian regime can continue to remain in power. Finally, it should be noted that the proverbial straw that breaks the camel's back is invariably withdrawal of support from an external sponsor. All of the military authoritarian regimes that collapsed invariably had their support withdrawn from the United States. The most dramatic case of the withdrawal of support was the case of Ferdinand Marcos when the United States flew him to safety in Hawaii, not unlike the assistance provided to the Shah of Iran to flee to Mexico in 1979.

In total, both the 1980s and 1990s witnessed very important developments in state-society and civil-military relations in Southeast Asia. After all, the region had been home to a number of strong military authoritarian regimes and these in turn impacted substantially on state-society relations. As a matter of fact, in many instances, like the case of Indonesia, Myanmar, Philippines and Thailand, the state had effectively been captured or certainly controlled by the military. Sometimes, in order to compensate for the technocratic skills that were typically lacking in the military, a marriage of convenience was arranged with a functionally more competent bureaucracy insulated from external forces within the state. However, one by one, all the military authoritarian regimes collapsed, the last being the downfall of the Suharto government in Indonesia in 1998. For the most part, countries that have shed their authoritarian past have progressed in the direction of democratic norms. This development is certainly true in the case of Indonesia and the Philippines and until the recent developments that led to the collapse of the Thaksin government in Thailand, was also true of that country.

Myanmar Exception to the Southeast Asian Experience?

A brief survey of Southeast Asian political history would indicate that Myanmar shared many historical experiences with its neighbours. Like most of Southeast Asia, it was colonized in the nineteenth century, although the country took much longer to subdue than the other countries the British had colonized. The three Anglo-Burmese Wars was certainly in stark contrast to the residential system of government that the British employed in Malaya or the trading protectorate status that they provided the states of Sabah, Sarawak and Brunei. In the case of Burma, political control was exerted throughout most of the colonial period from India. The country certainly did not evolve a unified identity, having been consciously divided into the lowland areas where the British exerted formal control and administration, and the highland areas that were nominally controlled by treaties and agreements. Similarly, the British spent neither time nor effort in containing the Burmese Communist Party unlike the Malayan case where they imposed a state of emergency that lasted from 1948 to 1960. There appears also to have been little interest in nurturing the Burmese economy for subsequent independence and the generation of surplus revenue for administration and development. Consequently, it is arguable that Burma at the time of independence was hardly prepared for cohesive and unitary administration.

In light of the collapse of most military authoritarian regimes in Southeast Asia, it might be legitimate to ask why the Myanmar case differs so drastically from those of its Southeast Asian neighbours. Why or how has the military junta in the country managed to insulate itself from regional developments? The answer to this question is located in part in the country's history, in part in the structure of society and internal socio-political developments, in part in the absence of domestic challenges and finally, in part in the measure of external political and economic support.

Historically, Burma experienced a very traumatic post-independence period. Shortly after independence, many of the ethnic minorities formed insurgent armies and rebelled against the state. These groups subsequently became ensconced in the highland areas that the British Government had traditionally found difficult to control. The ethnic insurgent groups were outward manifestations of deeper divisions within Burmese society between the majority Bamar peoples who were predominantly settled in the lowland areas and the highland minorities like the Karen, Shan and the Kachin. The British colonial government controlled the highland areas by recognizing a measure of autonomy and the 1948 independence agreement offered the right of cessation to two of these groups. Added to these internal problems was the presence of a large Kuomintang detachment of troops in the Shan states that the Burmese Government was unable to defeat. As a result of this external military presence, both the U.S. CIA and the Chinese military became involved in the conflict. The former supported the KMT as part of containing communist China while the latter clearly aimed to defeat the nationalist troops.

Against this troublesome backdrop of domestic political developments, the parliamentary government that was in place was unable to effectively cope with the duties of government. In 1959, the military set up a temporary caretaker government that lasted about six months. Subsequently, power was returned to the civilian government. Afterwards, in 1962, the military staged a coup against the government and usurped power. However, this usurpation was to last longer with tremendous consequences for internal and external developments. Internally, the military announced the formation of the Burma Socialist Party Programme (BSPP). Externally, the government, in light of the fighting involving the KMT troops in the Shan states, announced a policy of neutrality achieved through self-imposed isolationism. Hence, rather than the Swiss approach which was to steer a neutral course in international relations, the BSPP government decided to significantly lower dealings with foreign countries to achieve such neutrality. Nevertheless, countries like Germany and Japan continued to have reasonably cordial relations with the BSPP government. Consequently, from 1962 to 1988 when the BSPP government led by Ne Win was in power, Burma was significantly, though not entirely, cut off from the rest of the world.

The pursuit of isolationism and the deteriorated socio-economic situation led to the outward migration of skilled professionals and low levels of infrastructural development and service provision. Consequently, when countries like Thailand and Indonesia were experiencing an economic boom and the growth of a middle class, there was no such broad-based development in Burma although there were significant numbers of locals who benefitted from illegal businesses and black marketeering. The country remained isolated and steeped in a deep Buddhist tradition that appeared to offer some solace to the general public. Nonetheless, there was an awareness of the changes taking place in the region and around the world and a social movement of sorts demanding political change was forged by intellectuals, students and monks. The protest for political change on 8 August 1988 by this group was suppressed by force by the military and many activists were killed or imprisoned. Subsequently, leading members of the military formed the State Law and Order Restoration Council (SLORC) that was subsequently renamed the State Peace and Development Council (SPDC) in 1997. The significant event that took place during this transformation of the military regime was the national election held in 1990 that was clearly won by the National League for Democracy (NLD). Aung San Suu Kyi led the party despite not having contested the election herself. Nonetheless, the SLORC refused to honour the outcome of the elections and has detained a large number of NLD members and supporters. Arising from these developments, some activists and students forged a broad-based alliance with the ethnic insurgent groups to unite them in the common cause of opposing the military junta. Suu Kyi herself has been held under house arrest since May 2003, her term typically being extended on an annual basis recently although she has been previously freed intermittently.

So what happened in Myanmar that differed substantially from the situation in Indonesia, the Philippines and Thailand? Firstly, the military had been in total control of the lowland areas since 1962 with little challenge. This military regime that had been at least partially isolated from the world since 1962 and especially after 1990 truly believed, and indeed continues to believe, that the conditions of the Cold War obtain, at least in the country's relations with the West and in particular the United States. It has consistently argued for a set of indigenous cultural values that it deems to be appropriate and good for the country. By contrast, imported "Western" values like democracy are viewed as corrupting the country's values. In this regard, the military junta in

power regards Aung San Suu Kyi as quite simply an emissary of the
West rather than a native returned to her country. The junta appears
unprepared to turn over political power to the NLD on the basis of the
1990 electoral victory and in fact has become even more conservative in
its views since October 2004 when it purged Prime Minister Khin Nyunt
for corruption. Khin Nyunt had previously distinguished himself for
being much more liberal than the other senior junta members — Than
Shwe and Maung Aye. Hence the possibility of change within the ranks
of the military has been thwarted as has structural change through a
democratic process. Meantime, the xenophobic tendencies of the SPDC
only seem to have increased with the sudden shift of the capital city
northward from Yangon Pyinmana. Whereas the new location is
strategically more central, rumours have also abounded regarding fears
of an imminent U.S.-led military attack against the junta. Opaque political
systems naturally spawn rumours and these remain difficult to verify
or substantiate.

Opponents of the junta in the form of ethnic insurgents have been
temporarily lulled into silence on the basis of ceasefire arrangements.
These arrangements provide for control of contiguous territory and the
right to bear arms within this territory. In return, government troops will
not attack these groups. The largest and most powerful of the ethnic
groups have been brought into the national fold on this basis. In the
meantime, the SPDC has argued that a new constitution is required and
has pressed ahead with a National Convention to draft a new constitution.
It has claimed that all ethnic and minority groups are being included in this
new process. While these developments are taking place, the level of faith
in the armed groups representing the ethnic minorities is going down.
Individuals are attempting a way out of the situation by acquiring wealth
or migration. The ceasefire groups themselves have become lethargic and
are wary that this SPDC strategy may well be one of attrition.[16]

In light of all these developments, it is arguable that the developments
that occurred in the Philippines, Indonesia and Thailand cannot be replicated
in Myanmar. There are quite simply no opportunities present. The potential
actors are weak and demoralized and there is no incentive for the military
to turn over power to a civilian government. If anything, the SPDC
increasingly projects itself as the guardian of national values and sovereignty
and has gone to great lengths to advertise this conception of itself. It has
also warned its citizens not to be enticed by foreigners who seek to sow
discord and eventually control the country.

As for international pressure against the SPDC, the United States and the EU have spearheaded an international economic embargo of the country. The sanctions regime has been significantly expanded but these negative instruments appear to disproportionately affect the Myanmar population rather than the military regime in power. ASEAN nations that in the past favoured a policy of engaging rather than isolating Myanmar have given up and resigned themselves to the situation. Calls by ASEAN elite from Indonesia, Malaysia, the Philippines, Singapore and Thailand have simply gone unheeded.[17] Most regional actors appear resigned to the existing situation as the prospects for political change in Myanmar appear to dim more and more. China and India, for strategic as well as competitive reasons, have supported the SPDC thus far and indeed appear prepared to continue the course. Under the circumstances, it would appear that the democratic revolution that swept Southeast Asia has not been fully played out in Myanmar yet. In the meantime, the military continues to grow in size and sophistication, making the transition towards political change potentially more difficult.

Conclusion

State-society and civil-military relations in Southeast Asia have indeed undergone major transformations in the last two decades. For the most part, developments in the non-socialist countries actually validate the state-in-society approach put forward by Joel Migdal. Open societies with capitalist economies generally allow for such transformations and spillover effects arising from societal norms. However, for such norms to be malleable, structural features of the state must allow for both transformation at the level of popular culture that in turn interacts with the state. In this regard, it is arguable that even socialist states like Vietnam have realized the need to undertake a measure of structural changes in the economy. Whether economic changes will in turn spur political reform that tends in the direction of democratic change remains a moot point for social scientists. On the one hand, there is ample evidence from Northeast Asia that dominant party systems eventually succumb to implosion that in turn leads to systemic structural changes. Yet, there are countries like Singapore where dominant party systems have indeed survived and prospered. Nonetheless, it is arguable that open societies are generally more prone to change than closed ones. In this regard, it is obvious that Myanmar as a country remains even more closed than socialist states like Vietnam. Whereas the state appears to have withdrawn from its previously overwhelming presence in many Southeast Asian countries, the converse has occurred in Myanmar after the collapse of the BSPP government in 1988.

Civil-military relations are invariably a microcosm of state-society relations or *vice versa* in military authoritarian regimes where the military establishment is *primus inter pares*. Such regimes typically disallow challenges from other mass-based organizations and work to prevent any structural changes in society that will undermine their power or access to it. These classic features of a military authoritarian regime were certainly in place in Indonesia, the Philippines and Thailand. Yet the demands of developmentalism and the structural and social transformations that obtain from them invariably empower society at the expense of the state. Judging from the Southeast Asian experience, such confrontations may deteriorate into violence but such incidents typically undermine the legitimacy of the regime, if not immediately, in the foreseeable future. The outbreak of such violence was the harbinger of the collapse of such regimes in Indonesia and Thailand. It could be argued that such actions constitute the utilization of social capital against what is perceived as the hegemony of the state. Dissension within the ranks of the military and the withdrawal of external support further weaken the challenged regime. However, none of these conditions or changes has obtained in the case of Myanmar and appears unlikely to obtain in the immediate future. The ability of the SPDC government to stave off external pressures and yet retain the support of proximate neighbours like India and China has provided the military with significant leverage that other countries in the region were unable to obtain. Years of isolation and xenophobia as well as the attempt to disseminate this worldview into the domestic population has also seemingly buttressed the regime's position. Consequently, social scientists are reduced to crystal ball gazing and speculative thinking or *ex-post facto* judgments at best when it comes to dealing with Myanmar.

In as much as societies have claimed more space from the state in Southeast Asia in general, it is also true that technology and the demands associated with modern security have empowered the state. Hence, the nature of the relationship between state and society is indeed a dynamic one, though not necessarily unidirectional in terms of obtaining positive outcomes as liberal social scientists were previously inclined to think. In this regard, the interactions between state and society in Myanmar have yielded negative results for society. In fact, both internal and external security measures that have been put into place internationally to thwart terrorist attacks since 2001 have significantly impinged on fundamental liberties as we understood them. This new development has in turn allowed the state to regain a good measure of space that was previously surrendered to society. Southeast Asia has certainly not been insulated from such global developments and the balance of power between state and society is continually subject to change.

Notes

1. See for example Joel Migdal, *State-in-Society: Studying how States and Societies Transform and Constitute One Another*, New York: Cambridge University Press, 2001.
2. See for example Peter B. Evans, Dietrich Rueschemeyer and Theda Scocpol, eds., *Bringing the State Back In*, New York: Cambridge University Press, 1985, for the most influential work on state-society relations in the 1980s.
3. See Amos Perlmutter, "The Praetorian State and the Praetorian Army: Towards a Taxonomy of Civil-Military Relations in Developing Countries", *Comparative Politics* 1:3 (April 1969): 382–404 and Eric Nordlinger, "Soldiers in Mufti: The Impact of Military Rule upon Economic and Social Change in Non-Western States", *American Political Science Review* XLIV: 4 (December 1970): 553–76.
4. Robert D. Putnam, *Making Democracies Work: Civic traditions in modern Italy*, Princeton, New Jersey: Princeton University Press, 1993, and "Bowling Alone: America's Declining Social Capital", *Journal of Democracy* 6:1 (January 1995): 65–78.
5. See Perlmutter, "The Praetorian State and the Praetorian Army", and Nordlinger, "Soldiers in Mufti".
6. David E. Albright, "A Comparative Conceptualization of Civil-Military Relations", *World Politics* XXXII:4 (1980): 553–76 and Henry Bienen, "Civil-Military Relations in the Third World", *International Political Science Review* 11:3 (1981): 352–68.
7. The classis studies of this subject were Juan J. Linz and Alfred Stepan, eds., *The Breakdown of Democratic Regimes* (Baltimore: Johns Hopkins University Press, 1978) and David Collier, ed., *The New Authoritarianism in Latin America*, Princeton, New Jersey: Princeton University Press, 1979.
8. Guillermo o'Donnell and Philippe C. Schmitter, eds., *Transitions from Authoritarian Rule: Tentative Conclusions about Uncertain Democracies*, Baltimore: Johns Hopkins University Press, 1986 and Kostas Messas, "Democratization of Military Regimes: Contending Explanations", *Journal of Political and Military Sociology* 20:2 (Winter 1992): 243–55.
9. Samuel P. Huntington, "How Countries Democratize", *Political Science Quarterly* 106:4 (1991–92): 579–616. On the third wave see his *The Third*

Wave: Democratization in the Late Twentieth Century, Norman: University of Oklahoma Press, 1991. For a rebuttal of Huntington's causal model that privileges actors see Michael McFaul, "The Fourth Wave of Democracy *and Dictatorship*", *World Politics* 54 (January 2002): 212–44.

10. See the description of precolonial societies and patterns of interaction provided by Patricio N. Abinales and Donna J. Amoroso, *State and Society in the Philippines*, Lanham: Rowman and Littlefield, 2005, pp. 22–23.

11. See for example, Bernard Boland, *The Crescent and the Rising Sun*, The Hague: van Hoeve, 1958.

12. See Manning Nash, *The Golden road to Modernity: Village Life in Contemporary Burma*, Chicago: The University of Chicago Press, 1973, pp. 92–101.

13. See Murray Edelman, *The Symbolic Uses of Politics*, Urbana: University of Illinois Press, 1985.

14. One of the earliest books dealing with this subject was *Civil-Military Relations in Southeast Asia*, edited by David S. Gibbons and Zakaria Haji Ahmad, Kuala Lumpur: Oxford University Press, 1985. For a much more recent and exhaustive coverage of the subject, see *Coercion and Governance: The Declining Political Role of the Military in Asia*, edited by Muthiah Alagappa, Stanford: Stanford University Press, 2001.

15. One of the best studies of the Myanmar military is Mary P. Callahan, *Making Enemies: War and State Building in Burma*, Ithaca: Cornell University Press, 2003.

16. This was the general view of ethnic insurgents from the Karen National Union and the Mon State Party who were interviewed in December 2005.

17. Ibid.

References

Abinales, Patricio N. and Donna J. Amoroso. *State and Society in the Philippines*. Lanham: Rowman and Littlefield, 2005.

Alagappa, Muthiah, ed. *Coercion and Governance:The Declining Political Role of the Military in Asia*. Stanford: Stanford University Press, 2001.

Albright, David E. "A Comparative Conceptualization of Civil-Military Relations", *World Politics* XXXII no. 4 (1980): 553–76.

Bienen, Henry. "Civil-Military Relations in the Third World". *International Political Science Review* 11, no. 3 (1981): 352–68.

Boland, Bernard. *The Crescent and the Rising Sun*. The Hague: van Hoeve, 1958.

Callahan, Mary P. *Making Enemies: War and State Building in Burma*. Ithaca: Cornell University Press, 2003.

Collier, David, ed. *The New Authoritarianism in Latin America*. Princeton, New Jersey: Princeton University Press, 1979.

Edelman, Murray. *The Symbolic Uses of Politics*. Urbana: University of Illinois Press, 1985.

Evans, Peter B., Dietrich Rueschemeyer and Theda Scocpol, eds. *Bringing the State Back in*. New York: Cambridge University Press, 1985.

Ganesan, N. "Thai-Myanmar-ASEAN Relations: The Politics of Face and Grace. *Asian Affairs*, forthcoming.

Gibbons, David S. and Ahmad, Zakaria Haji. eds. *Civil-Military Relations in Southeast Asia*. Kuala Lumpur: Oxford University Press, 1985.

Huntington, Samuel P. *The Third Wave: Democratization in the Late Twentieth Century*. Norman: University of Oklahoma Press, 1991.

———. "How Countries Democratize", *Political Science Quarterly* 106, no. 4 (1991–92): 579–616.

Linz, Juan J. and Stepan, Alfred.eds. *The Breakdown of Democratic Regimes*. Baltimore: Johns Hopkins University Press, 1978

McFaul, Michael. "The Fourth Wave of Democracy *and* Dictatorship", *World Politics* 54 (January 2002): 212–44.

Messas, Kostas. "Democratization of Military Regimes: Contending Explanations", *Journal of Political and Military Sociology* 20, no. 2 (Winter 1992): 243–55.

Migdal, Joel. *State-in-Society: Studying how States and Societies Transform and Constitute One Another*. New York: Cambridge University Press, 2001.

Nash, Manning. *The Golden road to Modernity: Village Life in Contemporary Burma*. Chicago: The University of Chicago Press, 1973.

Nordlinger, Eric. "Soldiers in Mufti: The Impact of Military Rule upon Economic and Social Change in Non-Western States", *American Political Science Review* XLIV, no. 4 (December 1970): 553–76.

O'Donnell, Guillermo and Schmitter,Philippe C., eds. *Transitions from Authoritarian Rule: Tentative Conclusions about Uncertain Democracies*. Baltimore: Johns Hopkins University Press, 1986.

Perlmutter, Amos "The Praetorian State and the Praetorian Army: Towards a Taxonomy of Civil-Military Relations in Developing Countries", *Comparative Politics* 1, no. 3 (April 1969): 382–404.

———. "Bowling Alone: America's Declining Social Capital", *Journal of Democracy* 6:1 (January 1995): 65–78.

Putnam, Robert D. *Making Democracies Work: Civic Traditions in Modern Italy*. Princeton, New Jersey: Princeton University Press, 1993.

Scott, James C. *Weapons of the Weak: Everyday Forms of Peasant Resistance*. New Haven: Yale University Press, 1985.

3

Minorities and State-building in Mainland Southeast Asia

Rachel M. Safman

So wedded are we to the nation-state system that it is hard for most of us to envision the world in other terms or to realize how recently this conceptual framework came into being. The idea of a nation-state first emerged as a philosophical construct in the late eighteenth century and only became a reality in most parts of the world in the last century. Since then, the notion of a unique ethnic group wedded to a specific territory has come to be the primary basis of political and social organization around the globe. Nation-state status is a marker of legitimacy for those whose collective identities have come to define the places in which they reside, and its attainment one of the central goals and aspirations of those excluded from the "community of nations" through their omission from the map. This chapter examines the emergence of four of the five nation-states of mainland Southeast Asia (Thailand, Cambodia, Vietnam, Laos) from their ethnic hinterlands, that is, from the perspective of those who were *not* named when the world order established boundaries in this region. It focuses on how and why certain peoples came to be excluded — in part or full — from the nation-building project and examines what the consequences of this have been for majority-minority[1] relations in the present day.

The chapter begins with an examination of the concept of a nation-state and the forms of nationalism often tied to it. It then proceeds on a country-by-country basis through the region, looking at the roles of minorities in the nation-building process and at the place of these groups in the contemporary socio-political landscape. The ultimate goal of this analysis is to lay the groundwork for a discussion of a fifth case, the one country of the region not treated in detail, Burma/Myanmar, in which minority-majority relations have arguably been the most complex and conflictual and for which the nation-building process is, in some ways, least complete. One final preliminary note: Because the chapter's orientation is towards Burma/Myanmar where "minority" has come to be synonymous with the numerous groups inhabiting the geographic periphery and because their history in the region and relationship to the "majority" is often so different from that of other minorities, the "lowland" minorities — specifically the Chinese in all of the countries discussed, the Lao in Thailand and the Vietnamese in Cambodia — will be given scant treatment in this chapter. Several excellent works devoted exclusively to these groups and their experiences exist, among them Reid (1996, 1997) and Wang (1988, 1991) on the Chinese in Southeast Asia, Keyes (1995, 1997) on the Lao in Thailand, and Thion (1988) on the Vietnamese in Cambodia (this last case will receive some treatment here).

Nation-states and Nationalism

The concept of the nation-state has its ideological roots in the Enlightenment thinking of Europe where, as Christie put it, "the dynamic contact between ethnic consciousness and the concept of popular sovereignty ... led inevitably to the demand that ethnic identity be given a legitimate political expression" (1996, p. 4). In a context where dynastic empires were breaking down and feudal territories banding together in ethnic confederations, the notion that state legitimacy could be founded on the "natural right" of individuals sharing a common history, language and culture to lay exclusive claims to a territory had immediate resonance and utility. So from the middle of the nineteenth century, the peoples of Europe began to divide themselves up into largely ethnically homogenous blocks[2] with agreed upon boundaries and terms for mutual engagement. Indeed, as the nation-state movement became dominant it came to be a premise of international relations that only nation-states or their close analogues had a place at the diplomatic table (Tilly 1992), and this as much as ideology, has been a driving force for the acceptance of the nation-state model by many peoples the world over.

The nation-state model had implications beyond the reification of more durable international boundaries. Among other things, it fundamentally redefined the relationship between state and society, in the process redefining the individual himself as a "citizen" of the state, rather than as a member of a clan or a tribe (Geertz 1963). It also consolidated administrative control in the central government (Giddens 1984; Tilly 1992). Finally, the creation of a nation-state, in which legitimacy was bestowed by society rather than divine or customary right, also created a space for civic discourse — including space for the discussion of state legitimacy (Calhoun 1993*b*; Gellner 1983, 1997). In these ways the emergence of the nation-state and of nationalist movements (that is, movements to establish a nation-state in a given territory or on behalf of a specific people) are closely linked either temporally or causally to the advent of modernity (Hobsbawm 1990).

Those scholars who stress the linkage between nationalism and modernity over the sometimes competing discourse on nationalism and culture[3] point out that the nation-building project is often as much a rhetorical as a practical undertaking. In particular, the construction of a "majority" group — and consequent definition of "minorities" — has been shown to be an active and intentional project on the part of national elites, who have staked their claims *vis-à-vis* other groups and/or before an external (often former colonial) power on the basis of a shared identity which arguably came into being (or came into being in its stated form) as a product of the national movement itself (Gellner 1983). Anderson (1991) and Brown (1994) are among the authors who have tied this into the study of the emergence of national languages, literatures and (often fictive) histories. While I do not dispute these claims, these matters will also not be taken up in the discussion here on the nation-building projects of Southeast Asia.

Instead, this chapter will focus on a dimension of inclusion-exclusion which is frequently omitted from discussions of nationalism *per se*, but which has been shown to be an integral element of inter-ethnic relations in a Southeast Asian context, namely, control of resources (Vandergeest 2003; Li 2000, 2001; Peluso 1992). More so than any dimension of inter- and intra-national relations besides, perhaps, national security, resource control has been a concern regulating access to the mechanisms of governance in a mainland Southeast Asian context and also determining how strongly or weakly the state has (tried to) intervene in the lives of the peoples living within its borders.

With that as background, a discussion of the particular nation-building projects of the countries of mainland Southeast Asia begins with the case of Thailand, which was the first state in the region to undergo the transition from kingdom to nation-state.

Thailand

Thailand is distinctive among the states of mainland Southeast Asia in having never been governed by a European power. This is not to say, however, that Thailand escaped the effects of the colonial era. Instead, Thailand experienced what is often referred to as "internal colonialism" with the ruling monarchy adopting many of the policies and conventions common to European colonial rule (Brown 1994), and in the process redefining its relationship with its subjects, especially those most peripheral to the centre of power.

To understand the changes which the (now) Thai state underwent during the colonial and immediately post-colonial periods, it is useful to begin with an examination of the notion of the *muang* and the traditional models of kingship which prevailed in the Tai world before this transformation. The term *muang*, which occurs in some variant in most of the regional languages and has been the preferred form of reference to these polities until quite recently, is defined by Thongchai (1994) as follows:

> *Muang* ... refers broadly to a community, a town, a city, even a country that is, an occupied area under the exercise of a governing power but without specification of size, degree or kind of power, or administrative structure" (p. 49).

Significantly, the *muang* was defined relative to the people it encompassed, rather than the land area (Scott 1998). The Siamese king (like his counterparts in Chiang Mai, Luang Prabang, Sipsongpanna, Siem Reap, etc.) exercised authority over a vast network of feudal lords who, in turn, controlled vassals.[4] From these subjects, the king indirectly extracted taxes, generally in kind payments of rice from lowland farmers and timber and other forest products from upland residents, and corvée labour, which enabled military campaigns and infrastructure projects. Land figured into the calculation of a sovereign's power only indirectly in the sense that its extent and quality helped determine the people's economic production. The uncultivated or agriculturally marginal lands at the extremes of the kingdom populated primarily by tribal peoples were also seen as an asset to the extent that they provided a convenient source of labour and security buffer against invading armies (Jonsson 1998).

The arrival of European colonists in the region changed this calculus entirely. As the Siamese monarch watched the progression of French and

British troops into the areas surrounding his kingdom on either side, he realized that the only way to prevent further encroachment into his kingdom was to lay claim to both the land *and* the people which the Europeans had to that point left unclaimed (Keyes 1997). Pitting the interests of the French and British against one another and playing upon the reluctance of both to come into direct confrontation, the Siamese court managed to negotiate a boundary with the French which lay at the banks of the Mekong River. Negotiations with the British similarly staunched the latter's territorial "incursions" at the Tenasserim Range[5] and to the south at the sultanate of Kedah.[6] These boundaries, established in the early part of the twentieth century, have remained essentially unchanged since, notwithstanding the challenges of ethnic separatism which have erupted at various times in the three provinces of the extreme South (Yala, Pattani and Narathiwat) and with lesser force in the Northeast.[7]

The establishment of well-defined territorial boundaries is but one condition for the establishment of a European-style nation-state, and at the completion of the territorial negotiations, the Thai monarch found himself in control of a state but not a national state (following from Tilly's aforementioned definition). Lacking was any real sense of national identity or any effective means of attaining national integration. To address this void, the government promulgated a new vision of what it meant to be Thai, translated by then King Vijaravudh as "free" but arguably meaning "people of the *muang* (Pinkaew 2003). It was grounded on the three so-called national pillars: *Chaat* (acknowledgement of and identification with the sovereign and indivisible Thai state), *saatsanaa* (officially "religion," but in practice, Buddhism), and *phramahakaset* (subservience to the Siamese monarchy, now referred to as the "Thai king" in recognition of his egalitarian patronage over all the country's citizens). This formulation, which remains at the core of official Thai discourse on national identity (Mulder 1996), proved suitably broad to be accepted by the vast majority of Thailand's two largest non-Siamese groups: The Thai-Lao, whose numbers in fact exceeded those of the Central Thai, and the Thai Yuan or Northern Thai who comprised a smaller fraction of the national population (about one-quarter) but had a stronger sense of regional identity (Brown 1994).

Excluded from Vijaravudh's vision, however, were three distinct minority populations: The southern Muslims, who were excluded most pointedly because of their religion, also because of their non-Tai language and culture;[8] the primarily city-dwelling Chinese; and the so-called "hill tribes" (*chao khao*), a generic term only newly in use at this time

(Pinkaew 2003) which included the Karen, Lawa, Hmong, Lahu, Lisu, Akha, Htin, Khmu, and Yao. These groups were for the most part concentrated in the mountains of the Upper North, at the very threshold of the central state's cognition. Thus while it can be argued that the exclusion of Southern Muslims and even more pointedly, the Chinese, was undertaken deliberately as a means of consolidating the Thai elite's control over commerce and discouraging further Chinese immigration (Keyes 1997; Pinkaew 2003), the exclusion of the upland minorities was likely the product of neglect. They were not so much *excluded* from early state-building efforts as they were "not included".

For those who were included among Thailand's newly anointed "citizens", the rise of the new nationalism meant, most concretely, a dramatic expansion of the government's presence in their lives. The country's highway and telecommunications infrastructures were vastly expanded, facilitating the movement of not only goods and people but also ideas and political directives from Bangkok to outlying areas (Brown 1994). A system of primary schools, offering instruction exclusively in Central Thai (as was now the legal requirement[9]) was established nationwide and staffed by government-trained teachers, and public hospitals and healthcare facilities were created. As a result, for the lowland residents of the kingdom, particularly those residing in rural areas of the North and Northeast, this was therefore an era of tremendous modernization and "Thai-ization" (Pinkaew 2003). By contrast, for the peoples of the uplands, the first half of the twentieth century was largely a period of isolation with the biggest changes resulting from ecological or demographic rather than political forces.[10]

With the close of World War II and more significantly the eruption of the violence which accompanied the withdrawal of occupying troops from both Burma and French Indochina, the Thai state's view of the uplands and its people changed markedly. In the name of national security and on the advice of the American military, the Thai Government moved decisively to secure its borders to prevent communist insurgents from infiltrating the kingdom. Particularly targetted by the government's security measures were groups residing near the country's periphery, in particular the Thai-Lao farmers of the Northeast and the "migratory" hill tribes of the Northern uplands.[11] While both were subjected to military intervention (Brown 1994), the hill tribes were particularly targetted in a two-pronged effort in which the Royal Thai Army and Border Police were sent in to secure the border, thus sealing off a significant avenue of social and economic contact for the upland groups, while the Forestry Department and the

Ministry of the Interior were sent in to investigate and document tribal incursions into "protected" forest areas.[12]

In both these campaigns the Hmong, numerically the most significant of the upper-altitude dwelling minority communities, faired particularly badly (Tapp 1989). They seem to have been singled out as targets by the government for various reasons, among them the fact that they were relatively recent arrivals on the Thai side of the border, although the same could be said of the Lahu and Akha. They were also opium cultivators, a practice which was falling into increasing disfavour throughout this period. Finally, they were seen to be residing in especially ecologically and/or politically sensitive spaces (the two seemed to coincide with remarkable frequency), a trait which again was shared by other groups, but which gained the Hmong particular notoriety (Pinkaew 2003). As tensions grew between the Hmong and the military, the situation erupted into violence, the so-called Red Hmong Rebellion, which was only quelled when the king ordered the army to show restraint.[13] Nevertheless, in the wake of this confrontation, the authorities resolved to undertake a programme of forcible resettlement in which hundreds if not thousands of Hmong families were moved from their upland villages to agriculturally marginal but strategically less sensitive settlements at lower altitudes (Tapp 1989).

With the cessation of aggressions in former Indochina, the Thai Government backed down from its policy of military engagement with the peoples of the uplands, but the thawing of relations between the state and its most peripheral subjects — in most cases, not citizens — was slow in coming. One of the main hurdles to better relations proved to be a new joint initiative between the Thais and Americans, focusing on drug eradication. Opium cultivation was a practice with deep historical roots in the upland regions of Southeast Asia and had long been tolerated by both the traditional monarchies and the colonial administrations.[14] However, with the fall of colonialism and more so, the return of opiate-addicted soldiers from the conflict in Vietnam, the world community's view of the opium trade underwent a sea-change, and the Thai Government responded to international opprobrium by outlawing the sale of opium, an action taken on paper in 1959 but only gaining force on the ground from the early 1970s. Once again the residents of the uplands, and in particular the Hmong, were cast as obstacles to the state's advancement, but in this instance, the corrective took a subtly different form. Rather than simply disciplining the offenders or prosecuting them, the state began a highlands development campaign designed to wean the hill tribes from their "environmentally and socially destructive" practices of swidden culture and opium cultivation through the introduction of improved agriculture and substitute crops. From the perspective of those in the uplands, this new campaign differed little from those which had preceded it. In both cases their livelihood strategies were disrupted and their communities subjected to unwanted and intrusive interventions by the state (Gillogly 2004). At a rhetorical and conceptual level, however, this new campaign *was* different from earlier efforts in that it implicitly recognized the state's obligation for the welfare of the people in the uplands,[15] who were now being referred to with increasing frequency as "ethnic minorities" rather than "hill tribes" (McCaskill 1997).

The rhetoric of "development" and hence inclusion, of minority groups, has in recent years, come to be the dominant discourse of engagement between the Thai state and its most peripheral inhabitants (Gillogly 2004), though in the case of the upland minorities, this embrace has stopped well short of full acceptance. Indeed, full citizenship, the ultimate currency of inclusion in modern society, has consistently been denied to the vast majority of the minority residents of the Thai uplands — this despite numerous campaigns which were ostensibly aimed at facilitating their attainment of this status.[16] State interventions have also fallen short in their efforts to create or even approximate conditions under which highland residents could enjoy an economically viable existence while remaining intact in their communities. Instead, the government's development strategy for its upland minorities has been, and continues to be, to give them the means and incentives to move out of the hills and into the lowland society where they can integrate with the larger nation (Brown 1994). The primary (some might argue, only) real brake on this effort has been the immense revenue boon which the government — and the economy more broadly — has realized through the growth of ecotourism and trekking, an industry dependent on the preservation of at least a fragmentary remnant of the minority communities with their distinctive customs and tribal garb. These most innocuous expressions of ethnic difference are thus tolerated or even encouraged in the state's interactions with upland minorities, while more "problematic" practices like shifting cultivation, an established land use pattern in non-irrigable areas, are being phased out.

It is thus unclear what the ultimate endpoint of Thailand's state-building project will be for the people most removed from the political centre, both geographically and culturally. The fact that this is still an ongoing project is in fact evident by the active debate which has recently surrounded discussions of citizenship for Thailand's upland residents. Significantly, these discussions are no longer confined to the highland communities themselves nor to the government agencies assigned responsibility for "Hill Tribe Affairs". They have made their way into Thai mainstream and have been taken up by political activists who see the welfare of the people in the hills as irrevocably tied to that of politically marginal groups throughout the kingdom (Lyttleton, personal communication, *The Nation* 2005).

At the same time, continuing tensions along the Thai-Myanmar border, including a particularly brutal high profile stand-off between a small group of armed rebels and the Thai military in a hospital in Tak in December 2000, have driven a wedge between the Thai public and upland groups, including the Karen and Lawa, who had long been regarded as examples of "good" minorities who respected the environment and obeyed Thai law. It seems likely that so long as unresolved political and economic tensions within Myanmar perpetuate undocumented migration and illicit trade across this border, the status of border-dwelling population, most of whom are ethnic minorities, will remain somewhat in limbo.

Laos

Despite the striking similarities of their pre-colonial political and social structures, the modern state-building process in Laos transpired quite differently from that of Thailand. For while the Thai state evolved in an almost seamless fashion from the pre-existing pre-colonial monarchy, the Laotian state is, in the minds of most historians, "a construct of the modern period" (Jerndal and Rigg 1998, p. 811) having grown out of the colonial ambitions of French commanders who wished to cement their hold over land holdings on the northeast bank of the Mekong by incorporating it as a distinct territory (Evans 1999; Steinberg, et al. 1985). While a casual reader of history might see little difference between a nation-state created by an indigenous leader's efforts to ward off external territorial claims and one created through the efforts of these external actors to assert such claims, it is a distinction which in the eyes of some nationalist historians (see especially Gunn 1998, drawing on arguments put forward by Katay Sasorith 1953) and regional scholars dictates the very legitimacy of the resultant polities, as Neher (1991) has written:

> Laos might best be described as a quasi-nation, having emerged from maps drawn by European colonists rather than from a sense of territory and nationhood among united people (p. 197).

It is, however, both biased and unfair to conclude that the Lao People's Democratic Republic is something "less than a state" for having arisen relatively recently and on the basis of a deliberate initiative. Indeed, were historical longevity of the state-building process or organic expressions of ethnic sentiment necessary prerequisites for political legitimacy or equal inclusion within the "family of nations", one might question how many of ten members of ASEAN,[17] or for that matter, the 192 members of the United Nations, would actually qualify for inclusion.

Rather, as Evans (1999) has insightfully suggested, the process of state-building in Laos should be seen as a historically path-dependent *alternative* to the "organic" model of state-building which prevailed in continental Europe and was most clearly replicated among Southeast Asian nations in Thailand. Indeed there are, as Evans has enumerated, remarkable parallels between the state-building processes of these two Southeast Asian countries, both of which in the process of modernization effectively re-organized their internal social relations from those of a traditional *muang* to a modern nation-state.[18] As a case study, therefore, Laos poses an interesting contrast to Thailand and — precisely *because* of its more clearly deliberative origins — an important model of the ways in which "majority" populations in Southeast Asia have incorporated "minority" groups in forging a national identity.

The notion of a nation composed of "majority" and "minority" groups is itself a bit of a misnomer in the context of Laos, a state in which the dominant pseudonymous group comprises no more than forty-five per cent[19] of the total population (Evans 1999). Indeed, since the overthrow of the royalists in 1975, the Laotian Government has rejected the use of terms like "majority," "minority," and "indigenous" on the grounds that these terms might be seen to be pejorative or to unfairly privilege certain groups in this society in which there is official equality and unity among groups (Ovesen 2004). Instead, most official government discourse has described the country's ethnic composition with respect to three large sub-populations, namely: "Lao Loum" (lowland Lao), "Lao Theung" (midland or slope Lao) and "Lao Sung" (upland Lao).[20] In this way all Laos' people — except arguably the Vietnamese — are shown to be equally "Lao".

Whatever the message implied by the official discourse, it would be wrong to assume that all members of the Laotian population are equally reflected in the composite "national culture" or that they have been included on equal terms in the nation-building project. It is far from coincidental that the names of the modern nation-state (officially, the Lao Democratic People's Republic) and its people (the Lao or Laotians) correspond so closely[21] to that of the group which has wielded greatest political authority both contemporarily and historically.

In the pre-colonial era the relative power of the ethnic Lao was expressed through the collection of tributary payments from other lowland and, particularly, upland groups — the latter of whom were referred to collectively as *kha* or "subservient ones".[22] The Lao kings also engaged in road-building and other infrastructural projects, though on a much smaller scale than the Khmer, using corveé labour provided by both their Lao and non-Lao subjects (Condominas 1980). However, the relationship which existed among the subjects of the Lao monarchs and between the Lao and other ethnic groups in the period before French colonization did not cohere to our understanding of a nation-state or even proto-nation-state. Tributary relations were not unique — the same subjects were often taxed by multiple overlords, resulting in discontent and even revolts in some instances (Gunn 1998) — nor binding in terms of identity. Furthermore, monarchical control was understood to be associated with the people themselves rather than the land which they inhabited, although the taxation of the products of that land did imply some connection (Reid 1988; Wolters 1982).

The arrival of the French in the late nineteenth century both solidified the Lao's advantage over the other ethnic groups and transformed the understanding of these social and spatial relations. Among the first changes which the French effected in Laos was the introduction of a European notion of territoriality into the relationship between the Lao and Thai — or more accurately, the Lao people residing on the East bank of the Mekong *versus* those on the West — by negotiating a "firm" boundary dividing the region controlled by the Siamese monarch from the French protectorate. Then, over time as the French administrators perceived the need to more sharply divide the Lao from the Thai, they began a campaign designed to instil a "national spirit" among their Lao subjects (Jerndal and Rigg 1998). As part of this effort, they replaced the Annamese functionaries (many of whom had been transferred to Laos from Vietnam to serve in this role) with ethnic Lao, established a rudimentary system of public education and constructed a limited system of roads which linked lowland agricultural regions to markets in Vietnam (Ivarsson 1999). Importantly, however, the

French efforts to create (or revive) a national culture in Laos never extended significantly beyond the lowland populations. The highland peoples were, for the most part, invisible and irrelevant.[23]

There is one interesting and historically significant exception to the general neglect of uplanders during the Franco-Lao state-building period. The Hmong, an upland group from southern China whose arrival in Southeast Asia only slightly predated that of the French, had nevertheless achieved a prominent position in the regional opium trade in that time. Given the centrality of this trade to the colony's finances (Gunn 1990) and the demonstrated willingness of the Hmong to prosecute their interests even to the point of armed rebellion, the French colonial officials not only engaged in direct negotiations with the Hmong (rather than working through Lao intermediaries) but eventually granted them a near-autonomous status within the colony, freeing them from taxation and oversight by lowland overseers.[24] In this sense, the Hmong were arguably the first people in Laos to enjoy a form of self-government defined along ethno-national principles, though these institutions were still contained within the larger governmental structures of French Indochina.

The outbreak of hostilities at the start of World War II marked an important breakpoint in the Lao state-building project.[25] For a period of approximately thirty years while external pressures for national consolidation were at bay, the peoples of Laos more or less fell back into many of the patterns which had characterized their lives in the pre-colonial era. Political and social relations became far more parochial again, and there only the colonial legacy of territorial boundaries and the externally acknowledged sovereignty of the Lao monarch based in Luang Prabang kept the polity from dissolving back into a fragmentary state. However, this interstice of apparent inactivity provided the opportunity for the growth of a new nationalist movement informed not only by the experience of French colonization but also the spread of communism through the region.

The vanguards of this ideology among the Laotians, the Pathet Lao, had both practical and ideological reasons for extending their campaign to the uplands, where local inhabitants who had been (re-)defined as *kha* by the royalists, tended to give the insurgents a sympathetic ear. The Hmong, in particular, having been deprived of their semi-autonomous status through the restitution of the monarchy were often quite willing to lend support to a movement which promised them "liberation" from state taxation and oppression.[26] In moving their campaign into the hills, however, the revolutionaries were forced to confront the ethnic heterogeneity of Laotian society in a manner that prior regimes never had, and the nationalist rhetoric which emerged from the conflict (in which the Pathet Lao ultimately prevailed) was one of inclusion and ethnic balance.

This rhetoric notwithstanding, there have been, and remain, many aspects of the post-communist nation-building project in Laos (a project still very much in progress) that brand it as a "Lao" rather than "Laotian" campaign. Not only is the Lao language the only official language and Lao script the official script (and only language which the government has invested resources to standardize), but Buddhism, a religion practised almost exclusively by lowland Lao (Lao Loum) is the state religion and Lao dress and customs are promoted in the national curriculum (Evans 1999; Ovesen 2004).

Likely more troubling than these symbols of Lao cultural hegemony for most Lao Theung and Lao Sung citizens, however, are the more concrete manifestations of a lowland bias in terms of the way that state development programmes are managed and state resources distributed. The Lao Government, operating within the constraints imposed by the lowest GDP per capita of any country in Southeast Asia, has left many aspects of infrastructural development to the respective provinces which, in turn, have generally opted to create road systems which linked established population centers to international markets, thus by-passing the significant portion of the population (particularly upland peoples) who reside in sparsely populated areas and/or have few resources of value to trade internationally (Jerndal and Rigg 1999). Service delivery, in turn, tends to be confined to the more accessible regions of the country, meaning that those cut off from the highway infrastructure are also deprived of educational and medical services and other social benefits (Lyttleton 2005). They are effectively excluded from participation in the larger economy and society and, not surprisingly, have tended to express their frustrations through participation in vigilante activity such as the hijacking of vehicles travelling on roads traversing remote areas (Gunn 1998).

With the relaxation of communist strictures on trade and the expansion of cross-border trade throughout the Greater Mekong Sub-region (GMS), in which Laos occupies a central position, the road system in Laos has been extended and the access to markets and the consumer goods they offer extended to an ever wider share of Laotian society. But to enjoy the benefits of these improvements, members of traditionally upland-dwelling groups are frequently forced to relocate to lowland areas, a move which comes at substantial physical, psychological and cultural costs, as Lyttleton (2005) has documented. The upland peoples of Laos are thus increasingly faced with a dilemma, whether to become more completely "Lao", meaning to move down from their high altitude communities, take up social and agricultural practices characteristic of their lowland neighbours and, by doing so, reap the benefits of increased access to schools, healthcare, consumer goods and labour markets, or to remain in their traditional enclave communities in the hills where their relative disadvantage is likely to become more pronounced but their cultural and social distinctiveness may remain intact. Whatever their choices as individuals and collectively as a community, the Laos of the future seems likely — whatever the rhetorical position of government authorities on ethnic diversity — to be a country based on a narrower range of ethnic expression integrated more tightly into a national and international community.

Cambodia

Although the overarching structure of the state-building process in Cambodia is not dissimilar (though, unfortunately, a great deal more violent) than that in Laos, the place of minority peoples in this process is quite different and, in this sense, quite instructive. Indeed, with respect to minority experiences, the case of Cambodia occupies a rather idiosyncratic position in the panoply of Southeast Asia. Alone among the upland minority groups of the region, the Cambodian hill tribes or *montegnards* have enjoyed a privileged position in the national consciousness, elevated — at least, rhetorically — to a position on par with or even superior to the majority Khmer (Ovesen and Trankell 2004). Of course, given the small numbers of people involved — estimated at about 100,000 or 0.1 per cent of the total population — and their low visibility even relative to this fraction, it can be argued that this semantic concession has come at almost no cost to the dominant majority and in fact may even have reified their dominant position. Nevertheless, it is interesting to consider how upland "Khmer" may have come to occupy such a celebrated place in the national consciousness.

For most of the period from the fall of the Angkor civilization (1431) through independence, the people occupying the territory now known as Cambodia were under the suzerainty of others (Thai /Siamese, Vietnamese and ultimately, French). Yet the absence of a separate polity does not seem to have been a hindrance to the formation of a well-defined, if somewhat porous[27] definition of "Khmer" identity. The notional sense of the Khmer nation's boundaries, which seems to have predated colonial contact,[28] was given clearest articulation by Prince Norodom Sihanouk following the establishment of the post-colonial Kingdom of Cambodia. His conception of a greater Khmer identity encompassed not only the dominant majority, who comprised about ninety per cent of the population, but also religiously and culturally distinct minorities including, among others, the predominantly Muslim Cham,[29] who were incorporated into the national fabric under the rubric of "Khmer Islam", and the Austronesian-speaking Jarai,[30] who were among the groups collectively known as "Khmer Loeu" or "upland Khmer". Indeed, the prince's vision of the nation extended even beyond the nation-state's borders to include the Khmer-speaking inhabitants of the Mekong delta (in Vietnam) who were designated Khmer Krom ("lowland Khmer") (Collins 1996).

Pointedly excluded from the post-colonial vision of Khmer-ness — and later subject to the political, economic and social consequences of this exclusion — were two minority groups who, both historically and contemporarily, have played a significant role in Cambodian society: The Chinese and the Vietnamese. The presence of both these groups in the area now comprising Cambodia can be traced back to at least the thirteenth century, and their integration into Cambodian society is demonstrated by the participation of the Chinese, in particular, in the religious life of the Buddhist majority, while the Vietnamese had established themselves in the floating villages which lined the Mekong River and Tonle Sap and were thus well integrated into trading networks and the food supply. Both groups were nevertheless classified by Prince Sihanouk and enshrined in law at independence as "foreign residents", and while their legal status has since changed, the popular perception of the Vietnamese, in particular, remains that of untrustworthy "outsiders" (Chheat Sreng 2006).

The decision to draw the boundaries of Khmer-ness so as to include groups located both physically and culturally at the society's margins, while excluding others who were in both senses more central, is in many ways counter-intuitive and thus deserving of further attention. The remainder of this discussion attempts to discern the underlying logic of Cambodian nationalism and in doing so, to elucidate the way in which the Khmer majority — and potentially, other dominant groups in the region — have situated themselves relative to other ethnic groups with which they are in contact.

Ovesen and Trankell (2004) in an excellent examination of the roots of Khmer (and non-Khmer) identity in Cambodia attribute the majority's relatively positive characterization of the upland minorities to the society's obsession with its historic roots in Angkor. The consequences of this reification of a (by necessity) agrarian past is a tendency to lionize those cultures based around the cultivation of (preferably, paddy) rice and conversely, a suspicion of those engaged in commerce or other urban-centred enterprises. This prejudice, they claim, was played out in a macabre way through the Khmer Rouge's persecution of urban residents and intellectuals among whom the Vietnamese and Chinese figured disproportionately. The Vietnamese were also specifically targetted for abuse because of the long history of conflict along the Vietnamese-Khmer border and the recurrent occupation of portions of "Khmer" territory by the Vietnamese.

By contrast to the experiences of the Chinese and Vietnamese minorities, the majority Khmers' rural bias worked overwhelmingly to the advantage of the upland groups who "represented the Khmer ideal of purity because they were the least contaminated by foreign influences" (Ovesen and Tankell 2004, p. 248). So, ironically, the very technological "backwardness" and isolation which in other national contexts has made upland peoples the target of ridicule and exclusion, worked to their political benefit in modern Cambodia.

Having said this, the experience of being incorporated into the Cambodia state has been far from painless for the upland minorities — or any minority groups in this country. While the Pol Pot government rhetorically lauded the upland groups for their simplicity and freedom from outside "contamination", it also expected members of these groups to conform to the same cultural practices which would mark them as members of the national whole. There have thus been pressures applied to the minority groups to adopt Khmer language and dress — traditional costumes have all but vanished except for special "cultural presentations", which are now as likely to be carried out by ethnic Khmer in tourist venues such as the "Cambodian Cultural Village"[31] outside Siem Reap. The animist groups in the hills, who comprise a majority in these areas, have also been "encouraged" to forsake such "extravagant" and "barbaric" practices as animal sacrifices which have been a mainstay of community ritual life (Bourdier 1996). Even the "primitive" agricultural practices which first endeared the hill peoples to their lowland neighbours, have come under assault with the rise of a new "environmental consciousness" which has identified swidden rice cultivation as an ecologically destructive practice and sought to replace it with more sustainable (if not better adapted) forms of horticulture.

Vietnam

While the discussion to this point and, indeed, the very structure of this chapter has tended to treat the upland minorities of the mainland Southeast Asia region as an undifferentiated and conceptually unified group within each national context, it is only in Vietnam that the upland peoples themselves have forged such a united identity and sense of common purpose *vis-à-vis* the state. The emergence of a common "Montagnard" ("hill people") identity among Vietnam's highland minorities, who together constitute about eight per cent of the national population (Michaud 1996), like the creation of a national consciousness among the country's lowland population was in large part the product of the Vietnamese peoples' long and complex relationship with various outside groups which at different points in time took an interest in these peoples and their land.

While the origins of most, if not all, of the dominant majorities in mainland Southeast Asia are believed to lie in ancestral homelands beyond the region,[32] the movement of the Kinh or Viet people, from southern China and the Red River valley in the far north of contemporary Vietnam down through the coastal plains to the Mekong delta, figures more prominently in the contemporary consciousness of the Vietnamese than it does in other countries of the region. This is probably because the displacement of the Austronesian and Mon-Khmer peoples — in particular, the Cham and Khmer Krom — who once dominated the Central and Southern Vietnamese lowlands was somewhat more recent than the other major population movements in the region. In addition, the Kinh's progression towards the Mekong delta echoed a well established trop in Vietnamese history, that of invaders from the North overcoming populations to the South.

Indeed, for more than a thousand years, the majority of the areas which is now Vietnam was governed as a remote province of China. The incorporation of North and Central Vietnam into the Chinese empire was so complete that by the time the Chinese forces were decisively routed the Vietnamese had themselves adopted such characteristically Chinese features as a strongly Mahayana-influenced form of Buddhism (as compared to the

Theravada Buddhism practised elsewhere in the region), a Confucian social order (complete with an annual examination to enter government service), a system of writing derived from Chinese characters (Nom) and a system of terraced agriculture with complex irrigation systems also more characteristic of Southern China (and its social organization) than of other parts of mainland Southeast Asia (Keyes 1995). As such, the Vietnamese were by the fourteenth century, already quite distinct from the peoples residing to their south and west in the area which Coedès (1968) famously referred to as the "Indianized states of Southeast Asia", and these cultural and historical differences were arguably sufficient to have given rise to some sense of "boundedness" which lay at the heart of the pre-colonial Vietnamese consciousness. As Woodside (1979) has noted, the traditional Vietnamese elite saw themselves as "the cultural cynosures of a society surrounded by subversive barbarians" (quoted in Keyes 1995, p. 193).

Given the comparatively late movement of the Kinh themselves into the region and the states' relatively recent separation from the multi-ethnic Chinese empire, it is unsurprising that the pre-colonial Vietnamese polities were ethnically diverse. All three of the ruling dynasties — the Lê in Central Vietnam, the Trinh in the North and the Nguyên in the South — governed populations which included a substantial number of non-Kinh. In particular, there was a large and distinct ethnic Chinese population, whom the Vietnamese referred to as Hoa, spread across the three kingdoms but concentrated predominantly in urban areas and trading centres within each region (Châu 2004). In addition, pockets of Cham and Khmer Krom remained in the Centre and South, respectively (Keyes 1995). Finally, living on the periphery of the kingdoms were the forty or more upland groups to whom the Kinh referred collectively to in a derogatory fashion as *moi* ("savages"). The *moi* paid tribute to the rulers, sometimes in the context of somewhat ritualized displays of subjugation (Keyes 1995, Woodside 1971), but were in other respects all but invisible to the peoples of the lowlands, as evinced by their glaring absence from contemporary Vietnamese and Chinese historical accounts (Michaud 1996).

Initially the arrival of the French colonists did little to change status of the Montagnards or "mountain people", as the upland peoples were known to the French. The resident system of indirect rule meant that the Montagnards had little if any direct contact with the colonists and remained at the periphery of the state's consciousness. This changed, however, in the period following the expansion of France's territorial holdings to include the region to the north and west of mountains, namely Laos and Cambodia.

Recast in the context of a larger "French Indochina", the Vietnamese highlands were suddenly seen as "central" (Christie 1996), a designation which has ironically outlived the colonial project itself. In any case, from the last years of the nineteenth century to the outbreak of World War II, the upland regions of Indochina, and Vietnam in particular, came into administrative focus as they never had before.

One can only imagine that an increase in state attention would have been perceived as, at best, a mixed blessing by the upland peoples whose interactions with the lowland state to date had been premised on violent and compulsion (Woodside 1971; Christie 1996). But the French, who were wary of setting off a(nother) revolt in the highlands[33] and desirous of establishing trade relations with local opium producers (Michaud 1996), tried to achieve "pacification" of the highlands by peaceful means, building relations with the local tribal leaders and extending basic social services such as education and healthcare to at least some of the mountainous communities, especially around Darlac (Christie 1996). Missionary efforts in the region also increased, resulting in the first serious attempts to document the local languages and codify tribal laws (Michaud 1996). A precedent was thus established for winning over the Montagnards through persuasion rather than coercion, and this legacy of French rule persisted, to some degree, beyond the colonial period.

This is not to say that early efforts to more fully incorporate the uplands and its people into the larger polity were entirely sanguine. Not only did increased French interest in and control over the upland areas result in increased efficiency of taxation and heightened demands for corvèe labour (which to that point many Montagnard groups had escaped), it also led to a vast expansion of the transportation and communications infrastructure which linked the uplands to the coast. This development, coupled with the introduction of plantation agriculture and forestry, which redefined the "marginal" slope areas as economically desirable, led a dramatic rise in the migration of Kinh settlers to the hills, a trend which continues to this day (Christie 1996). Political inclusion thus quickly translated to greater physical inclusion in the Vietnamese polity and the erosion of the geographic barriers which had separated the Montagnards from the Kinh.

The French colonial project in Southeast Asia was dealt a death-blow by the onset of World War II. While the French attempted to reassert their control over the region following the withdrawal of Japanese forces, they never again exercised effective control over the territory.

Nevertheless, their actions in the twilight period of their administration, specifically the period from 1946–54, were again decisive in setting the tone of highland-lowland relations in Vietnam. In an ironic twist of fate, the French — who had always feared that the uplands could become a hotbed of resistance to colonial rule — deliberately fostered a rift between the Montagnards and the lowland nationalists. They oversaw the creation of a semi-autonomous territory (which they themselves conveniently co-administered) encompassing a significant portion of the upland region and installed Montagnards there as low-level functionaries (a level of political incorporation thus far unprecedented). They also trained members of the Hré minority as a guerilla force whom they deployed to counter Viet-Minh (nationalist) advances on French holdings. The nationalists, for their part, countered the French efforts by trying to persuade the Montagnards to unite with other "Vietnamese nationalities" against the French. They too succeeded in building a network of supporters in the highlands, a move seen as increasingly central to maintaining a political and military hold over Vietnam.

The implementation of distinct policies governing affairs in the upland regions might have served as a force distancing rather than integrating the Montagnards into the affairs of the Vietnamese state — as such policies, in fact did in Laos, where the semi-autonomous status granted to the Hmong later served to sever them from the Pathet Lao's post-independence nation-building project — but historical circumstances conspired to avoid this development in Vietnam. As nationalist forces among the Vietnamese themselves evolved into anti-French sentiment (a development which never transpired among the Lao), a battle for the "hearts and minds" of the upland peoples — who had again come to be defined as a strategically pivotal group — grew up between the opposing factions and when this happened, there grew among the Montegnards themselves an awareness of their political potential. Efforts began, mainly among Montegnard leaders who had fled into Cambodia, to organize an inter-ethnic coalition (FULRO) which could serve as an advocate on behalf of the various upland communities (Christie 1996). However, this movement was eventually swept up by larger political forces and the minority communities, through the collaborative alliances endorsed by their community leaders increasingly found their fates bound up with the fate of the communist forces, which came to see the highlands as a secure and strategic base from which to launch assaults on the nationalist strongholds along the coast.

During the period of the Indochinese wars, Montagnard communities suffered bitterly as a result of this alliance. Their losses, both in terms of casualties suffered as well as economic devastation to the region, were vastly disproportionate to their numbers or the degree of their actual commitment of forces. However, with the VCP's victory in 1976 it seemed that their gamble had paid off. The newly installed communist regime promulgated a constitution which for the first time guaranteed the country's citizens — among whom the upland populations were to be considered equals — access to state services including education, healthcare and enfranchisement. It also offered them protections such as the right to maintain their local languages, to select their own leaders and govern their communities according to traditional norms and customs — these were the protections enshrined in the constitution, but in practice the experience of independence and participation in a broader national community has been somewhat more mixed for most of Vietnam's upland minority peoples.

Although the constitutional protections and the shared wartime experienced which motivated and animated them did result in minority races being incorporated into the society and its governance to a much fuller extent than had ever been the case in the past,[34] they have also found themselves subject to many of the same social and economic impediments faced by other residents of distant, resource-poor areas. As the national economy has expanded and become more competitive and their opportunities to participate in it from their marginal perch have become increasingly impoverished by comparison (Christie 1996). There have also been encumbrances which are specific to minority communities. For example, while the state has guaranteed them the right to pursue traditional "cultural" or "social" practices, other aspects of traditional life deemed to be predominantly "economic" in nature or to have "environmental" implications have come under assault. Swidden agriculture and other indigenous approaches to managing forest resources have been deemed "unproductive" or "degrading" of the resource base, and the traditional long-house based social structure of the Austronesian groups, has been termed "backward" or detrimental to socialist values and so replaced by individual dwelling units — all under the rhetoric of effecting "national development" and "improvement" of the Montagnards and the lands they have traditionally inhabited (McElwee 2004).

As an interesting contemporary footnote highlighting the extent to which nation-building is an ongoing project, particularly in the more peripheral areas of the Southeast Asia region, a movement is now afoot within many upland communities in Vietnam to resist some of the more unpalatable aspects of national integration. Politicians representing minority communities have advocated for the national government to make good on its as yet unfulfilled promises of extending healthcare and educational facilities in equal measure to upland communities and to see to it that the latter are supportive of education in both the national and local tongues (McElwee 2004). More ominously, there have been instances of armed uprisings in some of the minority communities in which usurpation of land and other resources by Kinh settlers have been especially intense. The Vietnamese Government has responded cautiously to these expressions of unrest, quelling the violence, forcibly, in most instances, but at the same time providing greater surveillance of immigrant activity and granting requests for additional government services and protections.

Myanmar

Much of the story of state-building in Myanmar seems to have been excerpted from the experiences of the other countries in the region. But where ethnic difference, and in particular, tensions between "majority" and "minority" groups have exerted a comparatively minor or intermittent impact on the development of state-society relations as a whole in other mainland Southeast Asian countries, this impact has been greatly amplified in the case of Myanmar where the proportion of "minority" members in the population is larger than that of any country in the region other than Laos.[35] The divisive effect of ethnic diversity is a rather ironic outcome of Myanmar's history if one regards, in particular, the role which ethnicity played — or perhaps more accurately, failed to play — in the early years of the society's development. But as was the case in every country in the region which underwent a period of colonial subjugation, the experience of living under a foreign power which had little vested interest in the local implications of its policies (Taylor 1987), had a profoundly disruptive and, in Myanmar's case at least, destructive effect on the cohesion of the polity resulting in a contemporary political and social climate too often characterized by disunity.

Early archeological evidence suggests that the Burmans likely migrated to their present location from some indeterminate point of origin to the north — much as the Siamese, Lao, Khmer and Kinh peoples came to settle in their current locations. Unlike many of these "majority" groups (the Khmer and Kinh most pointedly), however, the Burman did not, in the course of their migration south, simply drive off the peoples who had previously resided in the lowland plains and deltas but rather, established a civilization which existed alongside some of these groups, the Mon and Rakhine being the clearest examples of other peoples whose civilizations co-existed with the Burmans in a relationship which was at times antagonistic and competitive, but in other instances cooperative and integrative.[36] Indeed, by the time that Alaunghpaya established the Konbaung dynasty in 1752, the lowlands of what is now Myanmar seem to have become, culturally speaking,[37] an ethnically variegated but essentially unified area the boundaries of which were defined in the minds of the inhabitants (and those with whom they had recurrent interactions) by a social organization based around wet-rice agriculture and a similar interpretation of Theravada Buddhism (Lehman 1967; Silverstein 1997; Landé 1999).

The political influence of the Konbaung monarchs, like that of many of the lowland political elite who had preceded them, extended beyond this cultural zone into the uplands, a region characterized by a greater diversity of agricultural practices (mostly forms of swidden cultivation but also different forms of dry-land agriculture and forest-based resource management), belief systems (an array of ancestral and animist beliefs as well as forms of Buddhism which differed significantly from those of the plains), and languages.[38] The societies of these upland areas tended to be organized around more localized communities and lineage groups but maintained tributary relationships with the kingdoms of the plains — not only those of the Burmans (or Mon or Rakhine) but also the Siamese, Yuan (northern Thai, whose kingdoms included Lanna and Haripunchai), Yunnanese Chinese (in Sipsongpanna), and Lao (Luang Prabang). There is furthermore evidence of significant political interplay and intrigue among the upland groups and between them and the lowland rulers, who depended on the upland peoples to supply manpower and provide a strategic buffer, particular in times of elevated tension between peoples based in what is now Myanmar and those in contemporary Thailand (Jonsson 2001). As such, the upland peoples, tributary payments notwithstanding, were never understood to "belong" to any of the lowland kingdoms, but rather, to occupy a distinct political and cultural space in the traditional worldview (Leach 1954).

Of course, the European model of territorially bounded states and peoples, which the British carried with them when they arrived in the early 1800s, did not admit to the possibility of a politically or socially "unbounded" space of this nature. Hence the dawn of the colonial era, brought about for the people of Myanmar through the invasion of British forces based in India, signalled the end of the traditional set of relationships. That said, especially for those residing furthest from the point of initial penetration, the transformation of traditional relationships occurred sporadically and incompletely. Indeed, the British annexation of Myanmar was itself a staged and conceptually staggered project, which Smith (1999) has succinctly described as "unpremeditated". It was not with the hopes of achieving significant political or economic gains that the British forces first invaded the land which they knew as Burma — though both of these explanations were later invoked to explain the extension and expansion of their campaigns (Tarling 2001). Rather, the colonial army was first sent across the Irrawaddy from British India to put an end to armed incursions by Burmese troops (Silverstein 1997). Having first occupied Arakan and Tenasserim and subsequently all of Lower Burma, the British forces found themselves enmeshed in a protracted campaign to put down resistance which arose insidiously throughout the region (Aung-Thwin 1985). As time dragged on, the British commanders found themselves in the *de facto* position of having to make policy for the territory, a problem which they solved initially by simply treating their newly acquired holdings as an extension of their Indian holdings (for which they truly had colonial ambitions) (Taylor 1987; Tarling 2001).

One can only speculate on how Myanmar's state-building process might have progressed had the British influence in the region been limited to the role they assumed in this early period. Tarling (2001) has presented documents suggesting that at least within the colonial administration there had been floated the idea of occupying the lowlands while allowing the uplands — which remained "unpacified" throughout the 1800s and in some instances essentially never fell completely within the control of the colonial regime — to exist as a "buffer zone" separating the British holdings in India from the French holdings in Indochina (a role which Thailand was later to assume). In any case, the actual method by which the British occupied and administered the area which they came to refer to as "Ministerial Burma" or "Burma Proper", that is, the alluvial plains and delta region, was consistent with the forms of colonial administration which in other parts of the region gave rise to indigenous notions of nationhood and a sense of national identity consistent with a nation-state model (one need look no further than Laos to see how this transpired even under circumstances where such ideas were entirely absent in the pre-colonial era). There was, for example, a centralization of power in the hands of the authorities, which in the case of Myanmar meant, unfortunately the centralization of power in the hands of a largely imported class of Indian bureaucrats but nevertheless required that the administrative mechanisms of taxation, administration, juridical proceedings, etc. be established and extended even to rural communities.[39]

There were also economic developments which accompanied the imposition of the colonial project in lowland Myanmar. The delta region, once a comparative backwater, was transformed into a thriving agricultural zone producing rice for export to India and other parts of Asia and, following completion of the Suez Canal, also Europe and the Middle East (Tarling 2001). Infrastructure was developed including roadways, rail lines and oil pipelines, all of which also served over time to connect the lowlands to the uplands, but which were more effective conduits for moving people and goods within the lowland areas themselves. Finally, there was significant investment in the construction of social institutions such as hospitals and schools,[40] with public education, in both English and Burmese, made available to children throughout much of the lowlands (Silverstein 1998). While the level of educational development, in particular, was never on par with that of British India, it was nevertheless sufficient to give rise to the next generation of Burmese intellectuals and political elite who were eventually to replace the British as the state's decision-makers (Silverstein 1960; Taylor 1987).

If this was the experience of colonialism for the peoples of lowland Myanmar, the experience of the peoples in the uplands, an area which the British referred to as "Frontier Burma" or the "Excluded Areas", was dramatically different. The British, who were reluctant administrators of Ministerial Burma, had even fewer ambitions (at least at first) for the Frontier. This area was essentially "inherited" from King Thibaw, the last Konbaung monarch, when he was deposed in 1885 — as tributaries, a position consistent with the British understanding that they were to assume a position as the new "monarchs" of Burma. In fact, it is unclear that most Myanmarese, whatever their place of residence or ethnicity, ever bought into this notion of British authority (Taylor 1987; Aung-Thwin 1985). But certainly among the upland communities, who had traditionally manipulated their relationships with lowland powers in such a way as to maximize their own position and advantage (Jonsson 2001), the transferal of allegiance was far from automatic. Rather, almost from the outset, some of the larger and better organized of the upland communities, the Shan being a prime example, began bargaining with the British authorities, agreeing to cede certain resources and refrain from forming cross-border alliances with the Siamese in exchange for recognition of the localized authority of their traditional leaders, the *sawbwas* (a set of terms which was, in fact, granted). Over time the British came to conclude similar agreements with many of the upland communities, relegating themselves to a position of indirect authority in exchange for a promised end to hostilities,[41] resource concessions, especially for gems and timber, and other forms of tribute or labour, resembling those of the pre-colonial period. Within upland communities then, social and political relations remained somewhat more intact, when compared to the pre-colonial period, than they had been in the lowland areas. However, the relationship between lowland and upland communities was cast in entirely different terms — now as a contractual, rather than personalized tributary relationship (Aung-Thwin 1985; Taylor 1987).

Importantly, too, since the British with their passion for classification and order, understood themselves to have negotiated these political relationships with the official or, at least, officially acknowledged spokespersons for each of the ethnic groups to whom they understood specific upland regions to "belong" (building on the nation-state model under which territories pertained fully and uniquely to a distinct "nation" which resided in that area), they sub-divided Frontier Burma into distinct ethnic "states" each of which was assigned to a specific ethnic group (Chin, Kachin, Kayah, Mon, Karen, Shan, Rakhine). Whether the decision to refer to these distinct regions as "states" rather than "divisions", the term used to refer to administrative subunits in Burma Proper, was consciously intended to imply this sort of nation-state assignment, or whether that idea instead grew up in the wake of subsequent political developments, it has nevertheless imparted to these internal boundaries a level of sensitivity and political salience disproportionate to the somewhat arbitrary fashion in which they were drawn.

Just as the colonial project had economic implications for the lowland populations of Myanmar, the imposition of British control and, in particular, British commercial ventures in the uplands, had significant implications for the ways in which these regions were developed. The primary focus of British attention in Myanmar's periphery was its vast timber reserves which concessionaires began harvesting rapaciously almost as soon as claims had been made to the territory (Tarling 2001). The extraction of the timber, and also the gems which were being mined further north, required large numbers of workers comprising a mix of upland natives, lowland Burmans and imported Indian labourers, as well as infrastructural projects such as the construction of roads, bridges, railway linkages from Mandalay to Myitkyina and, on a more localized basis, timber camps. The hills were thus no more an isolated backwater.

Related to this, there was another change that went on in Frontier Burma that had parallels in upland areas of French Indochina but not in the lowlands, namely, the rapid growth of Christian missionary activity targetting the "oppressed minorities".[42] The preachers cum teachers and in some cases, scholars, who infused even quite remote regions of the uplands, brought with them not only religions teachings but also support for education — often in local languages which they helped codify for the first time — and the chance to participate conceptually and sometimes literally in a global community of like-minded believers, an unprecedented experience for individuals who had always been located (even in their own minds) on society's periphery (Lehman n.d.). They can thus be credited with helping lay the seeds of the imagined national communities which would sprout forth from these ethnic enclaves (Taylor 2005).

The outbreak of World War II is credited with bringing about the end of British colonial rule in Myanmar, and indeed it was Japanese forces who routed the British from their colony. However, while the Japanese invasion was, in other parts of Southeast Asia, essentially a global drama played out on local soil, in Myanmar, it was an expression of the society's own fracturing. The disparities which existed within colonial Burma, not only between the uplands and the lowlands, but also between different ethnic, political, and social factions within each region were, by the 1930s, coming to be expressed in the form of organized violence directed not only at the British authorities but also the groups whom the British rule had favoured, namely, the Indians and the Karen who unlike other ethnic groups, were permitted to serve in the army and hold preferred government positions (Smith 1999).[43] Unsurprisingly, then, when the advance of Japanese forces through the Asia-Pacific began to threaten the European powers' hold over their territories there, the peoples of Myanmar were of various minds as to whether this was a positive or negative development. As it happened, when the Japanese actually arrived at Myanmar's borders, it was Burmese nationalist forces under the leadership of the charismatic General Aung San who escorted them in, overpowering other Burmese and Indian forces who remained loyal to the British. As an indication of just how volatile sympathies and alliances were in this period however, it was also General Aung San (now leading a somewhat different alliance) who three years later led the campaign to drive the Japanese out of Burma (Steinberg, et al. 1970).

Far from being a transient interlude in the colonial project, the war proved the breaking point of British hegemony over Burma (Silverstein 1960; Taylor 1987), not only laying waste to significant proportions of the infrastructure which the British had established, but also throwing open the question of how the country would be governed, what territory would be included and what the involvement of the local peoples would be in governmental institutions. Although these queries were first expressed in relation to the prospect of continued (renewed) British involvement in the colony (an option which was quickly removed from the table), these issues in fact became the impassable morass in which nationalist debates in the country would founder for the two decades which followed. Attempts were made to build broad consensus by structuring the definitional elements of the proposed union in minimalist terms, essentially reducing the terms of belonging to the following principles:

1. The unity of Myanmar's people and integrity of its territory;
2. The right of the country's various constituent groups to express their ethnic, cultural and religious differences;
3. Equality for all the state's ethnic groups.

Inoffensive as these terms may appear to an outside observer, they proved highly contentious for those involved in the process, especially as these broad principles came to be translated into actual policy statements.[44]

As the debate dragged on and the various parties grew increasingly fractious and disenchanted with the process, the theme of ethnicity began to emerge ever more pronouncedly in the discussions. This is perhaps an unsurprising development given the significance which ethnicity had been assigned under the colonial regime. However, the implications of mapping ethnicity onto territory and political alignments were less pronounced in an era when *all* ethnicities and territories were essentially subjugated beneath the colonial regime (Taylor 1987). Now in the post-independence era, it was potentially the right of a given ethnicity/territory/political faction to pull out of the discussions and succeed from the union — a course of action which was threatened almost from the start. However, in adopting this stance a national/territorial/factional spokesperson was now making a statement which had significant political and economic ramifications for persons who did not necessarily share all these affiliations in common. Indeed, never was the fallacy of the British administration designations clearer than in the post-independence era when it became clear that not only were all the persons residing in, for example, the Chin state, not necessarily Chin, but that Chin-ness itself was not a unitary, well-defined characteristic with unambiguous political implications. One might go so far as to state that in the two decades following the end of World War II the peoples of Myanmar, and in particular, those residing in the country's periphery, were suddenly vaulted from a quasi-feudal era through the modern age and directly into a condition of post-modernity.

The disunifying forces within Myanmar society, which in the decades following World War II had also had disastrous consequences for Myanmar's economy, reached their pinnacle in the early 1960s when the complete dissolution of the union seemed an imminent possibility. Stepping into the breach, as they had in many states in the region during periods of (perceived) crisis or political uncertainty, was the military — in this case the so-called Revolutionary Council under the leadership of General Ne Win. Where the provisional governments which had preceded the Revolutionary Council had attempted, however ineffectively, to draw the country together by consensus and the articulation of loosely defined terms of affiliation, the military regime took the opposite approach, attempting to impose order through force. Administrative control was centralized within the regime itself, thus reversing the trend among previous post-independence governments towards recognition of regional authorities and devolution of control. There was furthermore a nationalization of productive assets, which included not only the manufacturing and agricultural apparatus of the lowland areas, but also the natural resources of the upland areas.

Unsurprisingly, these changes were met with fierce resistance, including both acts of passive defiance amongst the rice producers in the fertile delta region and armed uprisings in many of the border regions whose ties to the union had become progressively frayed in the years leading up to the military coup. Not just one but multiple administrative bodies, each claiming legitimacy within a specific territory or on behalf of a specific people, sprang up throughout the areas populated predominantly by ethnic minorities. As a result much of the country's periphery quickly became a "no-go zone" for government personnel, including not only military forces but also bureaucrats and civil servants who might otherwise have been extending basic services or ensuring administrative access in these regions. They remained a part of the union only to the extent that the government continued to prosecute its claims over these lands and peoples, and to employ military force to seek to retain and, indeed, reintegrate them. In the absence of an agreed upon basis for peaceful, productive cooperation among Myanmar's people, conflict thus came to be defined as the currency by which the country's various constituent elements retained some degree of engagement with one another.

Surprisingly in the last few years since around 2000, the armed conflicts which had come to define the primary linkages between Myanmar's centre and much of its periphery in the past four decades have abated, with ceasefire agreements having been concluded in most, although not all, areas of conflict. That said, the state-building project in Myanmar is clearly far from complete. The ongoing National Convention, convened in 2005 and still unresolved, is but the latest in a series of attempts to define "Burmese-ness" or "Myanmar-ness" in terms which are minimally acceptable to enough of the country's citizens to allow other aspects of the state-building project to carry on. For in the years when armed struggle has consumed the bulk of the collective resources and collective efforts of the country and its peoples, other aspects of state-building have not gone on. Not only is there still no consensus on what it means to be Myanmarese, but in much of the country, there is no functioning school system in which this ideology could be perpetuated if consensus were reached. The physical infrastructure needed to connect the country's citizens to one another and to encourage them to develop markets more strongly linked to the country's interior than to the countries that border it, is lacking in many areas, as are a functional system of finance and banking, or such vehicles for building political legitimacy as a healthcare system or comprehensive set of social and legal protections. Many of these challenges are shared by Myanmar's neighbours, especially those countries whose financial resources are most limited and infrastructural capacity most skeletal. So, there is in the region a community of countries struggling with more of less similar issues. However, these similarities remain largely irrelevant so long as Myanmar's people remain at odds in defining the boundaries of their own belonged-ness.

Notes

1. In the context of this paper the term "majority" will be used to refer to the dominant ethnic group within each of the eponymous states of the region, irrespective of the actual proportion of the national population which they represent. All other groups in the country will be referred to as "minorities".

2. Gellner captures the gap between the rhetoric and reality of "nationalism" when he defines it as "a theory of political legitimacy which requires that ethnic boundaries should not cut across political ones and, in particular that ethnic boundaries within a given state — a contingency already excluded by the principle in its general formulation — should not separate the power-holders from the rest" (1983, p. 1). The complexities inherent in constructing world system around nationalist principals became evident during the division of Europe itself into nation-states. Most innocuous among these "problems" was the persistence of multi-ethnic states such as Belgium and Switzerland in which groups with different languages or cultures could not — or did not desire to be — separated politically. Of greater consequence has been the plight of minority groups in Europe who were either geographically dispersed (for example, Jews and Romanies or gypsies) or distributed across established nation-state boundaries (for example, the Basques in France and Spain and the Irish in Great Britain) and thus not granted their own sovereign territory.

3. Many scholars of nationalism (Connor 1994; Eriksen 1993; Smith 1996) and most nationalist movements stress the centrality of a shared culture to national identity, and this becomes the basis of the claim of various peoples to "deserve such 'national' states as a matter of right" (Calhoun 1993, p. 217). Tilly (1990) makes a cross-cutting argument by distinguishing rhetorically, but not in degree of legitimacy, between nation-states, which have such a shared linguistic and cultural heritage, and "national states" which Calhoun summarizes as those which "attempt to extend direct rule to their entire populations and expand their capacity to organize the lives of the members of those populations, whether for purposes of warfare of economic development" (1993, p. 217).

4. It should be pointed out that in this system the monarch's control was neither absolute nor necessarily exclusive. He could press his demands only to the extent that his underlords or their subjects conceded to meet his demands, and his subjects — especially those at greater distance from the centres of power — might well be paying tribute to more than one monarch simultaneously (Raendchen 2004).

5. From the perspective of the Siamese court both of these negotiations involved the renunciation of tributary claims. To the French were ceded principalities in the vicinity of Luang Prabang and other areas on the East bank of the Mekhong. To the British were given the Malay sultanates of Trengganu, Kedah and Kelantan (but significantly, not Pattani) as well as a small population of Thai-speakers, living on the western side of the Tenasserim range.

6. An extended discussion of the process of defining and negotiating Thailand's national boundaries can be found in Thongchai (1994).

7. An excellent discussion of separatist politics in Northeastern Thailand can be found in Raendchen (2004).

8. The majority population in Thailand's three southernmost provinces of Thailand (Yala, Pattani and Naratiwat) are ethnically Malay and speak a Malay dialect.
9. Vajiravudh's reforms outlawed the use of languages other than Central Thai in schools, the media or other publications, and the conduct of "official" business (that is, in courts, hospitals, district offices, etc.).
10. The first half of the twentieth century was likely a period of significant population growth in the Thai uplands due to the migration of high altitude dwelling tribal groups (Hmong, Lahu, Lisu and Akha) from southern China, Laos and Burma and the movement of landless peasants from the Northern lowlands to mid-altitude slopes (Michaud 2000).
11. It is interesting to note that certain "hill tribe" groups, most pointedly the Karen and Lawa were explicitly excluded from the military's containment efforts during this period. Pinkaew (2003) suggests that this was because of their more sedentary settlement and cultivation practices which rendered them "civilized" in the eyes of the Thai state.
12. Note, the "forested" areas of Thailand were brought under royal protection during the 1960s and 1970s through a series of cadastral surveys which were used to demarcate land, purportedly on the basis of certain ecological and topographical conditions. These surveys had the effect of progressively excluding the traditional forest-dwellers or cultivators from areas to which they had historically had access while effectively opening the land to commercial forestry and plantation crops (Vandergeest 2003).
13. Ironically, the hostilities between the Hmong and the Thai military, referred to as the Red Hmong Revolt, appeared to have less to do with anti-state or communist sympathies than with resentment at the state's intrusion on the Hmong opium trade (Cooper 1979).
14. To say that the colonial states "tolerated" opium is, in fact, an understatement. For many years, most of the colonial administrations maintained a lucrative monopoly over the sale of opium in their respective domains, as did the Thai state (Renard 1997).
15. My point here is not that the highland development efforts of this period were motivated primarily by a desire to ensure the well-being of the upland minorities. It was clearly a concern for the indirect effects of opium production and upland forestry practices on lowland residents that spurred the government's actions. But, it is significant in my mind that the avenue selected for achieving these goals was one that tacitly acknowledged the social and economic needs of upland populations, as well.
16. Successive waves of registration and documentation efforts have created a patchwork legal framework in which persons of minority origin (indeed, even members of the same community or family) might be arbitrarily assigned any of more than a dozen legal statuses, many of which abridge their rights

     to travel within or beyond the kingdom, restrict their access to education and health care and deny them political representation. A more detailed discussion of this issue can be found in Toyota (2004).

17. The Association of Southeast Asian Nations whose members include Brunei, Cambodia, Indonesia, Laos, Malaysia, Myanmar, Philippines, Singapore, Thailand, and Vietnam.

18. Evans comments that whereas in Thailand the transition was made "first by constructing a form of absolutist state which then made the transition to a modern state", in Laos "this transition was overseen by colonialism" (1999, p. 23).

19. The oft-cited (and politically convenient) proportion of 55 per cent is based on an estimate of the total "Lao Loum" or "lowland Lao" population of the country. However, this classification includes not only Lao but also Phuan, Lue, Tai and other Lao-Thai peoples (Ovesen 2004).

20. This three-fold division of Laos constituent ethnicities came into official usage with the rise of the communist authorities and was employed consistently until 2002 when the government suddenly broke with this classification scheme claiming that it was promoting an "incorrect" understanding of the country's different ethnic groups. Official documents and discourse now refer to each of the 60 to 80 identified ethnic groups separately, a move which Chamberlain and colleagues (quoted in Ovesen 2004) claim is intended to splinter the Lao Theung and Lao Sung politically.

21. Note, in English it is correct to use the term "Lao" to refer either to the to the speakers of the Lao language or the citizens of Laos (independent of language/ ethnicity). Many politicians and authors, however, will preferentially use the alternative term "Laotian" when referring specifically to the political identity. In Lao, the terms for the people (*khon Lao*) and the country (*Pathet Lao*) are identical.

22. The term *kha* has frequently been translated as "slaves" but Ovesen (2004) has convincingly argued against this understanding of the term, which is nevertheless clearly derogatory.

23. "Irrelevant" in the sense that the whole purpose of the nationalist project in Laos was to more closely bind the Lao to the French and divide them from the ethnic Lao residing on the Thai side of the border (Evans 1999; Jerndal and Rigg 1998). Interestingly, while the French administrators themselves were thus blinded to the ethnic diversity of Laos, their Franco-Lao counterparts were not. A prominent nationalist leader from this period, Kathay Sasorith, wrote "Although Lao and Thai are closely related, it is necessary ... that each of us should live within our own natural limits," but he continues, "To form a single nation it is not absolutely necessary to speak the same language, to worship the same God or to practice the same religion," an indication that

among the Lao involved in this nation-building project there was a greater awareness of the existence and importance of non-Lao groups (quoted in Evans 1999).

24. For a more detailed account of the Hmong rebellions against the French and the economic and political concessions which resulted, see Gunn (1990).

25. Ivarsson (1998) has disputed this claim and argued that the period of Japanese Occupation was actually a period of solidification of gains in terms of national consciousness and establishment of a national press and language. However, historical evidence, such as the reluctance of the Lao monarch to accept independence when it was proffered by the Japanese at the conclusion of hostilities would seem to substantiate the majority view.

26. Indeed, the Hmong were sympathetic to essentially any party who promised them increased recognition and autonomy and the American CIA agents also enlisted large numbers of Hmong supporters to the royalist cause by promising them an independent state once the communists were defeated.

27. Oversen and Trankell (2004), Mabbett and Chandler (1995) and Kiernan (1996) have independently attested to the ease with which individuals of Siamese or Cham ancestry could enter into (and possibly, leave) the Khmer mainstream merely by altering their manner of custom and dress, suggesting — according to Oversen and Trankell — that the local understanding of "race" had as much a cultural as biological interpretation (p. 255).

28. Note, Edwards (1996) has argued to the contrary that the racialized understanding of being "Khmer" that exists today emerged as a product of the French colonial experience.

29. The Cham are believed to constitute the remnants of the historic kingdom of Champa. They are estimated to comprise about 2.3 per cent of the Cambodian population.

30. In addition to the Jarai whose language is related to that of the indigenous inhabitants of Polynesia and New Zealand, the term "Khmer Loeu" is also applied to groups such as the Tampuan, Brao, Phnong, Kui, Pear, Chong, Samre, Saoch, Kreung and Kravet, all of whom are speakers of Mon-Khmer languages and in this sense, at least, less distant from the lowland majority (though in most cases still animist and practising swidden culture) (Bourdier 1996; White 1996).

31. Those unfamiliar with this genre of national expression might be tempted to interpret the Southeast Asian "cultural villages" as sites of preservation of traditional languages and practices. But in fact, in most instances they serve more as showcases to display the "quaint cultural practices" of the ethnic minority communities for the benefit of the dominant majority and foreign tourists. This is clearly the case in Cambodia.

32. A more complete account of the movement of the migration streams through

which most of mainland Southeast Asia's Mon-Khmer and Austronesian indigenous groups were displaced and the lowlands settled by Tai-Lao and Tibeto-Burman peoples see Keyes (1995).

33. A history of the violent uprisings against lowland powers originating in (and to this point in history, largely confined to) the Indochinese highlands can be found in (Hickey 1982).

34. The most celebrated example of this is the case of Nong Duc Manh, former chairman of the National Assembly and a member of the Tay ethnic group (McElwee 2004).

35. It is difficult to cite demographic characteristics of Myanmar's population with any precision since the last systematic census of the country's population was carried out in 1931. However, it has been estimated that the total size of the population is approximately 48 million, of which about two-thirds are members of the eponymous majority known alternatively as Burmans (the term adopted in this chapter), Bamah or Burmese (Nicholas and Singh 1996).

36. The conventional periodization of Burmese history based on the efforts of British colonial scholars including Hall and Furnivall has characterized pre-colonial Myanmar as essentially a succession of warring ethnic states. However, this characterization has been challenged by more recent scholarship by, among others Aung-Thwin and Lehman, who insist that political and social relations during the early period were ethnically more nebulous and cooperative.

37. Silverstein (1997) has argued that far from being a mere historical accident or artifact of extended contact and exchange, the social and cultural incorporation of the Mon and Rakhine into the "Burman" kingdom was the result of a deliberate campaign by the ruling monarchs to more fully integrate them.

38. The estimated 135 ethnic groups (or "national races") of Myanmar include speakers of languages belonging to the Tibeto-Burman (for example, Burman, Lahu, Lisu, Rakhine, Chin), Mon-Khmer (for example, Mon, Wa, Palaung), Tai-Kadai (Thai, Shan), Hmong-Mien (Hmong, Yao), and Austronesian (Salone) families.

39. A more detailed discussion of how this was accomplished "on the ground" can be found in Taylor (1987) and Aung-Thwin (1985).

40. As evidence of this, between 1868 and 1878, the number of primary schools in Burma increased from 141 to 3,075 and the number of students attending school similarly grew about thirty-fold (Saito and Kiong 1999).

41. In fact, armed conflicts with "intransigent" upland groups, most notably the Wa, continued to plague the British throughout the colonial period and remained unresolved as the state moved into its post-independence period.

42. Missionaries had been present in Burma prior to the fall of the Konbaung dynasty, but their numbers and level of activity increased markedly following annexation.

43. The most virulent expression of anti-British sympathies was the Hsaya San Rebellion which lasted from 1930–32. Not long after this was put down there erupted a spate of anti-Indian riots which extended throughout much of the decade (Silverstein 1960, 1998).
44. For example, equality translated to the promulgation of a state constitution which, in turn, ensured that the leadership of the various regions would be selected through a comparable process. This undermined the authority of the traditional leaders among the Shan and Karenni who were, in fact, themselves participants in the constitution drafting process (Taylor 1987).

References

Anderson, Benedict R. *Imagined Communities: Reflections on the Origin and Spread of Nationalism*. London: Verso, 1991.

Brown, David. *The State and Ethnic Politics in Southeast Asia*. London and New York: Routledge, 1996.

Calhoun, Craig. "Nationalism and Ethnicity", *Annual Review of Sociology*, 19 (1993): 211–39.

Callahan, Mary P. "Language, Territory, and Belonging in Post-Socialist Burma", in *Boundaries and Belonging: States and Societies in the Struggle to Shape Identities and Local Practices*, edited by Joel S. Migdal. Cambridge, UK; New York: Cambridge, 2004.

Christie, Clive J. *A Modern History of Southeast Asia: Decolonization, Nationalism and Separatism*. London: New York: Tauris Academic Studies, 1996.

Christie, Clive. "Karens: Loyalism and Self-determination" in *Turbulent Times and Enduring People: Mountain Minorities in the South-East Asian Massif*, edited by Jean Michaud. Richmond, Surrey: Curzon, 2000.

Cooper, Robert. *Resource Scarcity and the Hmong Response: Patterns of Settlement and Economy in Transition*. Singapore: Singapore University Press, 1984.

Duara, Prasenjit. "Historicizing National Identity, or Who Imagines What and When", in *Becoming National: A Reader*, edited by Geoff Eley and Ronald Grigor Suny. New York: Oxford University Press, 1996.

Duncan, Christopher R., ed. *Civilizing the Margins: Southeast Asian Government Policies for the Development of Minorities*. Ithaca: Cornell University Press, 2004.

Durrenberger, E. Paul. *State Power and Culture in Thailand*. New Haven, Conn.: Yale University Southeast Asia Studies, 1996.

Engelbert, Thomas. Kubitscheck, Hans Dieter, eds. *Ethnic Minorities and Politics in Southeast Asia*. Frankfurt am Main; New York: Peter Lang, 2004.

Eriksen, Thomas Hylland. *Ethnicity and Nationalism*. London: Pluto Press, 1993.

Evans, Grant. *Laos: Culture and Society*. Chiang Mai: Silkworm Press, 1999.

———. "Laos: Minorities", in *Ethnicity in Asia*, edited by Colin Mackerras. New York: Routledge-Curzon, 2003.

Gellner, Ernest. *Nations and Nationalism*. Oxford: Blackwell Publishers, 1983.

———. *Nationalism*. London: Phoenix, 1997.

Goudineau, Yves. "Laos and Ethnic Minority Cultures: Promoting Heritage", in *International Expert Meeting for the Safeguarding and Promotion of the Intangible Cultural Heritage of the Minority Groups of the Lao People's Democratic Republic, 1996*. UNESCO, 2003.

Hechter, M, Okamoto, D. "Political Consequences of Minority Group Formation", in *Annual Review of Political Science* 4 (2001): 189–215.

Hickey, Gerald. *Free in the Forest: Ethnohistory of the Vietnamese Central Highlands, 1954–1976*. New Haven: Yale University Press, 1982.

Hlaing, Kyaw Yin, Robert H. Taylor and Tin Maung Maung Than, eds. *Myanmar: Beyond Politics to Societal Imperatives*. Singapore: Institute of Southeast Asian Studies, 2005.

Hobsbawm, E.J. *Nations and Nationalism since 1780*. Reprint (Canto imprint.) Cambridge: Cambridge University Press, 2000.

Howitt, Richard, John Connell and Philip Hirsch. *Resources, Nations, and Indigenous Peoples: Case Studies from Australasia, Melanesia, and Southeast Asia*. Melbourne; New York: Oxford University Press, 1996.

Hunter, Guy. *South-East Asia — Race, Culture and Nation*. London, New York: published for the Institute of Race Relations [by] Oxford University Press, 1966.

Jerndal, Randi, Rigg, Jonathan. "Making Space in Laos: Constructing a National Identity in a 'Forgotten' Country", *Political Geography* 17, no. 7 (1998): 809–31.

Kahn, Joel S., ed. *Southeast Asian Identities: Culture and the Politics of Representation in Indonesia, Malaysia, Singapore, and Thailand*. New York: St. Martin's Press; Singapore: Institute of Southeast Asian Studies, 1998.

Keyes, Charles F., ed. *Ethnic Adaptation and Identity: The Karen on the Thai Frontier with Burma*. Philadelphia: Institute for the Study of Human Issues, 1979.

Keyes, Charles. *The Golden Peninsula: Culture and Adaptation in Mainland Southeast Asia*. Honolulu: University of Hawaii Press, 1995 (reprint of 1977 edition).

———. 1997. "Cultural Diversity and National Identity in Thailand", in *Government Policies and Ethnic Relations in Asia and the Pacific*, edited by Michael E. Brown, Sumit Ganguly. Cambridge, Mass: MIT Press, 1997.

King, Victor T. and W.D. Wilder. "Southeast Asia and the Concept of Ethnicity", *Southeast Asian Journal of Social Science* 10, no. 1 (1982): 1–6.

Kunstadter, Peter, ed. *Southeast Asian Tribes, Minorities, and Nations. Volume 1 and 2*. Princeton, N.J.: Princeton University Press, 1967.

Lambrecht, Curtis W. "Oxymoronic Development: The Military as Benefactor in the Border Regions of Burma", in *Civilizing the Margins: Southeast Asian Government Policies for the Development of Minorities*, edited by Christopher Duncan. Ithaca: Cornell University Press, 2004.

Landé, Carl H. "Ethnic Conflict, Ethnic Accommodation, and Nation-Building in Southeast Asia", *Studies in Comparative International Development* 33, no. 4 (1999): 89–117.

Leach, Edmund. "The Frontiers of 'Burma' ", *Comparative Studies in Society and History* 3, no. 1 (1960): 49–68.

Lehman, F.K. "Ethnic Categories in Burma and the Theory of Social Systems", in *Southeast Asian Tribes, Minorities and Nations, volume I*, edited by Peter Kunstadter. Princeton: Princeton University Press, 1967.

Li, Tanya Murray. "Articulating Indigenous Identity in Indonesia: Resource Politics and the Tribal Slot", *Comparative Studies in Society and History* 42, no. 1 (2000): 149–79.

———. "Relational Histories and the Production of Difference on Sulawesi's Upland Frontier", *Journal of Asian Studies* 60, no. 1 (2001): 41–66.

Luce, G. H. *Phases of Pre-Pagan Burma: Languages and History*. Oxford: Oxford University Press, 1985.

Michaud, Jean. *Turbulent Times and Enduring People: Mountain Minorities in the South-East Asian Massif*. Richmond, Surrey: Curzon, 2000.

Mulder, Niels. *Inside Thai Society: Interpretations of Rveryday Life*. Amsterdam: Pepin Press, 1996.

Nation, The (Thailand). "Call to Change Clause Denying Rights to Thai-born Children of Aliens" 4 July (Section 1), 2005.

Nicholos, Colin and Raajen Singh. *Indigenous Peoples of Asia: Many Peoples, One Struggle*. Bangkok: Asia Indigenous Peoples Pact, 1996.

Oommen, T. K. *Citizenship, Nationality, and Ethnicity: Reconciling Competing Identities*.Cambridge, Mass.: Polity Press in association with Blackwell Publishers, 1997.

Ovesen, Jan, Trankell, Ing-Britt. "Cambodia", in *Ethnicity in Asia*, edited by Colin Mackerras. New York: Routledge-Curzon, 2003.

Peluso, Nancy. *Rich Forests, Poor People: Resource Control and Resistance in Java*. Berkeley: University of California Press, 1992.

Pinkaew Laungaramsri. "Ethnicity and the Politics of Ethnic Classification in Thailand", in *Ethnicity in Asia*, edited by Colin Mackerras. New York: Routledge-Curzon, 2003.

Rajah, Ananda. "Ethnicity, Nationalism and the Nation-state: The Karen in Burma and Thailand", in *Ethnic Groups across National Boundaries in Mainland Southeast Asia*, edited by Gehan Wijeyewardene. Singapore: Institute of Southeast Asian Studies, 1990, pp. 102–33.

Rajah, Ananda. "A 'Nation of Intent' in Burma: Karen Ethno-nationalism, Nationalism and Narrations of Nation", *The Pacific Review* 15, no. 4 (2002): 517–37.

Reid, Anthony. *Sojourners and Settlers: Histories of Southeast Asia and the Chinese*. St. Leonards, New South Wales: Allen and Unwin, 1996.

———. "Entrepreneurial Minorities, Nationalism, and the State", in *Essential Outsiders?: Chinese and Jews in the Modern Transformation of Southeast Asia and Central Europe*, edited by Daniel Chirot and Anthony Reid. Seattle: University of Washington Press, 1997.

Renard, Ronald. "The Making of a Problem: Narcotics in Mainland Southeast Asia", in *Development or Domestication? Indigenous Peoples of Southeast Asia*, edited by Don McCaskill and Ken Kampe. Chiang Mai: Silkworm Books, 1997.

Smith, Anthony. *The Ethnic Origins of Nations*. Oxford: Blackwell, 1986.

———. "The Origins of Nations", in *Becoming National: A Reader*, edited by Geoff Eley and Ronald Grigor Suny. New York: Oxford University Press, 1996.

Smith, Martin. *Burma: Insurgency and the Politics of Ethnicity*. Second edition. London: Zed Books Ltd, 1999.

Steinberg, David Joel, ed. *In Search of Southeast Asia: A Modern History*. Singapore: Oxford University Press, 1985 (Reprint edition).

Sutherland Claire. "Nation-building through Discourse Theory", *Nations and Nationalism* 11, no. 2 (2005): 185–202.

Tapp, Nicholas. *Sovereignty and Rebellion: The White Hmong of Northern Thailand*. Singapore: Oxford University Press, 1989.

Taylor Robert H. "Perceptions of Ethnicity in the Politics of Burma", *Southeast Asian Journal of Social Science* 10, no. 1 (1982).

———. "Do States make Nations? The Politics of Identity in Myanmar Revisited", *Southeast Asia Research* 13, no. 3 (2006): 261–86.

Thion, Serge. "Remodeling Broken Images: Manipulation of Identities. Towards and Beyond the Nation, An Asian Perspective", in *Ethnicities and Nations — Processes of Interethnic Relations in Latin America, Southeast Asia, and the Pacific*, edited by Remo Guidieri, Francesco Pellizzi and Stanley J. Tambiah. Houston: Rothko Chapel, 1988, pp. 229–58.

Tønneson, Stein and Hans Antlöv, eds. *Asian Forms of the Nation*. Surrey: Curzon, 1996.

Tooker, Deborah E. "Modular Modern: Shifting Forms of Collective Identity among the Akha of Northern Thailand", *Anthropological Quarterly* 77, no. 2 (2004): 243–88.

Toyota, Mika. "Subjects of the State without Citizenship: The Case of 'Hill Tribes' in Thailand", in *Multiculturalism in Asia: Theoretical Perspectives*, edited by Will Kymlicka and He Baobang. New York: Oxford University Press, 2005.

Vandergeest, Peter. "Racialization and Citizenship in Thai Forest Politics", *Society and Natural Resources* 16, no. 1 (2003): 19–37.

Wang, Gangwu. *Changing Identities of the Southeast Asian Chinese since World War II*. Hong Kong: Hong Kong University Press, 1988.

———. *China and the Chinese Overseas*. Singapore: Times Academic Press, 1991.

Wijeyewardene, Gehan, ed. *Ethnic Groups across National Boundaries in Mainland Southeast Asia*. Singapore: Institute of Southeast Asian Studies, 1990.

Winichakul,Thongchai. *Siam Mapped: A History of the Geo-body of a Nation*. Honolulu: University of Hawaii Press, 1994.

4

British Policy towards Myanmar and the Creation of the 'Burma Problem'[1]

Robert H. Taylor

Looked at historically or contemporaneously, the British Government has never actually had a policy as such toward Myanmar or Burma, the name the former colonial government gave the country. Rather, British policy has been the result of multiple accidents and the making of policy has been the result of contingencies extraneous to Myanmar. Some of these policies have been the result of geography, especially Myanmar's presence on the eastern borders of the British Indian empire, between China and French Indochina with Siam as a nominal British dependency during the nineteenth century. Some have been the result of historical contingencies, such as the Japanese Occupation which unleashed militant Myanmar nationalism and militarism leading to the decision to hurriedly grant independence in 1948. Others have been the consequence of human relationships, such as the decision of Daw Aung San Suu Kyi to return to Yangon from Oxford in 1988 to nurse her dying mother. All of these discreet circumstances, major or minor in the scales of human history, have had implications far beyond their immediate importance.

During the nineteenth century, British policy toward Burma evolved out of the advent of liberalism in imperial policy and the defence of Britain's growing influence in Asia more generally. The first Anglo-Burmese war, from 1824 to 1826, was the result of the clash of empires which occurred at the River Naaf as the British East India Company resisted the Konbaung dynasty's efforts to control anti-Innwa guerrilla forces. The consequent British administration of Rakhine and Tanintharyi which followed the defeat of the Myanmar forces was along standard company lines of the time. The Second Anglo-Burmese War of 1852 was largely the result of efforts to force British liberal trading policies on a recalcitrant mercantilist Myanmar state. Similarly, the Third Anglo-Burmese War in 1885 was prompted by the imposition of a fine on the Bombay-Burmah Trading Company by the Konbaung courts as well as concerns about the protection of general British economic and security interests in the region as French power was being progressively extended to the east of Myanmar.

The annexation of Myanmar to India which followed one month after the swift defeat of the armies of the last Konbaung king, Thibaw, found the British Government unprepared. It was only determined to impose direct rule, rather than a puppet prince on the throne, after lengthy and sometimes farcical considerations.[2] The options reviewed included turning Myanmar into a buffer state as a protectorate, a regency or even a religious kingdom with a Buddhist monk appointed by the Chinese emperor!

The annexation and the war which proceeded had, of course, to be justified to an increasingly "democratic" Britain. At least among the political classes of the day, the newspaper was gaining influence over public opinion and parliamentary debate. Prior to the third Anglo-Burmese War, and with echoes of contemporary media politics, "the Burma problem" was launched and momentarily resolved by the removal of King Thibaw. Subsequent British decisions began then to shape Myanmar's history. The Konbaung dynasty had failed to understand and respond in a timely manner to the media war which was launched against it prior to the actual invasion.

As H. Fielding-Hall wrote in 1899, when discussing the consequences of the encirclement of the Myanmar by the British prior to the war,

> This intensified the natural concealment and reticence of an oriental government. Looking upon us [i. e. the British] as foes, they did not care in any way to justify and explain to us their acts. Expecting us to wilfully misunderstand them and find evil where we could, the Burmese government and people saw no use in trying to make matters plain and put their conduct in a fair and clear light. Explanations would be weakness, and moreover useless to an enemy determined to see only the worst.[3]

Noting that the government was autocratic and hence likely to have many enemies, Britain's newspapers were consequentially full of "the tales of spies whose only concern was to speak evilly".[4] While Thibaw's friends remained distant and uncommunicative with his foreign opponents and friends, their "enemies were only too ready to pour their grievances and scandals into our, as they hoped, sympathetic ears, hoping thereby to obtain vengeance on those who had injured them."[5] Noting the propensity of the British, and for that matter most people, to think ill of that which they do not understand, Fielding-Hall went on to write,

> So partly through our own fault, partly through the fault of the Burmese themselves, the stories that obtained credence and circulation about the king and his people were to their discredit. It was in this way that arose the tales of the continual drunkenness of the king, of the bloodthirstiness of the queen, of the utter wickedness of the palace in general. Little sparks of truth were fanned into huge flares that lit the whole history of these years with lurid light. Tale-teller vied with tale-teller as to which could impute most wickedness to the palace, regardless of truth or even probability. Yet consider how improbable those tales were, how impossible of belief to any one who stayed a moment to consider them![6]

This poisoned atmosphere contributed to the ten years of chaos and conflict that the imposition of direct rule created in the country. The positive aspects of the system of administration which the British could have adapted and used to manage Myanmar as a buffer state, including the king's army, judicial system and administrative structures, were abandoned. Naturally, the dismissal of many government servants and their replacement with foreigners and individuals of lower social status whetted initial anti-British sentiments, creating strong nationalist sentiments before they could be expressed in modern political language.[7] The fateful decision, discussed below, to administer the Shan states and the rest of northern Myanmar separately from the remainder of the country, implemented two years after the annexation, shows how unprepared the British were for the tasks they had assumed in shaping the emergence of twentieth century Burma.

The Mapping of Myanmar and the Politicization of Ethnicity

Though this flies in the face of the official nationalist historiography of the country, it is no exaggeration to say that that the British made modern Myanmar. This was a result of the superior British Indian military power which defeated the armies of the kings of the Konbaung Dynasty in three wars during the nineteenth century. Those three wars resulted in the drawing of the map of Myanmar, establishing its borders with neighbouring states, and demarcating the internal conceptual and administrative structures of the modern state. Myanmar or British Burma was incorporated as a province of the British Indian empire until 1937 and its current international borders largely represent British imperial interests at the height of that empire's power. While the western reaches of Myanmar do not incorporate much of the territory that Myanmar kings had once included within their own empires, particularly the territories known as Manipur and Assam, the northern, southern and eastern reaches of the country extend into areas which Siamese kings and Chinese emperors would have claimed as their own had their military power been as strong as their territorial claims.

For various reasons largely to do with a lack of understanding of the nature of the various communities within the country and also parsimony, the British perceived the governance of Myanmar as requiring two different models of administration. Following the first war, the territories of Rakhine and Tanintharyi[8] were absorbed into the administrative structures of the British East India Company through its agents in Bengal. Rakhine had only been conquered by the founder of the Konbaung dynasty, Alaungpaya, in 1775 and elements of its population were resisting his successor's control when the British appeared on their frontier in Bengal. Equally, Tanintharyi had only come into the empire in recent years, having been an arena of dispute and overlapping claims between Myanmar and Siamese kings for many years. After 1826, however, they became the first elements of what eventually became British Burma and were directly governed by British officials with largely Indian staff.[9] The Bengali Muslim minority found today in this region is part of the legacy of that period.

The defeat of the Konbaung armies at the end of the second war in 1852 saw the delta of the Ayeyarwady River and its tributaries, plus the territory of the former Mon kingdom at Bago, brought under British Indian control. The delta was then largely a jungle of tall grasses and swamps but, as a result of a major programme of dyke and dam construction, soon was turned into arable land. This encouraged the migration of thousands of Myanmars from the central regions of the country still under the king's administration to the delta where they were given land rights on the payment of three years taxes. Also, there began at this time the migration of Indian labour, some permanently settled on what were effectively sugarcane and cotton plantations, and others as migrant workers on public works projects and the construction of Yangon from a sleepy fishing village to a major international port. It was following the second war that

Myanmar began to establish itself as the major rice exporting territory for India. The administrative model of British India was extended at this time to cover all of southern Myanmar.

The opening of the Suez Canal in 1869 and expanding demand for tropical products lead to heightened imperialist rivalry in South East Asia, eventually sealing the fate of the Konbaung dynasty in the third war in 1885. This resulted in the extermination of the Myanmar monarchy and the demarcation of the country to the north and west. The decision to abolish the monarchy, rather than to attempt to rule the country through indigenous institutions as the French did in Cambodia, Laos and northern Vietnam, or as the British did in the Indian princely states, much of the Malay peninsula, and Siam, had significant consequences for the majority Buddhist population of central and southern Myanmar. The king had been not only the head of state and commander of his empire but was also the fount of authority for the Buddhist monkhood or *sangha*. Without a king to maintain the monastic hierarchy, the monkhood was soon bereft of any internal disciplining institution. This led eventually to indiscipline in the *sangha*, stimulating sectarianism, wayward behaviour and involvement in nationalist political affairs, all in violation of the traditional principles of the monkhood. Not until 1980 would the Myanmar state once more regain administrative control over the monkhood such as Thailand had established nearly eighty years earlier.[10]

Moreover, the removal of the king in effect decapitated the existing social order in Myanmar. The monarchical state was hierarchical; some would argue caste-like in character. In the years leading up to the third war, the apparent inability of an inexperienced young king, Thibaw, to control his subordinates led to competition amongst princes and other potential claimants for power at regional and state level. This incipient war of all against all for control of the state by elements of the ruling elites was turned against the British when they took the capital, then at Mandalay, in 1885. There ensued ten years of sustained warfare between the British Indian army and a variety of pretenders to the throne and supporters of the old order. At the end of that decade of warfare, the British had created a military administration across all of central and southern Myanmar. In so doing, they inverted the old social order. Finding the former holders of power and authority to be untrustworthy or rebellious, the British sought those who would cooperate with them.[11] In central and southern Myanmar, these tended to come from the bottom of the social order, rich landowners, or from the ethnic minorities, especially some of the Kayin (Karen) population, who were the beneficiaries of the Christian missionary educational institutions which flourished in southern Myanmar under the auspices of the British.

However, in their new territory's mountainous border areas, largely populated by ethnic minorities, the British chose, for reasons of economy and simplicity of administration, not to overturn the existing social and political order, but rather, to harness it for their purposes. Therefore, rather than imposing a system of direct administrative authority manned throughout by British and Indian officials, the system of administration in the northern areas was referred to as "indirect rule". Here in the territory which soon became known as the Shan states and the Frontier Areas, to distinguish them from "Burma Proper", the British sought out and gave the imprimatur of authority to "traditional" headmen, chieftains and local lords, often known as Shan *sawbwas* and Kachin *duwas*. The *sawbwas* and *duwas* or other recognized figures became the recipients of synods which vested in them political and administrative authority over their subjects in exchange for their loyalty to the new British authorities in Yangon, New Delhi and London. In more sparsely populated territories, the British Indian army conducted periodic "flag marches" to assert their power over peoples and lands over which they held only nominal control. In the wake of the British came Christian missionaries who, especially amongst animist populations of the north, were able to make many converts.[12]

The sparse population of the northern and eastern hill areas and their low productivity made them economic liabilities for the British administration but their strategic importance on the Chinese and French Indochinese borders ensured that the army maintained control against their militarily inferior neighbours. The army, often through the agency of the Christian pastors who lived in some of the less remote hill areas, saw the populations of the frontier areas as potential recruits to the British Indian army and they soon developed a reputation as among the "martial races" of India in distinction to the lowland populations who were thought to be poor military material. Though the Bamar (Burman) populations of the lowlands who had formed the core of the king's armies were thought of as effective fighters, following the third war, their military potential was seen as a potential threat to British control.[13]

The administrative and military distinctions which the British used in their administration of Myanmar — lowlands and highlands, Burma Proper and the Frontier Areas — were only the beginning of the complexities which were soon conceptualized into an ahistorical "model" of the characteristics of Myanmar social formations. This has persisted inside and outside the country to the present day and bedevils clear thinking about the society's issues. Reified ethnicity, or "race",[14] has become the dominant expression of this model of Myanmar society for modern political purposes. Myanmar was colonized not only at the height of the power of the British empire but also at the height of racist conceptualizations of the moral meaning of ethnic diversity. While it would be wrong to say that ideas of ethnic difference did not play a role in pre-colonial Myanmar politics and statecraft, that role was muted and modulated by patron-client relationships, trade and military relationships, and religious bonds which overcame the potential saliency of other conceptualizations of societal relations.[15] Imperialism eventually undermined these premodern conceptualizations of social solidarity and replaced them with reified ethnicity which in time generated new forms of social and political action and reaction. The multiple nationalisms of modern Myanmar was the result.

The British conceptual model of pre-modern Myanmar was one based on ethnic distinctions which had its model in the then current understanding of Britain's own history as having been created by various invaders who dominated the indigenous populations. This model of history by invasion and violence was transferred to Myanmar. Thus the central valley kings were seen as in a state of semi-perpetual war against ethnic communities which lived in the hills surrounding them. A history of ethnic antagonism was created rather than a history of ethnic cooperation and accommodation where hill and valley peoples exchanged goods and services in a mutually beneficial manner.[16] Even if the historical reality of the past was not one of harmonious cooperation between hill and plains peoples, a process of accommodation was possibly more the norm than one of continual ethnic conflict. The teaching of the conflictual model of Myanmar's history thus became part of the justification of the colonial order. For some, the colonizer turned himself into a protector of the minorities against the allegedly inevitable exploitation of the majority population group, the Bamar.

This version of history was adapted to fit the special characteristics or historical opportunities of various communities. The Kayah (or Karenni or Red Karen) were allocated a special "independent" status which meant they existed in an early "treaty" relationship with the colonial state. The tenacity of insurgencies in the poverty stricken Kayah state in their fight against the central government owes something to the ideological badge of their ancestors' alleged modern territorial statehood prior to the formation of modern Myanmar itself. Similarly, the belief among some members of the small Christian minority amongst Kayin (or Karen) that they are the lost tribe of Israel who had the book restored to them by the white missionaries, gained greater cogency for it being incorporated into the origin myth of the animist hill tribes of the eastern hills. The attempts by the Christian leadership of the Kayin National Union (KNU), the longest standing of the insurgent forces fighting the government, to create a Kayin nation out of the linguistic plurality of the Karennic speaking peoples of Myanmar, has its origin in the missionary's model of their past. The KNU harks back to these myths as part of their claim to political legitimacy.[17]

Similarly, the claim by Shan insurgent bands that they are fighting to re-establish a pre-colonial form of statehood rooted in similar historical reconstructions. These claims were first advanced in the 1930s by the Shan *sawbwas* when they claimed that they should have been recognized by the British as autonomous rulers on the model of the rulers of the Indian princely states or the Malay sultans.[18] This claim, which was rejected by the British, had its roots in the recasting of their historical relationship with the kings of central Myanmar from one of political client and symbolic emulator to one of an independent ruler fending off the imposition of the power of "alien" predatory invaders. While some of the *sawbwas* attempted to demonstrate the military independence of their states prior to World War II by somewhat feeble attempts to organise their own defence forces, more important for post-colonial politics was the recruitment of men from the Kachin, Chin and other smaller hill peoples into the British Indian armed forces during the colonial period. This reinforced the notion of the independence of the hill peoples from the historical kingdoms of the Ayeyawardy basin.

World War II itself served to heighten the political saliency of the British model of Myanmar's history. The recruitment of irregular anti-Japanese guerrilla forces in northern Myanmar by the British and Americans established a special position for some of the leaders of these peoples.[19] The violent potential of ethnicity in Myanmar's future was also made salient during and after the war in attacks by members of the Burma Independence Army in cooperation with the occupying Japanese on Kayin Christians[20] or subsequent protection of Kayin in the delta from Bamar opponents as well as the formation of a Kayin anti-Japanese resistance force along the Thai border.[21]

While the British denied the oft repeated claim by Myanmar nationalists that they were applying a policy of "divide and rule" in the colony, the effects of British policy created an impression that there was more that divided the people than united them. This was done by not merely denying that the peoples residing in the colony shared a common cultural symbiotic past, but also by ensuring that central and southern politicians could not gain ready access to the populations of the frontier areas in order to advance their nationalist claims. While the Frontier Areas remained largely undeveloped and cut off from the more vibrant political economy of the remainder of the country, so also the educational opportunities which were available in the towns and cities of the southern and central parts of the country did not exist in the minority territories except for a special school for the sons of *sawbwas* at Taunggyi.

As noted above, World War II was to have a dramatic impact on the Frontier Areas. Not only did British, American, Japanese and Chinese nationalist armies enter the territory, but the semi-permeable barriers that the British had created between the minority peoples and the ethnic majority, the Bamar, were removed during and after the Japanese Occupation. As it became apparent soon after the end of the war that Myanmar's political independence was not only inevitable but imminent, elites throughout the country began to make claims and counter-claims about the historic rights of "their people". Ethnicity now was transformed from an object of discussion and a principle of organization to political rallying cry. A plethora of nationalist claims were advanced. The "federal" constitution that the country adopted at independence in 1948 was the result of compromises that the British had encouraged, and General Aung San achieved, at the Panglong Conference in 1947. Then the logic of a unified state and economy came up against the realities of a highly divided society with a variety of unmet and often inchoate, ethnically perceived demands and expectations. The result was the widespread and armed ethnically motivated insurgency that is detailed by Martin Smith.[22] The state which the British bequeathed Myanmar politicians in 1948 had not been created to meet the expectations of the second half of the twentieth century. One of the primary requirements of the first constitution of independent Myanmar was to reshape the state to meet those expectations and in that it failed.

British Rule and the Rise of Myanmar Nationalism

The British, with the arrogance of power and the high imperialist notions of Caucasian racial superiority and *laissez faire* liberalism, denigrated indigenous institutions. Nationalists were to make much of these slights in later years, in particular European disdain for both the Buddhist faith and the military prowess of the Konbaung armies. These were to become the bedrock of many nationalist arguments along with the perception that Myanmar's society and culture faced inevitable deracination as a consequence of wide scale migration of Indian capital and labour into the colony which the British had encouraged. The economic principles of *laissez faire* liberalism were applied with a vengeance, resulting in extremely corrosive consequences for old social order.

The harshness of the initial years of foreign rule was exacerbated as a consequence of the fallacy of seeing Myanmar as an extension of India. Policies applied to Myanmar were often fit for the requirements of India, not the citizens of Myanmar, at least until 1937 when the country became an independent colony. At that point it came out from under the administration of the Viceroy in Delhi and subsequently the Governor of Burma reported directly to the Secretary of State for India and Burma in London. Prior to that time, Myanmar was perceived as not only a source of food for India and a destination for Indian labour and capital, but also as a financial milk cow for the central Indian treasury.

The abolition of the monarchy not only undermined the disciplinary power of the Buddhist hierarchy but also led to the displacement of Buddhism as the religion of the state. The British policy of "religious neutrality", though privileging to some degree Christian institutions,[23] meant that when the Konbaung dynasty was finally abolished in 1886, the faith no longer had a fount of authority in Myanmar. Monastic indiscipline faced little or no sanction and the behaviour of the monkhood changed, allowing members of it to become involved in secular activities, especially politics, in violation of strict Buddhist teachings. One of the key social roles of the Buddhist monkhood, the *sangha*, had under the kings been the provision of moral and literary education to the young, especially young men. The role was soon undermined by British educational policy which viewed the primary function of education as secular and functional, not religious and moral. The introduction of secular education proved to be popular for it was the root to advancement in the new institutions of the colonial state, especially in fields such as administration, commerce and the law. However, the new educational system was not only elitist, touching only a small minority of the indigenous population, but also an extension of the education then offered in the rest of India. For example, the much heralded University of Rangoon was in fact a branch of Calcutta University until 1921 and remained an offshoot of the Indian Education Service until 1937. Even then, only about half of the students who attended it were from Myanmar and none of the senior faculty was from the country.

As noted above, the incorporation of British Burma into the Indian empire led not only to the extension of the British Indian army but also the British Indian administrative and legal system to British Burma. This had a number of consequences, all of which added to the list of grievances that the majority of the indigenous population felt toward their colonial rulers. The use of South Asians as well as British administrators, doctors, judges, and police provided a daily reminder of the indignity of colonization. The administrative boundaries which the British drew, particularly at the village level, ignored natural economic and administrative units which had developed under the less formal administrative system of the kings. Indian legal codes, written in English, seemed arbitrary and often unfathomable to the local magistrates and those who appeared before them in court. Moreover, the British Indian codes privileged English or Christian and Islamic law in cases where Buddhists and members of other faiths were involved. This especially affected the rights of women in mixed marriages and was the first issue raised by politicians in the initial session of the legislative assembly elected in 1921.

As the indigenous population was displaced from any significant role in the colony's military or administrative affairs during the colonial period, so also were they dislodged from control of the economy and, in time, even ownership of much of the country's prime agricultural land. This was the consequence of the encouragement of large scale South Asian labour migration to British Burma as well as the superior economic resources that Indian capitalists brought to the colony. The rapid economic growth which British rule engendered turned British Burma into a labour deficient area. There was particularly a labour shortage in urban areas and Yangon, the capital, soon became a predominantly Indian city, alien to the indigenous population which came to study or conduct business there. The volatility of this situation was expressed during the Great Depression by not only the Hsaya San peasants revolt but also countless other attacks on British and Indian individuals as well as race riots fuelled by employment disputes in the capital.[24]

The British were not blind to the consequences of their rule, but were limited in their ability to respond to the pressures they had created by the larger politics of India as well as their own often racially loaded concepts. Their primary response was to attempt to introduce representative political institutions in the belief that this would provide an outlet for nationalist and other forms of political and economic discontent. Again, the model which was applied to Myanmar was that which was invented for India.[25] Not only were the minority "races" governed under different principles from the majority of the population, but from the formation of the first legislative assembly in 1921, parliamentary constituencies were based on ethnicity and religion. Ethnic differences were thus incorporated into the representative structures of the colonial state. This was to continue to be the case until the 1951 election, the first in independent Burma. Just as racial stereotyping was part of everyday discourse in Burma,[26] so also racial categories became the stuff of discussions about how to resolve the colony's social and economic problems.

Given the range of issues which colonialism had posed for Myanmar's society in the short years of British rule, it was not surprising that nationalists developed a complex and sometimes contradictory critique of foreign rule which emphasized all of the slights and attacks they perceived on their civilization and economy. The evolution of nationalist organizations from the beginning of the twentieth century saw attention shift from the attack on Buddhism which was perceived in colonial policies to concerns about education and the denial of military opportunities for the indigenous people to a Marxist-informed critique of the effects of imperialism on the Myanmar peasantry and small but politically important urban population. The first expression of widespread organized sentiment was evoked by the Young Men's Buddhist Association (YMBA) which took up the issue of British denigration of Myanmar Buddhist customs. Soon university and secondary school students commenced demonstrations over shortcomings in the colonial educational system.

They were followed in the 1920s by the leaders of the General Council of Burmese Associations (Myanmar Athin Chokkyi or GCBA), some of whom established volunteer paramilitary corps, while others drew attention to the relative economic disadvantages of the indigenous peasantry vis-à-vis the Indian shopkeepers, moneylenders and landlords with whom they dealt. During the 1930s, each of these grievances was taken up by a next generation of nationalist leaders in the Dobama Asiayone (We Burmans Association) or the *Thakin* (Master) movement as well as the All Burma Students Union. Culminating in the formation of the Burma Communist Party and the People's [Socialist] Party in 1939, on the eve of World War II, young men such as Thakin Aung San and Thakin Than Tun sought to protect Buddhism, encourage indigenous education, rescue the military reputation of the Myanmar people, and advance the economic interests of the indigenous peasants and workers. In their understanding of their opponent's tactics, they saw the British as deliberately manipulating indigenous and alien minorities to disadvantage and disempower the unified Myanmar nation which they sought to lead.

The Birth of the Myanmar Army and the Struggle for Independence

The colonial world that the most ardent Myanmar nationalists found unacceptable was dislodged initially not by their own actions but rather by a rival imperial power to that of the West, Japan. But the Japanese invasion of South East Asia in late 1941 and 1942 unleashed social and political forces which proved to be overwhelming for all foreign interests in the country. In the cause of Myanmar independence, long suppressed nationalist energies became organized in a broad but diverse political movement which the Japanese and then the British were unable to control. The result was Myanmar's independence from Britain only six years later following the determination of the British Labour government to grant India independence. World War II encouraged the birth and expansion of several political organizations which would compete for power in post-colonial Myanmar. Among these were the Burma Communist Party, the Socialist Party and the Myanmar army, the *tatmadaw*. Each, led by young men who had been active in Thakin and student politics during the 1930s, sought to champion the nationalist cause and thus end the humiliation which they felt the British had imposed on Myanmar.

The Japanese, seeking to gain the cooperation of Myanmar nationalists in their effort to hold Myanmar and push on into India, encouraged the formation of a Myanmar armed force prior to the war. This began with the famous Thirty Comrades, young men from the Thakin organization who gathered on Hainan Island for military training prior to the formation of the Burma Independence Army (BIA) on the cusp of the Japanese invasion. Among the Thirty Comrades, led by Thakin Aung San, were a number of the post-war political and military leaders, most particularly Thakin Shu Maung, who took the *nom de' guerre* of Ne Win. Their role in the BIA during the war has now become part of the Myanmar nationalist tale of heroism which all are taught and most accept. Like the heroic rule of students in Myanmar's nationalist movements in the 1920s and 1930s, the *tatmadaw* is seen as one of the leading pillars of the nation. Founded seven years before independence, the army preceded the independent Myanmar state and thus its leaders claim a supervisory role in maintaining the state's independence. Aung San's astute political manoeuvring toward the end of the war when the Myanmar national army turned on their Japanese mentors together with their Burma Communist Party and People's Party allies in the Anti-Fascist Organization (AFO), and joined forces with the returning British army, ensured a political future for the army which none of its rivals for power could match.

This is so much nationalism hagiography today, but developments at the time were much more complex. The communists, led by the Minister for Agriculture in the wartime government as well as Aung San's brother-in-law, Thakin Than Tun, organized the peasantry in large parts of the country. Other leftists who had formally opposed collaboration with the Japanese in what they described as the fascist war, also organized extensively among the peasant population and formed an underground resistance movement before the BIA turned against the Japanese. So too did the much smaller People's Party of U Kyaw Nyein and U Ba Swe which became the kernel of the post-war Socialist Party element of the first independent government. The extensive organizational work of these organizations resulted in what was effectively a nationalist uprising during the brief period between the defeat of the Japanese and the return of the British. Faced with the threat of armed revolt in post-war Myanmar, the British, having decided to grant independence to India (and Pakistan), had no choice but to do the same for Myanmar as they were dependent on Indian troops to put down any armed revolt in the colony.

The nationalist forces, military, communist and socialists, which came together in 1945 in the Anti-Fascist People's Freedom League (AFPFL), were only some of the political groups which became active in the chaos that followed the war. The leaders of the ethnic minorities who had stood aside from the nationalist struggles of the 1920s and 1930s, realized that the autonomous future that the British had promised them before the war would be undone in a unified, democratic Myanmar. They, like the lowland nationalists, began to organize to advance their interests and protect what their opponents and rivals perceived as their British-guaranteed privileges. While the established leaders of the frontier areas were persuaded to seek guarantees from Aung San and the leaders of the AFPFL that their interests would be recognized by a post-independence state, the Christian minority leadership of the Karen National Union (KNU) sought to unify all Karennic speaking peoples in a demand for an independent "Karenistan".

Myanmar on the cusp of independence faced an uncertain future. Without the power of the British Indian empire, which had grouped its various elements in a single state, to hold it together, but the perpetuation of the argument that these peoples had been historically antagonistic toward each other, Myanmar looked set to dissolve into chaos as political rivals took up arms to advance their claims to power. Within months of independence, the Burma Communist Party, which had been excluded from power in the months prior to independence, went underground in armed revolt, taking with it several thousand members of the new state's armed forces. By the end of the first year of independence, the KNU had also gone into revolt, taking many of the ethnic minority troops which had previously been part of the colonial armed forces underground with it. Soon the Socialist-dominated rump AFPFL government of U Nu, General Aung San having been assassinated in July 1947, backed by Ne Win's Fourth Burma Rifles, controlled little more than Yangon. Though the new government received some modest support from India and Britain during these months, it became increasingly dependent upon the Myanmar army to retain power and to retake control of the country.

British Policy toward Burma after Independence to 1988 and after

Little has been written on British policy toward Burma in the post-colonial era. This is partially the consequence of Britain's declining power in Asia but also of the underlying political economy of the relationship between the two countries during the previous century and more. For all of Myanmar's fabled natural resources, the country had been relatively unimportant for Western economic interests whereas for India, Myanmar had been a crucial source of rice and petroleum products as well as a place for surplus Indian capital and labour to find an outlet. But once India and Pakistan were independent, this was no longer a concern to the British and Burma's economic relationship with South Asia began to atrophy, having been severely disrupted by World War II, and nearly ended after 1964 following the government's nationalization of almost all economic activities.

British policy in Southeast Asia after the war was concerned primarily with its major economic interests in Malaya and Singapore, especially the dollar earning power of the Malayan rubber and tin industry. Moreover, Britain's declining military power and its economic weakness deterred the country from seeking obligations and interests in newly independent Burma. The decision by U Nu's government to reject membership in the then British Commonwealth underscored the weakness of the relationship. In as much as it was the British Indian army which had garrisoned British Burma, the major consequence of Burma's independence was a much sought after reduction in post-war expenditure. The wartime destruction and post-independence decline of several colonial era industries in Myanmar, such as oil,[27] timber and mining, and the restrictions that the post-colonial governments placed on foreign investment, meant that British commercial interests also rather withered away to be completely eliminated after the Revolutionary Council came to power in 1962.

Britain's initial post-independence relationship was primarily concerned with the defence of the country in the Cold War and the future of the ethnic minorities, for which some individuals felt a personal concern growing out of the alliances that many Kayin, Chin and Kachin had developed with the British forces against the Japanese. However, the Attlee Labour government which governed during the first years of Myanmar's independence, tended to ignore those concerns which were taken up by the Conservative opposition. When the Conservatives came to power in the 1951 general election, they also, however, tended to ignore the interests of the minorities for the maintenance of existing treaty and other commitments with the AFPFL government of U Nu. As a significant number of Burmese students continued to come to the UK during the 1950s, people-to-people relations remained cordial and eventually, to Britain's advantage as the country became a net importer of Myanmar doctors and other medical personnel.

The initial defence relationship, the Britain-Burma Defence Agreement, popularly known as the Let Ya–Freeman accord, negotiated in 1947, became a model for Britain in its subsequent decolonization efforts. Through a treaty reached with the transitional Myanmar authorities prior to formal independence, Britain undertook continuing but limited defence responsibilities for Burma. This "run-down agreement" provided a modest amount of security for the country until Burmese forces were organized as well as serving "to emphasize the amicable nature of the parting."[28] The joint services mission which Britain was committed by the treaty to send to Myanmar was to "provide instructional and other staff for service with the Burmese forces" as well as assist with procurement.[29] British support was implied also if Burmese were attacked by a hostile power, China being perceived as the major potential threat. The agreement was terminated

four years after independence, largely as a result of the belief by General
Ne Win and other members of the officer corps that the British were pro-
Kayin and not providing adequate support for the army.[30] Even before that,
however, the effectiveness of the British Services Mission was undermined
by their implication in the assassination of General Aung San and cabinet
colleagues, just months after the Let Ya-Freeman agreement was signed.[31]

As the Cold War developed in Southeast Asia following the Geneva
Conference on the future of Indochina and the American proposal in 1954
to establish the South East Asian Treaty Organization (SEATO) as part of
its policy of containment in Asia, Britain undertook to determine whether
the five member countries of the Colombo Plan, which included Myanmar,
would be interested in joining the organization. U Nu's government made
it clear, as did India, Sri Lanka, and Indonesia, that its neutralist foreign
policy precluded any such move.[32] The earlier formation of the Colombo
Plan had come about in part as a vehicle to assist Myanmar during the
initial years of the post-independence civil war without compromising its
neutralist credentials or expecting it to join the Commonwealth.

British relations prior to 1988 often were largely of a nostalgic nature.
As Britain's aid donations were dwarfed by those of Japan and Germany,[33]
and its potential military support withered, trips by Lord Mountbatten of
Burma or various personages from the British Royal family, as well as
General Ne Win's occasional visits to London, shaped the relationship.
Mountbatten, for example, visited Yangon on four occasions between
1956 and 1972, on each of which he met with U Nu or General Ne Win.
When greeted by Ne Win on the arrival in 1967 and being whisked away
from the airport in the Chairman of the Revolutionary Council's Mercedes
Benz, Mountbatten was impressed to find two Tommyguns on the floor in
front of his and Ne Win's feet.[34] The final visit largely concerned Ne Win's
temporary "divorce" from his wife Katie and Mountbatten's failed efforts
to convince the General of the utility of sending two Burmese children to
the United World College in Wales.[35]

As British relations ebbed away in largely symbolic and trivial
exchanges, diplomacy between the two countries was largely concerned
with the rituals of state to state relations. Ambassadors came and went and
the British consigned Myanmar even lower down its list of foreign policy
priorities. As for having a policy toward Myanmar, live and let live
probably would sum it up if anyone ever got around to articulating it. For
example, the referendum on and introduction of the 1974 one-party socialist
constitution was viewed rather benignly. Reports by Ambassador E. G.

Willan on the events were largely complacent and the Foreign Office's Research Department perceived the county was being governed by "a relatively benign form of dictatorship (probably reflecting the personality of Ne Win himself) ...."[36]

That was to change dramatically in 1988 as a result of the crisis that the government of Myanmar found itself in at that time. When Myanmar finally returned to British newspapers and televisions in a quiet news period, the months of August and September, 1988, the events in the country were front page news and lead items on the evening television news broadcasts.[37] Given the previous complete lack of recent and relevant information in the British media on political and economic conditions in the country, the sensational, and sometimes sensationalized, visual news which was coming often from Japanese sources tended to be interpreted through lenses borrowed from other recent Asian events.[38]

As far as making policy toward Myanmar, however, it would seem that the Thatcher government, then at the peak of its popularity, was unconstrained by media reports and popular pressures. While Prime Minister Thatcher always persisted in the belief that the military government in Yangon was a dastardly bunch, policy did not get overtly politicized until after she was out of office and the predecessor organization to the Burma Campaign UK and related activities began to generate a minor policy issue with which the politicians felt that had to be seen to be acting in consonance. Between 1988 and the mid-1990s, British policy was driven by an emotional response to events on the streets in Yangon but also a desire to increase trade and investment with Myanmar as a now more open economy with the potential to be a new Asian tiger.

The British ambassador in Yangon in 1988 was Martin Morland. He had served in Yangon in the 1950s and looked back on those days of his halcyon youth as rather gloriously free and democratic. The civil war, high crime rates and political intrigues which others remember from that period were eclipsed as he remembered the dances and societies that apparently existed side-by-side with the less desirable aspects of that decade.[39] Like his American counterpart, Bert Levin, he now doubtless reported on the brutality that he saw in the streets of Yangon and reports of events in the remainder of the country in understandable language. At that time even seasoned visitors to Myanmar often seemed to have forgotten their history. One such individual emotionally advanced the view that the army's firing on Bamar citizens was the first time that Bamar had shot Bamar in Myanmar's modern history! Lurid reports that the government had released the inmates of Insein and other prisons were believed without thought. The period of intense political activity in Myanmar brought out a kind of lunacy in discussions of the country in London.[40]

British policy tended, as it usually does, to follow American policy at the time. With the end of the Cold War, spreading American style democracy now returned to the centre of the United States Government's foreign policy agenda. Aid was terminated but otherwise nothing much changed except the Department of Trade and Industry's Southeast Asia Trade Advisory Group (SEATAG)[41] became very active, encouraging trade missions and investment advisory information for British firms, which were believed to have the advantage over other Western economic interests besides the residual "goodwill" that existed toward the former colonial masters. The British embassy in Yangon hosted two British weeks and a number of companies displayed their wares. As foreign investment began to grow, British firms or firms registered in British dependencies became major investors in the Myanmar economy. In the growing gas sector, Premier Oil became a junior partner with Texaco, Petronas, MOGE and PTT in the Yetagun project, eventually purchasing Texaco's interests and directly managing the project.

However, the atmosphere in London began to change, particularly after the release of Daw Aung San Suu Kyi and the encouragement she gave to exile and foreign student anti-investment and boycott campaigns. Aung San Suu Kyi, an Oxford graduate who was married to a Briton, was close to the family of the former head of the British Foreign Office and former ambassador to Burma and India, Lord Gore-Booth, was a natural (source of information?) for the unanalytical British media.[42] The Burma Campaign and others now found their access to media outlets was greatly enhanced by keeping Aung San Suu Kyi's name at the centre of their propaganda. Alternative views on how to achieve political change were no longer welcome. The government came under increasing pressure in the House of Commons and the House of Lords and began to withdraw their support for encouraging trade and investment in Myanmar.

Following the 1997 British election, when the Labour Party under Tony Blair's leadership gained power, the new Foreign Secretary, the late Robin Cook, announced that from then on Britain would have a foreign policy "with an ethical dimension". In keeping with the post-Cold War trend of American foreign policy, human rights and democratic government became an aspect of Britain's foreign relations. The government implicitly endorsed the anti-trade and investment, anti-tourism and consumer boycott campaigns the Burma Campaign organized by, for example, publicly as well as privately calling on Premier Oil to disinvest in Myanmar. However, the government was unwilling to go to the extent of passing legislation banning new foreign investment in Myanmar as the U.S. Congress had done as this would undermine support for it in the City of London and not be consonant with European Union policy.

The Burma Campaign UK and related movements have gained increased prominence not only by the receipt of the Nobel Peace Prize and other international prizes by Aung San Suu Kyi, but also by a number of high profile incidents involving Britons arrested for political activities within Myanmar. Rachel Goldwyn was one of those. She served two months of a seven-year term for allegedly singing a pro-democracy song on a Yangon street.[43] A master at self-promotion and campaigning was James Mawdsley who entered Myanmar thrice and was arrested each time. His family, joined by inveterate human rights protesters such as Lord Alton and Baroness Cox, generated massive mail flows to the Foreign Office during his year in prison in 1999–2000.[44] His claims that the regime was committing "genocide" in the border areas with Thailand was echoed and publicized repeatedly by organizations such as Christian Solidarity Worldwide which manages to keep the "Burma question" in the British press in remarkably emotional terms.[45] Such is the strength of the Burma issue in Britain the Burma Campaign could get all three major political party leaders in February 2004 to publicly avow that it is best to avoid tourism in Burma because of the alleged financial succour this provides the army government.[46] When it comes to discussing Myanmar in Britain, it is as if the political class has been gripped by a form of long distance millenarianism.

Within the European Union, former colonial powers have significant influence on the formation of policy toward various Asian, African and Latin American countries as it is believed that they have a superior understanding of the politics of their erstwhile subjects. Britain's hard-line stance on Myanmar thus became the EU common position. However, over time, the failure of that policy to produce political change within the country, and the damage the continued denial of aid and trade was doing not to the generals but to the people of the country, led a number of countries to begin to question the British position. As the British position is presented with a high moral tone, rather as it was in 1885, there is little public discussion of the EU position in other member countries. Now, of course, the British position is set and the Myanmar problem has been defined as freeing Aung San Suu Kyi and placing her party in power.[47] As that is not about to happen, the British have created a problem for themselves which is compounded by the nature of the responses it creates in Myanmar.

Notes

1. Sections of this chapter have been adopted from the author's essay "Pathways to the Present" in *Myanmar: Beyond Politics to Societal Imperatives*, edited by Kyaw Yin Hlaing, Robert H. Taylor and Tin Maung Maung Than, Singapore: Institute of Southeast Asian Studies, 2005, pp. 1–29.
2. See for a recent brief discussion of an oft written about subject, "The Introduction of British Administration in Upper Myanmar (1885–86)" in *Selected Writings of U Hla Thein* (Yangon: Myanmar Historical Commission, 2005), pp. 167–94. See also Kyan, *Mahawunshintowminkyi Okchokyei (1886–97)* [Chief Commissioner's Administration], Yangon: Myanmar Yatana Sapei, 2003.
3. H. Fielding, *Thibaw's Queen*, New York and London: Harper and Brothers, 1899, p. 7. I am grateful for being reminded of this volume by Stephen Lee Keck, "Another Look at 'Thibaw's Queen': A Challenge to Colonial Historiography", in *Essays in Commemoration of the Golden Jubilee of the Myanmar Historical Commission*, Yangon: Myanmar Historical Commission, 2005, pp. 357–78.
4. Fielding, *Thibaw's Queen*.
5. Ibid., pp. 7–8.
6. Ibid., p. 8.
7. See Thant Myint-U, *The Making of Modern Burma*, Cambridge: Cambridge University Press, 2001 for an elaboration of these arguments.
8. Including what is now the Mon state and part of the Kayin state.
9. J. S. Furnivall, "The Making of Leviathan", *The Journal of the Burma Research Society* XXIX, no. 3 (1939): 1–138.
10. See Donald Eugene Smith, *Religion and Politics in Burma*, Princeton: Princeton University Press, 1965 and Tin Maung Maung Than, "*Sangha* Reforms and Renewal of *Sasana* in Myanmar: Historical Trends and Contemporary Practice" in *Buddhist Trends in Southeast Asia*, edited by Trevor Ling, Singapore: Institute of Southeast Asian Studies, 1993, pp. 6–63.
11. See Thant Myint-U, *The Making of Modern Burma*.
12. See Herman G. Tegenfeldt, *A Century of Growth: The Kachin Baptist Church of Burma*, Pasedena, California: William Carey Library, 1974.
13. For a fuller account, see Robert H. Taylor, "Colonial Forces in British Burma: An Army Postponed" in *Colonial Armies in Southeast Asia*, edited by Karl Hack and Tobias Rettig, London: Routledge, forthcoming.

14. In contemporary Myanmar public discourse, individuals are referred to as belonging to a "national race", one of the country's many "national races".
15. Victory B. Lieberman, "Ethnic Politics in Eighteenth Century Burma", *Modern Asian Studies* 12, no. 3 (1978): 455–82.
16. See, for example, G. E. Harvey, *History of Burma*, London: Frank Cass, 1967 (reprint of the 1925 edition); S. W. Cocks, *Burma Under British Rule*, Bombay: K. and J. Cooper, n.d. [1920s?].
17. Ananda Rajah, "A 'Nation of Intent' in Burma: Karen Ethno-Nationalism, Nationalism and Narration of Nation", *The Pacific Review* 15, no. 4, pp. 517–37.
18. See the papers in the Burma Office File 1506/37, India Office Library and Archives, the British Library, London. See also Robert H. Taylor, "British Policy and the Shan States, 1886–1940", in *Changes in Northern Thailand and the Shan States 1886–1940*, edited by Prakai Nontawasee, Singapore: Institute of Southeast Asian Studies, 1988, pp. 13–62, esp. pp. 32–45.
19. See Ian Fellowes-Gorden, *The Battle for Naw Seng's Kingdom*, London: Leo Cooper, 1971; Jon Latimer, *The Forgotten War*, London: John Murray, 2004, p. 210.
20. Dorothy Hess Guyot, "Communal Conflict in the Burma Delta", in *Southeast Asian Transitions: Approaches through Social History*, edited by Ruth T. McVey, New Haven: Yale University Southeast Asia Program, 1978, pp. 191–234.
21. See Ian Morrison, *Grandfather Longlegs*, London: Faber and Faber, 1947.
22. See Martin Smith, "Ethnic Politics and Regional Development in Myanmar: The Need for New Approaches", in Kyaw, Taylor and Tin, eds., *Myanmar: Beyond Politics to Societal Imperatives*, pp. 56–85.
23. Making Myanmar an Indian province did require the colonial government to protect and propagate Christianity, but the Church of England primarily concerned itself with Europeans and only about seven per cent of the Christian minority in the country were members of that church.
24. For an important recent study of the Myanmar economy in the 1930s, and the social and political consequences thereof, see Ian Brown, *A Colonial Economy in Crisis: Burma's Rice Cultivators and the World Depression of the 1930s*, London: RoutledgeCurzon, 2005.
25. See Robert H. Taylor, "British Policy toward Burma (Myanmar) in the 1920's and 1930's: Separation and Responsible Self-Government", in *Essays in Commemoration of the Golden Jubilee of the Myanmar Historical Commission*, Yangon: Myanmar Historical Commission, 2005, pp. 149–75.
26. See, for example, George Orwell, *Burmese Days*, London: Penguin, 2001; first published in 1934.
27. See T. A. B. Corley, *A History of the Burmah Oil Company*, 1924–66, Volume II, London: Heinemann, 1988.

28. Phillip Darby, *British Defence Policy East of Suez 1947–1968*, London: Oxford University Press for the Royal Institute of International Affairs, 1973, p. 13.

29. Ibid.

30. Mary P. Callahan, *Making Enemies: War and State Building in Burma*, Ithaca and London: Cornell University Press, 2003, pp. 120, 166–68.

31. Ibid., pp. 103–04.

32. Darby, *British Defence Policy East of Suez*, p. 62.

33. For example, Japan provided on averaged US$150 million per year in foreign economic assistance between 1983 and 1987; West Germany, US$42 million per year; France and the USA, US$8 million per year; and the United Kingdom, nothing. Indeed, repayments on earlier assistance during this period meant that net payments were — US$2.5 million per year. OECD, *Geographical Distribution of Financial Flows to Developing Countries, 1986/87, reprinted in Thailand, Burma Country Profile, 1989–90*, London: Economist Intelligence Unit, 1989, p. 67.

34. Philip Ziegler, ed., *From Shore to Shore: The Final Years, the Diaries of Earl Mountbatten of Burma, 1953–1979*, London: Collins, 1989, p. 151.

35. Ne Win apparently thought the school, because of its American financial backing, was some sort of imperialist plot. Ibid., pp. 229–32.

36. See papers in Foreign and Commonwealth Office Files FCO 15/1896 and FCO 15/1870, UK National Archives, Kew. I am indebted to Derek Tonkin for bringing these to my attention.

37. The 8-8-88 demonstrations were coordinated across Myanmar thanks in part to the broadcasts of the BBC back into the country.

38. One interviewer, for example, insisted that I respond to his question on a live news broadcast that the result of the demonstrations in Yangon would be decided by "people power" as in the Philippines the previous year. When I insisted the army would decide the outcome, he was less than impressed with my knowledge of Myanmar affairs.

39. Remarks by Mr Morland at a seminar at St Antony's College, Oxford, 1995.

40. One of the stranger phenomenon was the emergence of the alleged Crown Prince or King of Burma, one Shwebo Mintha. A former senior lecturer in accounting at the then Central London Polytechnic who had not returned to Myanmar on completion of his state scholarship in the early 1960s but married an English woman and remained in the UK, Shwebo Mintha approached the author after seeing him on television. He made the extraordinary offer of making him his prime minister when he returned to take up the throne. In the meantime, I would have to write his speeches as his Burmese was a little rusty.

41. I was a member at the time.

42. It remains a mystery as to whether she has obtained British nationality. Her brother, Aung San Oo, is an American citizen.
43. When she returned to England and refused to denounce the regime and its human rights record, she was publicly vilified in a press release by the Burma Campaign UK on 8 November 1999. <www.burmaproject.org/110899BCU.html>.
44. See James Mawdsley, *The Heart Must Break*, London: Century: 2001.
45. See Benedict Rogers, *A Land Without Evil: Stopping the Genocide of Burma's Karen People*, Oxford and Grand Rapids, Michigan: Monarch Books, 2004.
46. The same erroneous argument was advanced on BBC World Service television without peradventure by a spokeswoman for an "ethical tourism" campaign in November 2004.
47. It should be noted, however, that Britain has in recent years begun to provide some "humanitarian assistance" *via* non-governmental organizations to the people of Myanmar.

References

Brown, Ian. *A Colonial Economy in Crisis: Burma's Rice Cultivators and the World Depression of the 1930s*. London: RoutledgeCurzon, 2005.

Burma Office File 1506/37. British Library, London.

Callahan, Mary P. *Making Enemies: War and State Building in Burma*. Ithaca and London: Cornell University Press, 2003.

Cocks, S. W. *Burma Under British Rule,* 2nd edition. Bombay: K. and J. Cooper, n.d.

Corley, T.A.B. *A History of the Burmah Oil Company*, 1924–66, Volume II, London: Heinemann, 1988.

Darby, Phillip. *British Defence Policy East of Suez 1947–1968*. London: Oxford University Press for the Royal Institute of International Affairs, 1973.

Fellowes-Gorden,Ian. *The Battle for Naw Seng's Kingdom.* London: Leo Cooper, 1971.

Fielding, Henry. *Thibaw's Queen*. New York and London: Harper and Brothers, 1899.

Foreign and Commonwealth Office Files FCO 15/1896 and FCO 15/1870, U.K. National Archives, Kew.

Furnivall, J. S. "The Making of Leviathan", *The Journal of the Burma Research Society,* XXIX, no. 3 (1939): 1–138.

Geographical Distribution of Financial Flows to Developing Countries, 1986/87, reprinted in *Thailand, Burma Country Profile, 1989–90*. London: Economist Intelligence Unit, 1989.

Harvey, G. E. *History of Burma*. London: Frank Cass, 1967 [reprint of the 1925 edition].

Hess Guyot, Dorothy. "Communal Conflict in the Burma Delta", in *Southeast Asian Transitions: Approaches through Social History* edited by Ruth T. McVey, New Haven: Yale University Southeast Asia Program, 1978, pp. 191–234.

Hla Thein. "The Introduction of British Administration in Upper Myanmar (1885–86)" , in *Selected Writings of U Hla Thein*. Yangon: Myanmar Historical Commission, 2005. <www.burmaproject.org/110899BCU.html>.

India Office Library and Archives.

Keck, Stephen Lee. "Another Look at 'Thibaw's Queen': A Challenge to Colonial Historiography", in *Essays in Commemoration of the Golden Jubilee of the Myanmar Historical Commission*. Yangon: Myanmar Historical Commission, 2005.

Kyan, Mahawunshintowminkyi *Okchokyei (1886–97). Chief Commissioner's Administration*. Yangon: Myanmar Yatana Sapei, 2003.

Latimer, Jon. *The Forgotten War*. London: John Murray, 2004.

Lieberman, Victory B. "Ethnic Politics in Eighteenth Century Burma", *Modern Asian Studies* 12, no. 3 (1978): 455–82.

Mawdsley, James. *The Heart Must Break*, London: Century, 2001.

Morrison, Ian. *Grandfather Longlegs*. London: Faber and Faber, 1947.

Orwell, George. *Burmese Days*. London: Penguin, 2001. (First published in 1934).

Rajah, Ananda. "A 'Nation of Intent' in Burma: Karen Ethno-Nationalism, Nationalism and Narration of Nation", *The Pacific Review* 15, no. 4, pp. 517–37.

Rogers, Benedict. *A Land Without Evil: Stopping the Genocide of Burma's Karen People*. Oxford and Grand Rapids, Michigan: Monarch Books, 2004.

Smith, Donald Eugene. *Religion and Politics in Burma*. Princeton: Princeton University Press, 1965.

Smith, Martin. "Ethnic Politics and Regional Development in Myanmar: The Need for New Approaches", in *Myanmar: Beyond Politics to Societal Imperatives* edited by Kyaw Yin Hlaing, Robert Taylor and Tin Maung Maung Than, pp. 56–85. Singapore: Institute of Southeast Asian Studies, 2005.

Taylor, Robert H. "British Policy and the Shan States, 1886–1940" in *Changes in Northern Thailand and the Shan States 1886–1940* edited by Prakai Nontawasee, Singapore: Institute of Southeast Asian Studies, 1988, pp. 13–32.

Taylor, Robert H. "Pathways to the Present", in *Myanmar: Beyond Politics to Societal Imperatives* edited by Kyaw Yin Hlaing, Robert H. Taylor and Tin Maung Maung Than. Singapore: Institute of Southeast Asian Studies, 2005.

Taylor, Robert H. "British Policy toward Burma (Myanmar) in the 1920s and 1930s: Separation and Responsible Self-Government", in *Essays in Commemoration of the Golden Jubilee of the Myanmar Historical Commission*. Yangon: Myanmar Historical Commission, 2005, pp. 149–75.

Taylor, Robert H. "Colonial Forces in British Burma: An Army Postponed", in *Colonial Armies in Southeast Asia*, edited by Karl Hack and Tobias Rettig. London: Routledge, forthcoming.

Tegenfeldt, Herman G. *A Century of Growth: The Kachin Baptist Church of Burma*. Pasedena, California: William Carey Library, 1974.

Thant Myint-U. *The Making of Modern Burma*. Cambridge: Cambridge University Press, 2001.

Tin Maung Maung Than. "*Sangha* Reforms and Renewal of *Sasana* in Myanmar: Historical Trends and Contemporary Practice", in *Buddhist Trends in Southeast Asia,* edited by Trevor Ling. Singapore: Institute of Southeast Asian Studies, 1993, pp. 6–63.

Ziegler, Philip, ed. *From Shore to Shore: The Final Years, the Diaries of Earl Mountbatten of Burma, 1953–1979*. London: Collins, 1989.

5

Between Democracy and Economic Development: Japan's Policy towards Burma/Myanmar Then and Now

Kei Nemoto

Introduction

It has been said that among all the Asian countries, Japan is in a position to exercise the strongest influence on the military government of Myanmar. The country has a deep history of "friendship" with Burma/Myanmar and the Japanese Government itself emphasizes that Japan is the only country which possesses the means for negotiating both with the military junta and NLD. However, the Japanese Government has been blamed by both human rights activists and Japanese business circles. Human rights activists criticize Japan as supporting the military junta through the provision of economic assistance, while Japanese business circles are dissatisfied with their government's policy to keep the amount of ODA at a low level by freezing the new yen loans since 1988. Additionally, after May 2003 when Aung San Suu Kyi was detained, Japan, in concert with the United States and the EU, also froze most of the economic assistance for a while. This more recent policy is a means of attempting to bring pressure to bear on the junta through a quasi-policy of economic sanctions.

Has Japan supported the military government? This is not an easy question to answer. Although the Japanese government emphasizes that it has been making all possible efforts at promoting both democratization and the economic development of Myanmar, actual policies seem to suggest a passive willingness to support the junta through economic assistance in order to foster change towards democratic norms. However, such intentions do not appear to have been met with any success yet. It would appear that Japan's position is vaguely between democratic and economic development. In order to understand the reason why Japan has been caught in this middling position, I will survey the historical nature of relations between the two countries before examining the recent situation. Finally, I will discuss the activities of Myanmar nationals residing in Japan and their impact on the bilateral relationship.

Japan-Burma Relations before 1988

The Second World War, Japanese Occupation and War Reparations

Japanese forces began their invasion of Burma with an attack on Tenasserim from Thailand in January 1942. The first British line of defence at Moulmein on the Salween River was defeated and they were then driven westwards along the coast. Subsequently, a second British defensive position was defeated at Pegu. Following the second defeat, the British decided to evacuate Rangoon in March and retreated to Prome.

The British continued fighting the Japanese on the Irrawaddy valley and had some assistance against the Japanese from Chinese troops along the Burma Road. However, this Anglo-Chinese initiative of establishing a line from Pyinmana to Allanmyo fell through. The British were then forced to retreat up the Chindwin valley towards Manipur. Nonetheless, the British contemplated a third line of defence in northern Burma. This attempt was, however, frustrated by the Japanese who attacked the Shan Hills from China. This third attack in turn led to the disintegration of the British forces defending Burma, into small guerilla groups with assistance from the ethnic minorities. By the end of May 1942, the Japanese had captured the entire Irrawaddy valley.

The Burmese generally expected that Japan would help gaining independence of Burma. There existed a small nationalist student groups that were trained in Japan. They were the core members of the Burma Independence Army (BIA) which advanced towards Burma taking different routes from the Japanese Army. The Burmese Thakin Party that had initially offered collaboration with the Japanese went underground and supported the Japanese. During the next three years of occupation, the

Japanese administered Burma with the help of the local administration that had been left behind. The Japanese utilized the English language for administration and ruled the country indirectly through political commissars. The Japanese attempt to build a railway connecting southern Burma to Bangkok, the so-called "death railway", is one of the most potent and symbolic reminders of the Japanese occupation of Burma. Thousands upon thousands of natives and Allied prisoners of war perished during the construction of the railway line. In March 1945, many of the Burmese nationalists shifted to anti-Japan and developed resistance against them (Anti-Fascist War).

After the occupation and the end of the war following the Japanese surrender in 1945, Japan retained a special place in Burmese political developments. The immediate reason for this sentimental attachment was the fact that it was Japan that had trained the "Thirty Comrades" who were the core of the Burma Independence Army (BIA) which actually fought against the British and contributed towards gaining independence. The short duration of less than two-and-a half years between the Japanese surrender and the declaration of Burma's independence in January 1948 meant that Japan was able to re-establish ties with Burma's post-independence elite rather swiftly. And although Aung San was assassinated very early on, members of the "Thirty Comrades" and in particular, Ne Win, who came to power after the military coup of 1962, ensured that Japan had special relations with Burmese political elite. This special relationship allowed Japan to craft the ambiguous policy that balanced economic aid and grants with political pressure on the Myanmar Government towards democratization.

Post-war relations between Japan and Burma officially started from April 1955, when a peace treaty was signed and an agreement on war reparations went into effect. It took nearly four years for negotiations to re-open formal diplomatic ties between the two countries, since Burma did not take part in the 1951 Treaty of Peace with Japan (also referred to as the San Francisco Treaty). However, even before these negotiations, unofficial relations through economic exchanges had existed since 1949, a year after the independence of Burma. Since Japan lost its colonies such as China, Korea and Taiwan, which had supplied a huge amount of rice in the pre-war period, the country was faced with a serious food shortage in the post-war period. Japan's agricultural sector was in a terrible situation after the war and there was no other way but to import rice from abroad to avoid domestic famine. Burma was among one of the countries that Japan imported rice from. In 1949, Japan purchased 70,000 tonnes of rice from Burma. Given the situation of not having any official diplomatic relations, Japanese buyers from trading companies utilized ex-members of the *Minami Kikan* (a special Japanese military unit which existed from 1941 to 1942 aimed at weakening British rule in Burma by clandestinely providing arms and military training to young Burmese nationalists such as Aung San, Ne Win and Let Ya) as go-betweens. Members of this unit had strong linkages with the Burmese nationalist elite during the wartime period and these elite subsequently became the leaders of newly-independent Burma. In order to persuade the Burmese Government to approve the sale of their rice to Japan, this unique wartime connection made by the members of *Minami Kikan* helped Japan a lot.

The amount of rice that was purchased increased sharply in the immediate post-war period. Japan bought 170,000 tonnes of rice in 1950, and the amount rose to 300,000 tonnes in 1954. Some of these purchases were undertaken without open tenders in order to arrange for prices lower than those at the international rice market. Although from Burma's point of view there was no reason to sell their rice by giving such special priority to a country with which it had no diplomatic relations, it responded positively to Japan's urgent request. This special arrangement indicated the existence of strong linkages between Japanese members of the ex-*Minami Kikan* and Burmese political elite after independence.

Following the resumption of official diplomatic relations between the two countries, the Japanese Government paid 72 billion yen (which was then the equivalent of US$200 million) over the decade spanning 1955–65 in goods and services in accordance with the agreement on war reparations. Japan also paid an additional US$50 million for technical assistance as well as investment in joint ventures between Japanese private firms and the Burmese public and private sectors. A new agreement between the two countries in 1963 called the Economic and Technical Cooperation Treaty provided for another US$140 million which was in reality a continuation of the war reparations (it was called "quasi-reparations").

A major portion of the Japanese war reparations to Burma was used for the construction of the Baluchaung hydroelectric power plant which was built along the Salween River in the Karenni (Kayah) state. Another major portion of it was used for the so-called "four major industrialization projects", which consisted of light vehicle production, heavy vehicle production, farming machinery production, and electrical machinery production. These projects began in 1962 and lasted until 1988 and changed in character from projects associated with war reparation to those of "quasi-reparations". It was then finally transformed into commodity loans from 1969 as a part of Japanese Official Development Assistance (ODA).

Official Development Assistance to Burma

Japan's ODA to Burma, which actually replaced war reparations, began from 1968 in the form of yen loans. The grant aid was also started from 1975. The amount of ODA towards Burma was small in the beginning as Ne Win, who ousted U Nu in a military coup in 1962, nudged the country towards self-sufficiency under a regime called the "Burmese Way to Socialism" (1962–88). However, from the latter half of the 1970s, Burma altered its position to actively receive ODA in order to overcome its seriously stagnant domestic economy. From the onset of this policy change, ODA from Japan rapidly increased. Burma received ODA funds for large-scale projects, mainly for the development of social infrastructure such as electric power, transportation and irrigation. It also received commodity loans such as the aforementioned "four major industrialization projects" which included funds for procuring parts from four specific Japanese companies: Hino (for truck assembly), Mazda (for small-sized automobiles), Kubota (for farm machinery) and Matsushita (for electrical appliances).

The total amount of Japanese ODA to Burma from the time Japan began its funding until 1988 amounted to 511.7 billion yen (18.4 per cent). This amount comprised 403 billion yen (78.8 per cent) for loan aid, 94.1 billion yen for grant aid and 14.6 billion yen (2.8 per cent) for technical cooperation assistance. This total figure is extraordinarily high compared with Japanese ODA to other countries. Burma ranked seventh in terms of aid receipts from Japan during this period. More than sixty to seventy per cent of the total bilateral aid which Burma received between 1978 and 1988 came from Japan.

Reason for the Huge Amount of Japanese ODA to Burma

As is well known, during the period of Ne Win's "Burmese Way to Socialism", Burma not only promoted inactive and neutral diplomacy but it also strictly regulated the introduction of foreign capital. In spite of this

Burmese predisposition, why did Japan continue to give extraordinary amounts of aid to Burma? And why did Burma receive it? For Burma, it was probably the critical state of its domestic economy in the middle of the 1970s that led to the acceptance of such aid. But why did Japan decide to give Burma a higher priority than other under-developed countries? And why did Burma prefer Japan to other donor countries when it sought foreign aid? The answer may lie in non-rational reasons, such as Japan's special consideration for Burma and *vice-versa*, rather than rational ones, such as the economic or political relationship between the two countries. It is difficult to understand that Japan's ODA to Burma was given as preceding "investment" for Japanese firms to do their business there (such as was the case in ODA given to Thailand, Indonesia and the Philippines).

Though it was mainly hidden from the public view, in the discourse among influential Japanese in diplomatic and economic matters, they constantly refer to a "special relationship between Japan and Burma", or the "historically friendly relationship" between the two countries. The thinking behind this discourse is that while Japan brought a great deal of inconvenience to Burma during World War II, it also made significant contributions to the country. Young nationalists such as the "Thirty Comrades", which included Aung San and Ne Win, were educated and trained by Japanese army officers of the *Minami Kikan*, leading to the birth of the Burma Independence Army (BIA). This army subsequently developed into the Burma National Army (BNA). Japan also accepted many Burmese students, providing them with scholarships during the war. Many such students (military and civilians) rose to positions of national leadership in post-independence Burma. Therefore, when these returnees were entrusted to build a new Burma, the general feeling of Japan's policymakers was they should be supported.

Takashi Suzuki, the former Japanese ambassador to Burma who was stationed there from 1971 through 1974, details this line of reasoning in his Japanese written memoirs on the history of Japan-Burma relations (T. Suzuki, *A Country Called Burma*, PHP Research Institute, Tokyo, 1977). He especially emphasizes the achievements of Burma's anti-colonial vanguard forces, The Thirty Comrades, and the BIA, then goes on to declare that "Burma is one country that is most worthwhile for Japan to support." He points out that

the people of Burma are friendly and good natured, sincere, thrifty, forgetful of past misery with their hearts of Buddhists, with good communication with the Japanese people and very little resentment towards Japanese, and that Japan had a special relationship with Burma from a historical perspective.

However, the memoir fails to consider other important elements that cannot be ignored when recalling the history of independence in Burma. Those are the anti-Japanese struggle in 1945 and the process of crucial negotiations for independence with British authorities between 1945 and 1947, both under the leadership of Aung San. Clearly, Suzuki and others of similar views share a one-sided interpretation of history.

At the same time, we need to realize that the Burmese did their part to foster this idea of a special relationship with Japan. According to a Japanese diplomatic document made public in 2003, when Brigadier Aung Gyi, and his team visited Japan in January 1963 as a representative of Ne Win's Revolutionary Council to negotiate for an increase in war reparations (which resulted in the "quasi-reparations" put into effect from 1965), he made a speech in front of Japanese officials and politicians on the first day of his trip. In the speech, he mentioned that his trip was not for the negotiation of war reparations but rather "as a younger brother" consulting about a certain family problem to his "elder brother". Using the metaphor of "younger brother" for Burma and "elder brother" for Japan had been a cliché in Burma during the Japanese Occupation period though it became a politically incorrect expression for Japan to use in the post-war period. However, the Burmese delegation did use this expression in 1963. This speech in turn made such a strong positive impression on the Japanese Government that it felt the need to reciprocate positively to the Burmese demand (Diplomatic Record Office of the Ministry of Foreign Affairs of Japan, E02-003-001-002).

Another example can be seen in the views of the Burmese Government regarding their struggle for independence as written in school textbooks after independence and particularly after 1962. These views centre around the *Minami Kikan* and the birth and activities of the BIA. Although the historical significance of the all-out revolt against the Japanese Army by the BNA in 1945 led by Aung San is strongly stressed, the *Minami Kikan*, which gave birth to and guided the BIA, is described as a group of Japanese people who understood the Burmese nationalists' aspiration for independence. This gesture of describing the *Minami Kikan* (which was actually no more than a one-time spy organization of the Japanese Army) positively, or at least not labelling the *Kikan* as fascist, came about owing to the friendly relationship that existed between the *Kikan*'s members and the Burmese Thirty Comrades. This view was meant to justify to the Burmese nation Japanese assistance in the creation of the National Army.

In 1980, the Ne Win government publicly announced the achievements of the *Minami Kikan* by decorating former members with the Order of Aung San. Also, in March 1983, during a visit to Burma by then Japanese Foreign Minister Shintaro Abe, Burmese President San Yu told him that, in one sense, Japan had helped Burma to achieve independence. San Yu also openly stated that the Japanese Army made it possible for the young Burmese nationalists to acquire political skills. At a later date, Foreign Minister Abe wrote that during his talks with important people in the Burmese Government, he could sense "their strong friendliness and great expectations with Japan". (In H. Sakuma, "Introduction", *Modern History of Politics in Burma*, Tokyo: Keiso-shobo, 1984). The reasons for such statements by the Burmese governments might include an attempt at obtaining as much aid from Japan as possible, but it in turn helped to justify the perculiar Japanese understanding of Japan-Burma bilateral relations. It is worth noting that every Japanese ambassador to Burma in the 1960s, 1970s and early 1980s enjoyed better access to Ne Win than ambassadors from all other nations.

Japan's Policy towards Myanmar after 1988

In 1987, a year before the nationwide uprising in Myanmar, Japan secretly tried to persuade Myanmar to gradually move towards an open economic system, but the effort ended in vain. In 1988, Myanmar witnessed the large anti-Ne Win regime mass movement, which then metamorphosed into the movement demanding democratic change as well as a capitalist economy. On 18 September, however, the army (*tatmadaw*) regained control over the movement and established the State Law and Order Restoration Council (SLORC). In November 1997 it changed its name to the State Peace and Development Council (SPDC) and reshuffled many of the members except the four major figures: Than Shwe, Maung Aye, Khin Nyunt and Tin U.

The Japanese Government was among the first nations to recognize the military junta in February 1989. Although Japanese ODA stopped temporarily during the time of the peoples' uprising, it was later resumed, but limited to a few ongoing projects, technical cooperation, and humanitarian assistance. A freeze was put on new loans. This policy has not been changed up to now. From the beginning, the basic Japanese posture towards SLORC (and SPDC) has been one of soft persuasion. It has not resorted to economic sanctions. Japan behaved as a good friend of Myanmar, persuading the military junta to open up Myanmar's economy as well as to move towards democracy and stop human rights violations. The Japanese Government expects the Burmese military regime to change on its own, even though it has sometimes been irritated by the regime's stubbornness. Although Japan does not ignore the importance of Aung San Suu Kyi and her political party, the National League for Democracy (NLD), it does not express strong support towards them either. In this regard, Japan has made a clear break from the severe attitudes against Myanmar adopted by the United States and the European Union.

However, it should be noted that Japan's purpose and motive in maintaining this soft and friendly approach towards the Myanmar military government does not derive from the remembrance of past historical friendship between the two countries anymore. The Japanese Government's soft approach is now based on their consideration of the importance of economic development rather than political development in the movement towards democracy. Even though their official explanation mentions that Japan has been supporting the democratization of Myanmar as well as its economic development, the former has generally been given at best secondary importance.

The Japanese Government has generally held this diplomatic position based on the presumption that economic development will in turn be followed by democratization. When they realized that the Burmese military government adopted the market-oriented economy in 1989, they thought it was a good opportunity to apply this presumption to Myanmar too. This presumption, which is debatable among scholars, is resonant with the Japanese business circles' "economy first" voice, which is accompanied by Aung San Suu Kyi bashing (since she denies this "theory"). Though the Japanese Government has restricted its ODA to Myanmar to low levels since 1988, it is clear that they are always seeking an opportunity for the resumption of full-scale loan aid projects. For example, Japan conducted a joint research project on the economic structural adjustment of Myanmar with Burmese counterparts consisting of members of the military junta and some civilian technocrats from 2000 to 2002. Members of the Japanese research team included individuals from business firms, and the project was considered as a precursor to the resumption of new full-scale yen loans to Myanmar. However, it was deadlocked by the junta's categorical refusal to accept any of the Japanese advice rendered in the final project report.

On the other hand, one cannot simplistically argue that "economic development first" is Japan's only active policy towards Myanmar. The keeping of ODA to a low level by freezing new yen loans since 1988 is a sort of compromise between "democratic" and "economic development first" position. The government cannot ignore domestic and international public opinion, which supports Aung San Suu Kyi and the NLD. Much of the Japanese domestic media reports Aung San Suu Kyi's painful position and her unyielding activities in rather sympathetic terms. Her mistreatment by the military junta always attracts the media's attention. Letters supporting Aung San Suu Kyi's activities, or those voicing concern about human rights violations in Myanmar sometimes appear in the readers' columns of various newspapers. Usually such letters insist that Japan's diplomacy towards Myanmar should pay more attention to the deteriorating situation of human rights and democracy. Taking this public opinion into consideration, the Japanese Government cannot decide to lift the freeze on new yen loans so easily.

Following the May 2003 Depayin incident in which many members of the NLD were attacked and killed by a pro-government mob rumoured to be affiliated to a junta-made mass organization the Union Solidarity Development Association (USDA), Japan suspended its ODA to Myanmar. This harsh response was motivated by the brutality of the incident and subsequent detention of Aung San Suu Kyi for the third time. Japan wanted to impress upon the military junta that it was irritated by these negative political developments. However, as Yuki Akimoto uncovered in her article on *The Irrawaddy* (October 2004), Japan resumed ODA to Myanmar just a year later (June 2004). The ODA was delivered in the form of human resource development scholarships and an afforestation project in the dry zone of Myanmar. This recent resumption of aid has, however, gone largely unnoticed by the public. This method of resuming ODA timidly can be invoked as proof that the Japanese Government has not shifted from its vague position between "democracy" and "economic development first" policy.

The Burmese in Japan: Their Influence on Domestic Public Opinion

Behind the public voice of Japanese people supporting Aung San Suu Kyi and the democratization of Myanmar, there exists the influence of activities of several Burmese political groups in Japan. The members of these groups mainly consist of Burmese refugees and those seeking refugee status. It has been said that nearly 10,000 Burmese passport holders are living in Japan since the 1990s. Most of them are so-called "over stayers" or people who work in Japan without fulfilling proper legal requirements. On the other hand, there are also several hundred activists living in Japan who were active in the mass democracy movement in Myanmar. Many of them have sought political asylum in Japan. The Japanese Government has practised a very strict policy towards these asylum seekers and very few of them were initially recognized as refugees. However, this hard position changed in 1998 and Japan started recognizing refugee status and gradually offered special residential permission. Since then and up to August 2006, altogether 117 Burmese were authorized as refugees and another 139 were given special permission to stay in Japan by the government. There still exist more than 170 Burmese seeking refugee status in Japan. It is worth noting that most of the authorized refugees accepted in Japan after 1998 are essentially from Myanmar (the exceptions to this rule of thumb are a few Afghans and Kurds). This changed stance of the Japanese Government seems to be the result of the strong position of both domestic and international opinion supporting democracy and human rights in Myanmar. However, we should consider the influence of the political and non-political activities of the Burmese community in Japan at the same time.

The first Burmese political organization in Japan appeared in September 1988 when the mass movement for democracy in Burma reached the peak. It consisted of 150 members and was named the Burmese Association in Japan (BAIJ), but their control over the Burmese people and agenda in Japan did not last for long. In the 1990s, various political groups were established separately such as the Burma Youth Volunteer Association (BYVA), 8888 Association, Democratic Burmese Students Organization (DBSO), Students Organization for Liberation of Burma (SOLB), Burma Women's Union (BWU), Burma Rohingya Association in Japan (BRAJ) and the Japanese Branch of the National League for Democracy–Liberated Area (NLD-LA). Though the number of members in each group is small (approximately between thirty to a hundred), all of these groups, except BRAJ and NLD-LA, were re-organized under an umbrella organization called the Burma Office Japan (BOJ) which was established in 2000. BOJ issues its newsletters in both Japanese and Burmese every month.

Relations between the Japanese people and these Burmese political groups are rather strong. BOJ has been financially supported by the largest Japanese labour union Rengo (the Japan Trade Union Confederation) since its establishment. Not only the member groups of BOJ but also BRAJ and NLD-LA have joined an NGO called the People's Forum on Burma (PFB), which was established by both Japanese and Burmese citizens in 1996. Many Burmese activists take part in the activities involving human rights issues in Myanmar led by the Japanese office of Amnesty International. Their representatives sometimes visit the Ministry of Foreign Affairs (*Gaimu-sho*) and call on the Japanese Government to stop or restrict its ODA to Myanmar. On various occasions they have organized signature-collecting campaigns and hunger-strikes, for promoting and supporting the democracy movement in Myanmar together with Japanese volunteers, and these activities occasionally draw the attention of the local media.

Non-political activities organized by ordinary Burmese residents (who are not refugees or asylum seekers) are more numerous. Since the beginning of the 1990s, Burmese residing in Tokyo hold a Burmese new year festival (*Thingyan*) every April and more than 5,000 Burmese and Japanese gather for each occasion. Similar gatherings are held in Osaka and Nagoya. Low-cost Japanese language classes are also organized in Tokyo by these residents with the cooperation of Japanese volunteers. Ethnic minorities such as the Karens, Kachins, Buddhist Arakanese also have their own cultural bodies. Christian Karens and Kachins have their own churches in Tokyo as well. More than twenty Burmese restaurants have appeared in Tokyo since the 1990s and many of them draw both Burmese and Japanese customers. In some area in Tokyo, there are also a few Burmese stores that sell Burmese foods, books, magazines, CDs, videotapes.

Conclusion

Japan's bilateral relationship with Burma/Myanmar has undergone some recent changes. Traditionally, Japan always claimed a special place in Myanmar for training the "Thirty Comrades" who subsequently led the Burmese independence movement and went on to hold important political appointments in the country. Apart from Aung San, this important group that served as a bridge between Japan and Myanmar also included General Ne Win who was in power from 1962 to 1988. Even after the political changes that occurred after Ne Win's retirement, Japan has had better access to military elite within the ruling junta. This access if a function of the lingering effects of an historically embedded special relationship.

Apart from advantageous access, Japanese policy towards Myanmar has traditionally retained a strategic ambiguity between the importance of economic development on the one hand and democracy on the other.

The Japanese claim to a special relationship with the Myanmar junta has however, significantly eroded in the last few years and especially after the violence against NLD members and the detention of Aung San Suu Kyi in May 2003. Since then and much more in line with the positions adopted by the United States and the EU, Japan has reduced more on ODA. This new position is also influenced by domestic political developments within Japan. Such developments include the granting of refugee status to Burmese asylum seekers and the generally sympathetic attitude of locals and the domestic mass media towards Aung San Suu Kyi and the difficulties endured by ethnic minorities in Myanmar. Myanmar nationals in Japan themselves have organizations that promote their cultural and political interests.

6

"Legitimacy" in Burma/Myanmar: Concepts and Implications

David I. Steinberg

> If policy is the eternal pursuit of ends, it is the eternal pursuit of legitimacy.
>
> John Kane[1]

Introduction

The use of the term "legitimacy" and its antonym are often indiscriminately employed both in the media and even in policy circles at the highest levels. Definitions are generally absent, and a vague commonality of understanding is assumed on the part of those who articulate either concept and those who are the audience for it. In both attitudinal and policy terms, this is dangerous, for it leads to false expectations, simplistic approaches, and perverted policies on the part of all involved. Little thought is given, however, beyond an emotional response to the complexity of that assessment, and, indeed, the views of those affected by the legitimate-illegitimate paradigm.

In the case of Burma/Myanmar,[2] this gap is especially important because it not only involves a government and its political opposition, but a virtual myriad of minorities, each of whom may have their own assessment of what constitutes legitimacy for their own or central government administrations. This is further complicated as world attention has been focused on that state, and thus concepts derived from abroad, which may or may not have been fully ingested in that complex of societies, are attributed to internal events. Even the name of the state, "Burma" or Myanmar," conjures up both concepts of legitimacy and illegitimacy depending on one's vantage point.

The purpose of this chapter is not to determine which among these contested legitimacies or any potential permutations of them is appropriate, for that ultimate decision must rest only with the peoples of that society. Rather, it is an attempt to analyse the diverse forces that have consciously or unconsciously, inchoately or rationally, been used in this struggle and in previous societal attempts to apply various symbols and tools to attempt to forge consensus toward the employment of power and the resultant imposed or acquiesced authority — that is, the legitimacy of regimes or institutions.

But if in the popular foreign conception the current confrontation is dyadic, between the military elite now called the State Peace and Development Council (SPDC) and the political opposition National League for Democracy (NLD), personified by Nobel laureate Daw Aung San Suu Kyi, the reality is more complex; the tension is minimally triangular, and even more multi-faceted. The diverse minority groups (some of which are split by linguistic, religious, or other desiderata), varying by ethnicity, language, social organization, religion, historic and historical memory real and mythic, clan, as well as geography, are intimately affected by this unfolding turmoil, yet they speak in differing tongues, obscuring the validity of those within any single group who purport to represent that community, as well as those who might represent the minorities as a whole to the majority Burmans of either the government or the opposition.[3]

Welded together in an artificial state under British colonial rule that established contrived boundaries ignoring ethnicity and based on geopolitical considerations and happenstance, and then separately governed under Ministerial Burma and the peripheral areas, the peoples on the eve of independence lacked the commonality of history, symmetrical memory imaged or real, and of aspirations. In spite of heroic efforts to create synthesis before and after independence in 1948, the results have been less than successful. If "imagined communities"[4] are sometimes created to service contemporary nationalistic needs, Myanmar suffers from a plethora of such communities, which often lack the symmetry of both history and goals, and are antithetical to other such constructs. Those problems continue negatively to prevent the state of Burma/Myanmar from becoming a nation with a shared set of positive ideals and a national ethos, as contrasted with apparent and seemingly widespread anti-foreign sentiments. Even if common ideals are lacking so that the term "nation" in any but a legal sense is a misnomer, nationalism is a primary element in this search for legitimacy. But as majority nationalism among Burmans has grown, so has minority and ethnic nationalism, and the recognition of such nationalism by outside institutions, including multilateral donor organizations. Myanmar is facing an intensified complex of issues heretofore unexperienced.

Taylor has aptly commented:

> The most fundamental clash of values currently perceived in Burma is over the basis of the legitimacy of the state and its ability to structure social and political relations. The SLORC [now SPDC] rests its claim to legitimacy on its ability to maintain and protect a number of values held dear by itself, and, it believes, by the majority of the population. These include nationalism, national defense, economic development, and the preservation of indigenous religious, cultural and social institutions. Opponents advance the argument, more familiar to those in the West, that legitimacy comes from the consent of the people as expressed through the ballot box.[5]

Definitions and Dilemmas

Discussions of the issue of legitimacy in the Burma/Myanmar context transcend normal analyses and may become simply political issues that retard objective exploration. Rather than construed as attempts to probe into the social dynamics of that set of societies, such discussions immediately assume political proportions as various groups seek to use them to support their positions or to vilify their opposition. In an important sense, then, any discussion of legitimacy inadvertently becomes both an analytical as well as a political statement, and one that succeeds on one account probably fails in the other. The writer recognized the inherent danger involved.

Framing the issue of Burma/Myanmar in terms of contested political legitimacy may seem an unusual approach to a seeming myriad of societal problems that have been addressed on a number of occasions, but most often in sectoral terms (agriculture/rural, health, education). Yet elevating the issue to a more abstracted level provides an overarching approach that may be helpful in allowing broader consideration of the dynamics affecting the society as a whole. In spite of, or perhaps due to, the vagueness of the term, legitimacy as a concept offers conundrums. "Research on legitimacy is particularly difficult because the key decision, choosing the right theoretical perspective, presents a dilemma for which there is no necessarily correct solution."[6]

"Legitimacy", derived from the Latin (*legis*-law) has similar origins in the Burmese language, based on the classical Pali of the Burmese Buddhist canon. The term "political legitimacy" is not normally used in Myanmar, although the language has terms for both politics and legitimacy, the former *aso* or *asoya* (govern or government) and "legitimacy" *tayah win* (from the Pali *dharma*-Buddhist law, and to enter into) and *ubade* (also law from the Pali). They may be used singularly or together for the term law or legitimacy, but most often used in connection with the legitimacy of a child or truthfulness. Some claim that legitimacy is also sometimes conveyed by the terms *ana* (authority or power) and *awza* (influence) used together, but others would disagree as the former is normally institutional while the latter is often personal. How much the Buddhist derivations affect present attitudes and give added emphasis to these words is unclear. Political legitimacy, even if lacking in some traditional phrase, is evident in traditional concepts, such as that of the "good king" (*min gaung*). the attributes of whom then describe in traditional terms what in the modern period we might call "good governance".

Legitimacy, as variously defined, is ephemeral both in concept and reality in and across societies. It is constantly redefined and reinterpreted, both to suit changed political conditions and emerging needs — to justify or condemn regimes or ruling elites, and even states. Although it may lack scientific or social science precision, legitimacy nevertheless is a concept that is both ubiquitously and popularly used to support or vilify regimes. Internally, it must continuously be refurbished or it will wither away, like the theoretical Marxist state. In external relations, it may be affected by other overriding considerations, such as security or national interests. The positive forces that legitimate one regime or group can either be turned on their heads, or their absence can be used to delegitimate their opponents.

The Western social science tradition has been awash for some two hundred years or so with varying definitions of political legitimacy. This literature has been expertly reviewed and summarized, especially in the context of Southeast Asia, by Muthiah Alagappa.[7] He postulates four essential criteria for legitimacy: [1] ascension to power through established norms; [2] adherence to established norms of governance; [3] appropriate levels of performance in supplying goods and services to the population; and [4] the assent of those governed. The absence of these in whole or in part, according to some arcane local standards that may lose something in international translation, determines whether a particular society (or elements of that society or state) regards a certain regime as legitimate. Those standards may be quite different from those with international cachet. What seems apparent, as Alagappa notes, is that the less that a regime's internal legitimacy is evident, the greater the coercive force needed to keep it in power. But, as in any universalistic or comparative focus, Alagappa neglects to consider some indigenous aspects of the Burmese Buddhist tradition that could influence how villagers relate to these issues, as well as the potentially varying views of the diversity of peoples, regions, and backgrounds within the state.

We should consider Alagappa's configuration of legitimacy as applying indigenously, that is, how members of that society consider any regime. The importance of avoiding external value-laden judgments on legitimacy when attempting to ascertain the attitudes of any populace toward its own government is evident, for imposition of foreign views as representing local opinions is destructive of both analysis and policy. Yet in the modern world there is rarely a fire wall between indigenous perceptions of legitimacy and those emanating from abroad, except perhaps in the case of North Korea where the population has been effectively insulated from external influences. No matter how nationalistic a people, and how opposed they might be to globalization of any kind, international criteria and views of a government's legitimacy are likely to seep into the society and affect at least some of the population's views of the legitimacy of their own regime. This may cause a backlash against such "external meddling in internal affairs", as a government might phrase the issue, and although rural and relatively traditional populations are less likely to be influenced, it is probable that urban elites and the middle class will be affected to some degree. So this is not an inconsequential element in the complex internal legitimacy equation.

How much influence internally or externally should one assign to the fact that the Burma/Myanmar governments since independence has signed various international protocols concerning the rights and duties of their state and citizenry, and whether the state has adhered to these rights? As a signatory to a wide array of United Nations documents (some seventy-six are listed in the UN index), as well as assenting to the UN General Assembly resolution on the Universal Declaration of Human Rights of December 1948, to what degree can any government be castigated or held accountable for failure to recognize the concerns of both foreign institutions and governments, as well as their own people, that such rights or obligations are being ignored or placed on a lower order of priority than, for example, the national interests or security, however interpreted? Are selective foreign concerns in this regard about some countries, such as Myanmar, "fair" approaches, or are they results of prejudice toward the political system/ regime of any particular state? And who determines "fairness"? Are such concerns, especially coming from developed countries with considerable economic and military power, a result of ethnocentric political and foreign policies? These issues demand consideration, although answers are likely to be highly controversial.

Yet it is not only a regime or a set of leaders or an economic system (note the two communist insurrections in Burma against a government they regarded as insufficiently Marxist) that may be regarded as legitimate or illegitimate; the state and/or its boundaries may be so regarded, and at least in the earlier years of Burmese independence various elements within some minority groups (for example, the Karen, the Shan, the Kayah, the Kachin, some Muslim groups) questioned the legitimacy of the territorial integrity of the Union of Burma as was then constituted. These previous attitudes have generally been superceded by ones reaffirming the unity of the state, but under varying levels of administrative unity and centralization that have yet to be determined. Yet the suspicion that lurking in the shadows of the federalism that some minorities espouse, and that the NLD endorses, lie remnant desires for independence.[8] This remains a potent force in military thinking far beyond any propagandistic cant.

Geertz, writing in 1963, effectively analysed the problem that continues to plague the state and that is intimately connected to the question that Taylor raised in 1998 about differential interpretations of legitimacy:

> Here the government is to a very great extent the obvious agency of a single, central primordial group [the Burmans], and it is faced, therefore, with a very serious problem of maintaining legitimacy in the eyes of the members of peripheral groups — more than one-third of the population — who are naturally inclined to see it as alien, a problem it has attempted to solve largely by a combination of elaborate legal gestures of reassurance and a good deal of aggressive assimilationism.[9]

Simplistically portrayed, the ruling military elite, the State Peace and Development Council (SPDC),[10] has held that the cardinal element of its legitimacy as rulers has been the unity of the country that only the military can guarantee. This, together with the perpetuation of state sovereignty, is the primary (public) *raison d'etre* of continuing military rule, for without the military in command (according to the SLORC/ SPDC) the state will disintegrate. In contrast, the major opposition legal political party, the National League for Democracy (NLD) whose charismatic secretary and effective leader, Aung San Suu Kyi, remains under house arrest at the time of writing, believes that its overwhelming victory in the May 1990 elections gave them the mandate to govern. They also now agree to national unity, however.[11]

If the immediate dilemma externally seems to be a dichotomy between the military state and the civilian opposition (although most of the key leaders of the opposition NLD aside from Aung San Suu Kyi are former military figures — indicating the past prominence of the military in Burmese society and its likely continuation at least over the near term), the internal dilemmas are uncertain and may be compounded, for the autocratic nature of governance in Myanmar precludes the general attitudinal polling that is so prevalent in many societies and on which politicians and political scientists alike depend to ascertain public opinion. External assumptions are still based on the results of the May 1990 elections, which had a record turn out of about 72 per cent of eligible voters, and in which the opposition NLD swept about 80 per cent of the seats and some 59.9 per cent of the votes. The popularity of the NLD, or the unpopularity of military rule, may still be valid today, but it is an assumption some fifteen years later. That assumption is compounded by the question of whether, if the opposition maintains popularity, that popularity rests with the NLD as an organization, or personally with Aung San Suu Kyi, or with both in some complex proportion. Indeed, one issue in interpreting that election is how much the vote was in favour of the NLD, and how much it represented a desire to get the military out of governance.

Complex as well are the attitudes of many of the multiple minorities toward a central government they may regard as illegitimate, and what constitutes the legitimacy of such an administration, any differences among the minorities, and, indeed, between any individual minority element and its leaders and people.

The external assumption that elections are the only or essential indicators of legitimacy seems broadly accepted in the West and in some other states, although others, such as China and some fellow members of ASEAN such as Vietnam, Laos, and Brunei, might question that statement. Some democratic states have subordinated that concept to perceived national interests (for example, India in the case of Myanmar, the United States with Pakistan or Egypt). If the military in Myanmar believes in elections as conferring legal governance, which is questionable even though they agreed to hold them in May 1990 not perhaps for a new government but for a representative body to write a new constitution, then such voting in their minds is subordinate to their conception of the national interest of state unity.[12]

The "Washington Consensus" postulates an intimate, causative relationship between democracy and economic development, the latter being understood to require a market economic system. This is questionable theory (Singapore, for example), but is nevertheless pervasive. As Taylor noted: "Conversely, the largely unquestioned thesis of most Western observers of the struggle for economic reform in Vietnam and Burma/ Myanmar inevitably links the holding of 'free and fair' elections and the creation of a pluralistic democratic system of government as a necessary, if not a prerequisite, condition for successful and lasting economic reform."[13] Taylor continues that elections in developing countries are essential legitimizing forces to the aid-giving countries on which much of the developing world depends; they were accepted by the new leaders of such states and by much of the populace, and are a means of allowing diverse views. In any case, elections in the simplistic media are portrayed as the equivalent of democracy, although they are only one, but essential, indicator of that complex process. Although written some fifty years ago, Nash's observations on the rural sector that peasants have the form but not substance of political power, and that there is a gap between national and local scene that prevents the formation of building political institutions may still be applicable:

> A regime of civil liberties and democratic institutions, combined with the urgent tasks of cultural modernization and economic development, may take many forms, but it must grow out of the experience of the plurality of the people with real and substantive political power.[14]

Whether in Myanmar today elections internally play the pivotal role in conferring legitimacy as they do in other states, and if so, among which groups, are issues to be discussed. Historically, the record is mixed. Internally, elections have been both pivotal and inconsequential in modern Burmese history. Since independence, they were titular legitimating efforts by the mass mobilization Anti-Fascist People's Freedom League (AFPFL), which in hindsight is difficult imagining losing at that time. Taylor has commented, "If elections provide legitimacy for governments, the 1951 election in Burma provided a mere fig leaf."[15] Under the constitution of 1974, they were a travesty — an anachronistic facade to "legitimate" a regime through a mandated single-party mobilization system on a Soviet or Eastern European model. In 1960, however, elections were significant in the transfer of power from the military "caretaker" government to one that was civilian and not to the liking of the military itself. Whether the elections of May 1990 are pivotal in terms of the transfer of power remains to be determined, however much they may be the focus of international and internal attention.

So legitimacy remains contested, actors and their supporters invoking the necessity for continuing rule by the military or condemnation of that government by the opposition. One important question is how this contested legitimacy is strengthened, manipulated, or diminished, and how culture and history are evoked, interpreted, and reinterpreted.

The Cultural Background to the Legitimacy Debate

Political legitimacy takes place in a cultural context that cannot be dismissed any more than today the international context can be ignored. The Universal Declaration of Human Rights of 1948 is a set of aspirations representative of that period, and such rights have been, and continue to be, expanded to incorporate, for example, those of the handicapped and sexual orientation. In the international context, the West in general has advocated political rights (including preventing assaults of torture, rape, and other violations of the person) while some other societies are also concerned about social and economic rights, such as the right to an education, healthcare, employment, and cultural autonomy.[16] These issues were debated in Bangkok and Vienna in regional and international meetings in 1993. There are still substantive differences in emphases.

This writer has no doubt that the issue of "Asian values", which excited extensive debate a decade ago, was a means by which some autocratic governments could justify their degree of repression or imperviousness to foreign criticism of their political systems. Myanmar was one such government which used this argument, although the most prominent was Singapore, which ironically has a well-developed, if essentially autocratic, election system. Even the term "Asia" has no intellectual justification beyond its simplistic geographic focus, for Asia is far too complex and its cultures too diverse to give the term any precision. There are, however, certain aspects of individual Asian societies that culturally and historically have an impact on how rights are defined and how they may be protected. This should not be interpreted to justify the Asian values argument as attempts to exonerate repression, but simply to point out the obvious — that societies have developed in different contexts and that these contexts help define contemporary issues. Although some are adverse to call this political culture, history and culture do matter but it should also be understood that cultures, and political aspects of cultures, do change and evolve over time with critical consequences for the internal political efficacy of regimes.[17] Political systems and attitudes toward such systems are pervious to change, and to reify them would be a mistake.

As Ingelhart has written:

> Any stable economic or political system has a compatible and supportive cultural system which legitimates that system. The people of that society have internalized a set of rules and norms. If they had not, the rulers could only get their subjects to comply with their rules by external coercion, which is costly and insecure. Moreover, to be effective in legitimating the system, cultures set limits to elite as well as mass behavior — shaping the political and economic systems, as well as being shaped by them.[18]

National character studies are out of vogue and such generalizations are even intellectually dangerous. At the same time, societies do exhibit tendencies that may help observers understand the dynamics of the past and present, and anticipate the future. Burman society may be characterized as one in which power is highly centralized in theory even if in reality it has been fragmented historically and under civilian governments. This tendency is a direct result of the underlying concept that power is finite and personalized in those who have *ana* (Burmese, authority, power).[19] There is, thus, a reluctance to share it either in terms of institutional authority or in personal relations. All governments since independence have attempted to centralize control, and these concepts date from the pre-independence writings of Aung San and his vision of a new Burmese state through military regimes that instituted a command and control system that reinforced this tendency. Even in the civilian period under the AFPFL, when there was a good deal of scattered authority and pluralism, the focus was on the centre mostly because the government was too weak to exert its imprimatur over the whole country in the face of multiple insurrections, local leaders, and a weak administrative system.[20] This fictionalized "Union of Burma" was dissolved following the coup of 1962. One scholar has controversially argued that real Burmese independence dates from this period.[21]

This tendency to mobilize centrally all aspects of power results in instituting systems of orthodoxy.[22] Thus, rigid censorship and restrictions on public and private activities are extensive. In spite of a revised ideology extolling the private sector, there seem to be strong, residual beliefs that, as it did in the colonial period, the private sector could easily go out of control, threaten the state, and perhaps fall into foreign hands once again if the invisible hand is not in an iron glove. It is deeply concerned that organizations that are autonomous of the state (civil society) will undermine it. This orthodoxy has also been apparent in the National League for Democracy and among some of the minorities, and dissident groups, both internal and expatriate, that splinter along personal grounds and that will not tolerate dissent. Power and authority, conceived as personally oriented, makes factionalism a predictable problem. As power is focused on a leader, an entourage develops with prebends flowing down and loyalty flowing upstream. When a purge of a leader takes place, an organization is sometimes decimated as the entourage is eliminated, as happened in military intelligence in 1983, and as seems apparent in a similar purge in October 2004. In turn, orthodoxy in terms of loyalty toward the leader, and thus toward his/her programme, becomes a requirement. A "loyal opposition" is an oxymoron when power is personalized. This personalism has long been noted, even since the Pagan period.[23] Loyalty was not to the monarchy, but to an individual monarch.

Burman society has been known for its individualism and autonomy (although the term "loosely structured" has not been applied to it as it once was to Thai society), exemplified by the custom in which everyone has their own name and surnames are traditionally unknown. Perhaps because of this centrifugal tendency and characteristic, fear of fragmentation and the resulting confusion and "chaos" (as the military has termed it) has been pronounced. The motivation for General Ne Win's "caretaker government" in 1958, the coup of 1962, and the *tatmadaw's* justification for the coup of 18 September 1988 to prevent such "chaos" are all evidence of this concern. The most heinous crime under the SLORC/SPDC, and the one under which Aung San Suu Kyi was first placed under house arrest in 1989, was that of attempting to split the military, which would seem to highlight their concerns about unity and control. Coupled with the constant worries of minority separatism, and "federalism" as its preliminary stage, the military has ensured that control remains in their hands and at the centre. Trager in 1974 summed up the military position that remains germane today, however disputed it may be:

> The military saw themselves as the only operative force which could end political chaos, reestablish administrative rule, and restrain all forms of popular, agitational politics. Furthermore, the military saw themselves

not only as the preservers of nationhood, but also as the only true interpreters of what was good for the country.[24]

The stress on the contemporary formation of a new constitution for the state through the National Convention (1992–96, 2004–06), and the concerns about those of both 1947 and 1974, may give the impression that in Burma/Myanmar the rule of law once was, and again may be, paramount.[25] This is a misapprehension. Constitutions in various societies may be a real indication of the rule of law, they may be aspirations of directions in which the society might move, or they may be cosmetics directed toward internal or external audiences, or some combination of all of the above. The cultural pluralism that the Burmese constitutions have espoused, and are likely to do so in the future, may be hyperbole, as Burman culture dominates. The British colonial experience may give the illusion that concepts of law were well developed, and indeed this was true among an exceedingly well-educated but small elite, mostly schooled in England. In contrast to the British in India, Burma was a colony for a relatively short period, and legal institutions and attitudes toward law were less well established. Under military rule in Burma, the normal legal institutions were abolished and rule was for long periods by decree (1962–74, 1988–present). There was no separation of powers. Law was executive fiat. "Policy" was substituted for law, which was anything the leadership wanted, and titular law, which has been important, became simply an instrument of state policy. Policy, in turn, was a product of personalized power of the leader and his coterie, and could be changed by will or whim. One of the major reasons for the lack of foreign investment in Myanmar (except for major extractive industries) was not only U.S. sanctions and the moral outrage and pressures on foreign businesses, but also the unpredictability of regulations (or "law") that provided no assurances to investors that there could be continuity. Foreign investors had to rely on influential (military) individuals for financial alliances or support. In a sense, foreign investment was a modern, internationalized aspect of the Weberian patrimonial system.

This personalization of power and the flexibility of regulations have also led to the problem of corruption, an element that was exemplified at an earlier period in George Orwell's *Burmese Days*. Myanmar has become, according to Transparency International, one of the most corrupt societies in the world. At a lower level, this is understandable, as salaries, in spite of raises over the years, have not kept pace with the massive inflation that has become a characteristic of that country for decades. At a higher level, however, this has led to questions of the legitimacy of the ruling elite and the illegitimacy of governments, and rumors abound among the Burmese *cognoscenti* concerning the financial holdings of the children and grandchildren of the leadership and some of the minorities, especially the Wa. Prime Minister Khin Nyunt, along with many of his entourage, was arrested in October 2004 on tolerating corruption, and he was later found guilty but given a forty-four year suspended sentence. General Ne Win's son-in-law and grandsons have been found guilty of a purported coup, but observers believe the problems stemmed from the division of the spoils of economic activities.

One need not ascribe to Maung Maung Gyi's[26] characterization of Burmese society as rigidly authoritarian and impermeable to change to agree that these tendencies have been evident in Burmese history and that they have been illustrated as well in the contemporary period. This does not mean, however, that the society cannot change. One of the major debates has been whether the civilian period offers a cultural, intellectual, and institutional base for a new democratic government under the opposition, or whether older, more autocratic forms will persist.[27] This will be discussed below. Taylor has argued that no fully developed concept of state legitimacy can be derived from external sources, and although no explicit indigenous theory exists, such can be extrapolated from historical precedents and patterns.[28] Silverstein, however, argues that this civilian period does offer political experience on which democracy can be based.[29]

The Tools of Legitimacy: Uses and Misuses

If state unity (real or perceived) and elections are the two antipodal justifications of the legitimacy of each side, the question becomes more complex as various popular or conceptual elements are brought into play to support each side's contention of legitimacy and to deprecate or question that of their political adversary.

If the need for the unity of the state legitimates the military, as it claims, then it has done so because, according to the same sources, there is no other institution that could provide such guarantees. The strength of the military lies not only in its inherent coercive power, but in the weakness of other societal institutions.[30] Civilian organizations that might have been important (such as a legislature or court system or local civilian governments, or even an independent media acting as an "early-warning system" to inform the government when problems were arising), have all been smothered. So in a sense the military is correct in stating that theirs is the only present organization that could unify the state. But that statement has to be modified by indicating that they have eliminated all others that might have played a role in this regard, and that present status does not necessarily imply immediate or future capacities.

Nationalism — real, manufactured, invented, and mythified — has been a critical element in the explicit and implicit drive for legitimacy. Although the province of all politicians prior to the coup of 1962, under the military's Burma Socialist Programme Party (BSPP) government, nationalism was incorporated into Party rationales. But under the SLORC/SPDC it has been co-opted by the state, and denied to any other group— the NLD and the minorities included. Nationalism has not only been used to legitimate the military, but to delegitimate the NLD, and especially Aung San Suu Kyi, as married to an alien and under the sway of foreigners and thus is not authentic.[31] Indirectly, nationalism has been used by the government to Burman audiences and against the minorities, charging that they are out to split the country. Arguments appealing to nationalism have been used against foreign negative comments, interference, or intervention into what the military regard as internal state affairs, such as political and other human rights. But the mythification of nationalism in relation to the predominant institution in the state — the military — has been stressed so that the military's role historically has been reinterpreted as the embodiment and emblem of nationalism to endorse and strengthen its claim to power.

Nationalism has also been artificially invented or exaggerated. The most recent incident was the 2001 border dispute with Thailand and the clashes between the United Wa State Army and the Shan State Army (South). Anti-Thai emotions that can only be described as hysterical were encouraged in the media, and massive national demonstrations and mandated flag flying were instituted, so that the military could demonstrate that their predominant role was required for the preservation of the state and its unity. Nationalism has been compounded and invoked against the role of other foreign states, especially the United States that have imposed restrictions or sanctions on the military regime. State rumours of U.S. military intervention into Myanmar regularly surface.[32] A staple of the controlled press has been the republishing of all the excesses and problems conferred by foreigners (especially British and Indians) on that country during the colonial period, with the implicit intent of demonstrating that foreign opinions and actions are inherently antithetical to the well being of the Burmese people, whom foreigners cannot "love".

If Burman and military nationalism has risen, so has ethnic nationalism. Minorities have a greater sense of their own potential and the leverage to demand certain rights because of the spread of international communications, allowing easy contacts with ethnic cousins across boundaries, and with the increased worldwide interest in the plight of minorities and the institutions that monitor those situations. This complicates the role of the Burman majority that has treated the minority peoples with a certain cultural (and in some cases religious) disdain. Part of that attitude is based on a belief in the superiority of Burman culture, but part of it is also related to religion. During the period of relative international isolation under the BSPP, it was the Burmans who were most isolated, as the minorities had contacts with their ethnic cousins across the frontiers and some (Christians and Muslims) with their religious counterparts.

Religion has been, as in so many other countries of various theological persuasions, a prime element in the support of the legitimacy of both the regime and the opposition. Buddhism has been a major enthymeme for both the military and Aung San Suu Kyi. This is not new in Burma/ Myanmar, as U Nu effectively used Buddhism to win the elections of 1960 both by promising to make Buddhism the state religion and because of his exemplary and real devotion.[33] The traditional practice of building pagodas, repairing them, purifying the *sangha* (monkhood), and make appropriate offerings to the Buddhist clergy has been a characteristic of all Burmese governments, and those since 1988 have been no exceptions. Ne Win built a pagoda, and Than Shwe has built two, Maung Aye has built one, while General Khin Nyunt was in charge of the repairs to the Shwedagon, the most revered Buddhist shrine in Southeast Asia. Scarcely a day goes by without someone in the top military leadership portrayed in the *New Light of Myanmar* (the official press) paying homage or in some way demonstrating his, and the regime's, devotion to Buddhism.

The convening of an international meeting on Buddhism in December 2004, which was attended in part by the Thai and Lao prime ministers, is simply the expansion of the concept to an international arena. Burma/ Myanmar has always been active in the World Federation of Buddhists from the inception of the Republic. The procession of a Buddhist relic, donated by China, across the country served dual purposes in addition to its religious significance: it demonstrated Chinese goodwill and a benign foreign policy, an image of singular importance to China whose economic penetration of Myanmar has been profound and has caused some disquiet, and it showed both the international efficacy of the Burmese regime while appealing to the Burmese citizenry in their devotion. That U Nu convened the sixth Buddhist synod in the early 1950s and built the Peace Pagoda was not only an effort to legitimate the rule of the AFPFL and his own role, but that of the nation itself, as it was under siege from diverse insurrections. The military may regard their 1980 registration of the *sangha* and the invocation of control measures on it after 1988 as part of the tradition of *sangha* purification that has been historically perennial. Related to Buddhist legend has been the importance of the white elephant as a symbol of Buddhism and the legitimacy it brings. The military have found three in the jungles, although sceptics say that only two are white, but among the populace these symbols are revered and may have some impact.

The NLD has also used Buddhism, but with less effect because of a lack of access to the media. The first trip outside Rangoon by Aung San Suu Kyi after her first house arrest, was to a Buddhist monk in Pa-an. When her husband died, she had a Buddhist memorial service conducted in her compound. She has also written about Buddhism as the basis for political legitimacy, invoking the ten duties (Buddhist values) of the kings.[34] This is not to imply that religion has only been a political statement on either side, but rather to indicate that it has its political usefulness. Smith has posed an essential question:

> The question of legitimacy is closely related to the psychological problem of identity. Can Buddhism provide the values needed to create a modern Burmese national identity? In the attempt to solve the problems of political legitimacy and national identity through religion, what happens to the religious minorities and the delicate fabric of national unity? [35]

If Buddhism has been one of the pivotal points of legitimacy among Burmans, Christianity has played an important positive role among some of the minorities while enabling the military to use it to delegitimate some individuals and groups. Minority contacts with the international Christian communities (both Catholic and Protestant) have encouraged them in both their faith and indirectly in their status, often in rebellion against a government perceived as unsympathetic to their needs. Christianity has been a legitimating and unifying force among the Karen National Union in what has seemed like perpetual revolt against the central government. Yet this very unity provided the disastrous loss in 1992 of their headquarters at Manerplaw in the Karen state when a segment of their forces staged a Buddhist revolt against the Christian leadership and allied with the (Buddhist) Myanmar military. In the Chin state, which is said to be some

80 per cent Christian, there have been charges of religious persecution and the official promulgation of Buddhism. That glass ceilings exist for Christians (as well as for minorities) in the military has been evident for some time. The military has also constructed pagodas in what seems unlikely areas — in the Rakhine State (Arakan) in what is a virtually complete Muslim region near the Bangladesh border, and in a similarly completely Christian area in the northern Kachin state near the China border. Some observers believe that these have been constructed not to appeal to the faithful but to demonstrate the authority and sovereignty of the central government over peripheral areas; thus pagodas become the surrogate indicators of central control. That the minister of culture for the first time since independence visited numerous pagodas and archeological remains in the Rakhine area in December 2004 may be a further indication of asserting central control over peripheral areas.[36]

The titular protection of the cultures of all the ethnic minorities has been a cry of all governments, and has been included in both constitutions. Yet Burma has been called an "ethnocratic state".[37] The evidence that the various governments have denied the critical elements of indigenous minority cultures, however, is apparent by the refusal to allow local languages to be taught in schools as part of the official curriculum. Although Burmese as the internal language of mobility and of building nationhood seems to be a requirement, the prevention of instruction and official textbooks in local languages denies to the minorities what many have mentioned — their very identity, which is closely related to language and literature.[38] There has been a continuous and Burman, not simply military, "Myanmafication" of culture — the interpretation of cultural protection as being that of the dominant Burman majority.[39] Yet, the charge that foreigners are intent on subverting Burmese culture is a continuing theme of the military. They denied the tourist trade under the BSPP to protect Burmese culture, citing the Thai cultural destruction as evidenced by Bangkok as an example to avoid, but later under the SLORC/SPDC, they encouraged it as a means to garner foreign exchange. Yet the fears, probably a mixture of both real and contrived emotions, are *leitmotifs* in regime pronouncements through the controlled media.

If the military and civilian government and political opposition have used religion as a legitimating force, the military at an earlier period realized that it would be divisive in relation to the minorities. Since there was a strong, virtually universal Burmese need to get the economy back under indigenous hands, as it had been earlier controlled by the British, the

Indians, and the Chinese, socialism was a natural, secular, and acceptable means to elicit legitimacy. In the period around independence, the two communist parties that went into revolt against the government claimed that the democratic and moderate socialism advocated by the U Nu government was inadequate. After the coup of 1962, the military engaged in a thorough attempt to pursue socialism with disastrous effects on the economy and the society. In essence, this was an antidote to the use of Buddhism — it was a secular legitimation appeal that had widespread backing when it was implemented in moderation.

If socialism was the secular attempt to provide a legitimating ideology for the society as a whole, a new and more subtle effort seems to have evolved since the coup of 1988. This is the use of the military itself as the legitimating force and institution in the society. It transcends the use of the military as an implementing agency for legitimating actions, such as its capacity to ensure national unity and upholding national sovereignty, as well as delivering goods and services to the population, but is directed toward transforming the military in the public's eyes as the premier institution on which the country has historically depended. The roles of the great unifier kings of the Burman dynasties are extolled, museums established, palaces rebuilt, pagodas refurbished, and statues erected all implying that relationship between the present and past military glories of the society. The military's embellished role in its fight against colonial rule has been rewritten, and its struggle against insurgents of the left (the communists) and those among the minorities have been stressed. Thus, there is an attempt to make the military into the quintessential organization in the society. If in Thailand triangular loyalties are the monarchy, the nation, and Buddhism, in Myanmar they would be the military, the nation, and Buddhism.

To this end, history has been transformed and embellished; museums have been built extolling the far-reaching and positive effects of the military in realms beyond their supposed military accomplishments but also in their economic activities as well. Not only has there been a reinterpretation and rewriting of history, but some history has been destroyed. The 1962 blowing up by the military of the Rangoon University Student Union building, with all its historical memories from the nationalist movement of the 1930s and 1940s, resulted in the destruction of the physical evidence of the history of student activism, even if it may not have been the intent.[40]

The *tatmadaw* (armed forces), instead of being the agency for legitimating activities, has itself become the embodiment of legitimacy.

The far-flung influence of the military in the society has become pronounced, with its own schools and hospitals catering to its dependents, with its monasteries and temples with special relationships to the military, with commissary and other facilities, and even factories, available for supplies and employment for families, the military world has become effectively divorced from the society. The military have been called a "state within a state", but this is a misnomer. It is the military that have become the essential state, with a subordinate civilian mass population. This may be the most militarized society in the contemporary world.[41] This partition into two states — a military and civilian one — is not as complete as it appears, however. In rural areas, with budgets inadequate to sustain a bloated military establishment together with the costs of foreign purchase and maintenance of relatively sophisticated armour, the military has had to rely on local communities to help feed and support outposts through expropriation of land, forced labour, and financial extractions, all of which are much to the detriment of the local people, as this has become a type of taxation on the local peasantry.[42]

A sub-element of the *tadmadaw's* preoccupation with its own legitimacy is the continuous use of its massive infrastructure construction to justify its role. In a sense, it is legitimacy through construction. There is little question that the military has built more roads, railroads, dams, bridges and irrigation systems since 1988 than all the governments since independence. There is considerable pride in these accomplishments that are continuously touted in official speeches and in unofficial conversations with high-ranking officers (also regularly screened in the local television).[43] These accomplishments have been ignored by foreign governments and even private groups. Although one might question the probable printing of currency to pay for such construction and thus adding to inflation, the use of *corvee* labour, the negative economic rates of return on many of the larger bridges and projects, and the deleterious environmental impact of some dams and other construction, the dedication with which these projects have been pursued has been remarkable, if not always efficacious.[44]

The National League of Democracy's views of legitimacy, both stated in party documents and through the writings of Aung San Suu Kyi, are at diametrically opposed poles from those of the military. The NLD starts with the primacy of democracy and the recognition of the election of 1990, after which economic and distributive policies and justice will follow. In general, the NLD calls for civilian control of the military, some type of federal government with a significant degree of power shared with minority governments, and a market system. Although its tendency for control and orthodoxy are also likely to be apparent, it seems evident that there would be a more open society, and less restrictions on the media and civil society. Although foreign investment would be encouraged, but not until power has shifted, Aung San Suu Kyi has said that she does not want investment that is solely directed towards exploitation of the low-cost labour market. She discouraged tourism, and rejected for some years the operations of international NGOs in Myanmar, but since this could have been seen as a politically indefensible support for continuing poverty, and she was so charged by the junta, she changed her position. She has stated, "The real duty of non-opposition is a reminder that the legitimacy of government is founded on the consent of the people, who may withdraw their mandate at any time if they lose confidence in the ability of the ruler to serve their best interests."[45] The NLD is effectively led by Aung San Suu Kyi, even when under house arrest. Her followers have tried to turn her birthday into a Women's Rights Day, emphasizing her "unique" role in the feminine assertion of power, even though traditionally in Burma, the role of women has been far superior to their status in India or China as well as in the Middle East and, indeed, in Europe until modern times.

Legitimacy, however, is more complex than a singular force. It can be multiple and diverse, not simply between a civil-military axis or between or among ethnicities, but also by locale.[46] A government may be considered legitimate or illegitimate at the centre and quite differently in peripheral areas. Local officials who protect the local people and who have their interests in mind may be regarded as quite legitimate, even if the central government is abhorred. The reverse is also quite true. In minority areas, the local military commander's or officials' attitudes and actions could negatively influence the perception of the legitimacy of the central government. Some minorities simply want an absence of state interference with their normal pursuits, and that would be sufficient in the minds of some to confer legitimacy on an administration. This is not simply an issue for the minorities. One of the five traditional "evils" in Burman thought was the government, and the function of the traditional headman was to keep the government away from the village.[47]

The Principles of Legitimacy and Their Efficacy

If one examines Alagappa's four principles of legitimacy: (1) ascension to power through established norms; (2) adherence to established norms of governance; (3) appropriate levels of performance in supplying goods and services to the population; and (4) the assent of those governed, then by external (Western) standards, the military regimes have continuously been deficient in all categories of rule. The military have three times come to power through coups — contrived or imposed. The established norms of governance have been bent out of Western intellectual shape. The regimes have been remarkably inefficient and inept in supplying the goods and services to the bulk of the population while ensuring the military's own elevated position and status. Finally, the assent of those governed, at least at the time of the May 1990 election, has been denied.

Yet from a Burmese, or more precisely, Burman vantage point, the picture is less clear. In Burmese historical terms, coups or revolts against authority in classical times and against colonial rule have not been uncommon. Succession to the Burmese throne was never institutionalized. There have been many military revolts against the various Burmese administrations since independence, and only one change of government in modern Burmese history has taken place by elections (1960). Furthermore, the concept that military coups are inappropriate is a modern, largely European, phenomenon, and this may mean that such activities are more easily accepted in other societies. The stigma of coups engendering illegitimacy may be less severe in Myanmar.

That the military has not adhered to the established norms of governance is a statement that may be questioned. The appeals to Buddhism and nationalism are the established norms in modern times, and the military has been assiduous, perhaps overzealous, in their appeals to the populace in these terms. Although that rule has been undemocratic, this is not new, for even in the civilian period scholars have questioned whether the administrations at the local levels could be so considered. Governments have been denounced as one of the five evils (along with fire, floods, famine and thieves), and some may argue that from the grassroots perspective, the military has in effect been little different from previous regimes, no matter how much the educated Burmese elite might differ (and although the *tatmadaw* may be more adept at control than the civilians).

The performance criterion is the least defensible from a Western or comparative perspective, when one examines the per capita incomes of the states surrounding Myanmar, and which were either poorer or equal in income two generations ago. Now all have surpassed Myanmar. Yet internally, in the rural sector of Burma Proper (that is, in the areas that are ethnically Burman), the subsistence villages exist much as they have for centuries, and although some new technologies have entered into those societies, the bulk of the 67,000 villages (two-thirds of which are likely to be Burman) that make up the country are largely self-sufficient and intent on keeping away any government — civilian, military or foreign. The urban areas and the relatively sophisticated elites that have access to the outside world through television and cable networks recognize how little the society has economically progressed, and may resent or grudgingly accept such relative deprivation. Yet a large (but unknown) percentage of such extended families have members either within the military or in civilian bureaucratic positions where some of the subsidized goods and services trickle down to them.[48] So the international picture of virtually universal poverty may be overstated, although there is no doubt that it is dire. Moreover, that perhaps two-thirds of the economy is underground or unrecorded (and not only smuggling activities) means that for many the statistical data may portray an inadequate picture of reality. So if many suffer and remain at or below the poverty line (perhaps half the population), many more may have done poorly by regional standards but are not in abject need.

The role of karma as assuaging discontent and undercutting the concept of the state's obligation to provide goods and services should also be considered. As Spiro wrote:

> So far as the social order is concerned, the karmic message, then, is very clear. Inequalities in power, wealth, and privilege are not inequities; rather, they represent the inexorable and just working of a moral law which guarantees that (in the long run) everyone received and will continue to receive his true deserts.[49]

How great a role this attitude might play in the more traditional realms of the state is unknown.

If the life of the average citizen remains negatively affected by the present administration, one must note that no matter how ineffective macro-economic policies and implementation may have been, the state has moved from near bankruptcy in 1987 (in December of that year, foreign exchange holdings were about US$30 million when Burma became a UN designated "least developed nation") to a far more sustainable position in 2005 (approximately US$721 million), and with prospects of far greater assets through further gas and mineral sales. The claim that the regime is on the verge of collapse, which has been the mantra of some of the expatriate Burmese opposition, is far from accurate.

The assent of the governed was denied in the May 1990 elections. As discussed earlier, how much of this assent remains in the opposition's camp is unclear, but it would be prudent to estimate that at least a substantial groundswell for some opposition is widespread. A positive response for the opposition or the negative reaction to continued military rule may still be unclear, but it is evident that the *tatmadaw* itself has come to realize that it must ensure widespread support to overcome the disastrous defeat it suffered in the May 1990 elections. In its own terms, it has come to repair the support problems it encountered in misjudging the elections of both 1960 and 1990. It has done this through the delays in moving toward a new constitution, now perhaps on track to whatever end whenever that may take place, and the attempts to mobilize the society through the Union Solidarity and Development Association (USDA), with its membership of over 16 million,[50] as well as a variety of other extensive government-controlled networks. This would give the military the legalistic indication of the support, or at least the acquiescence, of the population in a constitutional referendum in a new configuration of governance in which the military (according to the principles established at the first session of the National Convention drafting the new constitution) would continue to play the leading role.

Conclusions

Each of the two main actors in this complex drama has attempted to reinforce their claim to legitimacy, while the minority cease-fire groups have been attempting to gain as much local authority as possible. Part of the issue is the hardening of positions since the May 1990 election based on positive or negative expectations — the NLD believing it has the mandate to govern, the military fearful of NLD or non-military control, and the United States generally backing the election results, and thus unequivocally the NLD and Aung San Suu Kyi. This has meant that room for compromise has been seriously eroded. Yet compromise is a critical element of any democratic or power-sharing administration but such compromise undercuts the moral authority of those in power. Both the SPDC and the NLD have systems of orthodoxy, and in the case of the former a command system that effectively prevents alternative views reaching those in authority. The NLD supporters around the world, who have their own brand of orthodoxy, have called for a simple return to the May 1990 election results, and although most would probably accept compromise if acceptable to Aung San Suu Kyi, their orthodoxy may be even more pronounced than those in Rangoon. In an official letter dated 23 December 2004 from the Chairman of the NLD, U Aung Shwe, to

Senior General Than Shwe, Chairman of the SPDC, the former called for the Buddhist virtue of forgiveness as part of *metta*, or loving kindness, and suggested reconciliation of two-way forgiveness. The response to that letter, if any, is not known at the time of this writing, but the offer has been repeated.

Internally, the *tatmadaw* seems to have been planning on the National Convention and its production of a new constitution as being the legitimating force in Burmese society. After the arrest of General Khin Nyunt in October 2004, the SPDC has reaffirmed its intention of proceeding with the convention and producing a new constitution.[51] Without the NLD in the convention, internal legitimacy will even more depend on how the minority demands or requests for greater autonomy are resolved. If they are denied significant concessions, the legitimacy of a new government will be limited, and some cease-fire groups may return to the jungle.[52] The military has attempted to provide economic incentives to some of these organizations to stay within what it calls the "legal fold", and some groups (or at least their leadership) have profited from this new relationship with the Burman centre.

In addition, the opening of the borders to legal trade has undermined some ethnic groups' economic monopoly on smuggling that supported the rebellion.[53]

As the special rapporteur has written concerning the convention, recessed until November 2005:

> If the inherent procedural restrictions are not amended and the representatives of the democratic opposition are absent from the National Convention, any Constitution which emerges will lack legitimacy and thereby credibility. Such impediments serve only to further postpone the democratic process in Myanmar. The Special Rapporteur reiterates his previous opinion that the National Convention will remain illegitimate as long as it fails to adhere to minimum democratic standards and fails to fairly and adequately represent the people of Myanmar.[54]

If present patterns hold, it seems unlikely that the NLD could agree to the constitution as is likely to emerge, although the government, through control of its mass mobilization organizations, could effectively guarantee the approval of any constitution through a referendum, even one in which vote counting was free (but mobilization controlled). Such an instrument might have the reluctant acceptance of the people, because from their viewpoint, it would be better than the present rule by decree.[55]

The National Convention has minimal external legitimacy, and a new constitution emanating from it would likely have a mixed international reaction. The United States and probably the EU would not accept the results of a referendum on it, but it is probable that Japan would do so, and more than likely that ASEAN would. ASEAN's own reputation for democratic governance has certainly been historically mixed, and today Vietnam, Laos, and Brunei (30 per cent of the ASEAN states) have no claim to such governance, and that of Cambodia is quite shaky.

If the military continues its patterns of intervention into the society, it may well lose authority. Traditionally, to paraphrase, the state that governs least governs best; benign neglect seems to have been desired. As McCloud wrote:

> Functional legitimacy of the state was based on the need to maintain the stability of the kingdom, which in turn provided protection and service so that village life could continue largely uninterrupted…but when village life was interrupted by banditry or foreign military incursions, legitimacy was lost. When the king and his court intervened too frequently, requiring corvee labor or military support or levying taxes too heavily, legitimacy was lost and peasants drifted away.[56]

Legitimacy may also be related to hope in the society. How much this operates in the Burmese context is unclear, but in Westernized societies such hope is linked to middle class aspirations. These are limited in Myanmar. The military in Myanmar has monopolized all avenues of mobility, and thus hope. In the civilian period, Burma (the Burman areas) was an open society, perhaps more open than most if not all other Asian societies. The pre-colonial elite did not re-emerge, as it did in a number of other Asian societies. Mobility was pronounced through free higher education, through the *sangha*, through mass political organizations and civil society, and through the military. This has now changed, with the military controlling all avenues of advancement, including activities in the private sector that need the protection of military figures, and with limited access to capital. By cutting off or vetting all such changes, the military have made themselves essential in social realms, and thus control the legitimating process, as well as controlling all coercive power in the state. For changes in military control and the broadening of legitimacy access, alternative means to military advancement and employment and access to power must be found. South Korea and Thailand are examples of two states that have differentially provided alternatives to direct military rule by enabling those in their societies who aspire for advancement to have alternative, non-military, paths to success.[57] No such routes now exist in the Burmese context.

Legitimacy issues are faced with the classic dilemma of what comes first. The NLD claims that democratic politics comes before economics and social improvements, as well as minority affairs. The *tatmadaw* claims that peace, stability, and economic progress should precede political change. At least some among the minorities have stated that "race" (ethnic) survival must come before democracy.[58] The dilemma is compounded when internationally other states create expectations and exert influence on these choices. If this seems inappropriate, and in some sense it is, then the question of the development of Myanmar, and thus fulfilling the aspirations of all concerned groups, is dependent on the external world and the process of globalization that Myanmar cannot escape. Thus foreign relations become directly related to both internal realities and aspirations.

Although some form of transparent electoral process seems to be required (or promised) for legitimacy for any group in Myanmar in the future, it is necessary to consider that elections do not necessarily bring instant democracy or even instant economic growth. As Collier and Hoeffler wrote, "Electoral competition can be introduced with great speed even in the most unpromising conditions such as Afghanistan." Checks and balances, however, a critical element of the democratic process, require time to develop, so that the concept that elections produce instant democracy is likely to be erroneous. "Being discrete simple events, elections get intensively reported. Citizens in the developing world have inevitably come to see an election as the defining feature of democratic legitimacy. Not only does international reporting spread a model which local populations follow, it enables them to harness the power of international pressure."[59] So those who expect instant democracy, "disciplined" or free, are both likely to be disappointed.

President Bush's 20 January 2005 inaugural address in which he called for a virtual crusade for freedom and democracy around the world, will create issues in Myanmar/Burma, as will Secretary of State Rice's specific mention of Myanmar as one of the six "outposts of tyranny". The fear of some in the *tatmadaw* that the United States will actively seek "regime change" will be exacerbated, however unrealistic in reality this may be, and the opposition will draw encouragement from it. But it would be a mistake, should the SPDC crack down on real or potential dissent even further in response to this, or should the opposition attempt to take action in the expectation of U.S. military support. More than moral support to the opposition is unlikely.[60]

Foreigners, however, equate the role of democracy and the NLD with that of Aung San Suu Kyi. It is also evident that the NLD, at least during this writing, is effectively paralysed without her leadership. So she has become the single determinant of U.S. policy and views on the legitimacy of any regime in Rangoon. This is a situation that has personalized policy to a degree that seems undesirable for any foreign policy position, and it further strengthens the military's appeal to nationalism and as the NLD has little institutional strength (which the military has intentionally decimated). Whatever prevalent internal attitudes may exist, externally legitimacy seems likely to continue to be denied to the government. And without internally and externally perceived legitimacy, a secure peace in Myanmar is likely to be denied.

Thus, the prognosis for how the mantle of legitimacy will evolve, on which group(s) it will be placed, and how peace may evolve all remain in doubt. The foreign observer can only wish the people well in times that are inadequately described as unfortunate.

Notes

1. John Kane, *The Politics of Moral Capital*, Cambridge: Cambridge University Press, 2001, p. 15.
2. In 1989, the military government changed the name of the state from Burma to Myanmar for all historical periods. This was never accepted by the political opposition, and the use of either has become a surrogate for political preference and even legitimacy. Without any political intent, in this chapter Myanmar is used for the period since 1988 (the start of the SLORC/SPDC) and Burma for all previous periods. Burmese is used for all citizens of that state, Burmans for the majority ethno-linguistic group, and Burma/Myanmar for continuity of periods.
3. There is considerable mistrust among the minorities themselves. See International Crisis Group, "Myanmar Backgrounder: Ethnic Minority Politics", Brussels: Report 52, 7 May 2003.
4. The concept is from Benedict R. O'G Anderson, *Imagined Communities: Reflection on the Origins and Spread of Nationalism*, London: Verso, 1991.
5. R.H. Taylor, "Political Values and Political Conflict in Burma", in *Burma: Prospects for a Democratic Future*, edited by Robert I. Rotberg. Washington, D.C.: Brookings Institution Press, 1998, pp. 34–35.
6. Weatherford, M. Stephen, "Mapping the Ties that Bind: Legitimacy, Representation, and Alienation", *The Western Political Quarterly* 44, no. 2 (June 1991): 251.

7. Muthiah Alagappa, *Political Legitimacy in Southeast Asia*, Palo Alto: Stanford University Press 1995.

8. The concern over federalism on the part of the military was reinforced by the Mannerplaw Agreement of July 1992 calling for a federal union of Burma. The problem has been exacerbated by the 17 April 2005 declaration by a Shan leader of proposed independence for the Shan state.

9. Clifford Geertz, ed., *Old Societies and New States. The Quest for Modernity in Asia and Africa*, New York: Macmillan, 1963, p. 136. One might also add, with a good deal of coercive force, especially since that was written.

10. This superceded the State Law and Order Restoration Council (SLORC) in 1997, but the top military leadership remained the same in both.

11. For example, see the Aung Shwe-Than Shwe letter of 23 December 2004, noted below. The NLD denounced the Shan independence statement of 17 April 2005.

12. This writer believes that although the military from 1988 was (and remains) adamant that it would retain essential power, whatever the facade, the leadership agreed to the May 1990 election because of the need for external legitimacy, and really thought that the SLORC of that period could be transitory. The military perhaps thought that it could manipulate the results of that election and keep power through allowing the proliferation of 235 parties (of which 93 parties participated in the elections) that would split the vote. They completely misjudged the mood of the society at that time.

13. R.H. Taylor, ed., *The Politics of Elections in Southeast Asia*, Washington, D.C.: Woodrow Wilson Center Press, 1996, p. 3.

14. Manning Nash, *The Golden Road to Modernity. Village Life in Contemporary Burma*, New York: John Wiley & Sons, 1965, p. 289.

15. R.H. Taylor, "Elections in Burma/Myanmar: For Whom and Why?", in Taylor (1996) op. cit., p. 173.

16. In October 2005, the United States voted against a UN resolution to protect cultural rights, because it may have believed that it would limit the import of U.S. popular culture, such as the movies, to some countries.

17. For example, see Lawrence E. Harrison, ed., *Culture Matters. How Values Shape Human Progress*, New York: Basic Books, 2000.

18. Inglehart, Ronald, *Modernization and Postmodernization. Culture, Economic, and Political Change in 43 Societies*, Princeton: Princeton University Press, 1997, p. 15.

19. The traditional concepts of kingship, and therefore governance, come from Indian origins. See Heine-Geldern, 'Conceptions of State and Kingship in Southeast Asia, in John T. McAlister, Jr., *Southeast Asia: The Politics of National Integration*, New York: Random House, 1973, pp. 90–111. On the finite nature of power, see Benedict O'G Anderson, "The Concept of Power

in Javanese Culture", in *Culture and Politics in Indonesia*, edited by Claire Holt, Ithaca: Cornell University Press, 1972. Colonial rule only marginally modified these concepts.

20. "[the minorities] are catered to by a rather intricate and highly peculiar constitutional system that protects them in theory against the Burman domination that the party system tends to produce in fact." Clifford Geertz, ed., *Old Societies and New States. The Quest for Modernity in Asia and Africa*. London: The Free Press of Glencoe, 1962, p. 136.

21. Michael Aung-Thwin, "1948 and Burma's Myth of Independence", pp. 19–34, in Josef Silverstein, ed., *The Future of Burma in Perspective*, Athens, Ohio: Center for International Studies, 1974.

22. For an analysis, see David I. Steinberg, "Burma: The Roots of the Economic Malaise", in Robert Taylor, Kyaw Yin Hlaing, and Tin Maung Maung Than, eds., *Myanmar: Beyond Politics to Societal Imperatives*, Singapore: Institute of Southeast Asia Studies, 2005.

23. See Michael Aung-Thwin, *Pagan. The Origins of Modern Burma*, Honolulu: University of Hawaii Press, 1985.

24. Frank N. Trager, "Democratic and Authoritarian Rule in a Not So Newly Independent Burma", in Silverstein, op. cit., pp. 65–79.

25. For a fascinating, fictional account of the complex relationship among colonial rule, British common law, and local custom in Burma, see Nevill, *The Brothel Boy and Other Parables of Law*. London: Oxford University Press, 1992. The author, no Burma expert but a professor at the University of Chicago Law School, created dilemmas for the hero of George Orwell's Burmese Days as examples of the tensions between law and custom and colonialism.

26. Maung Maung Gyi, *Burmese Political Values. The Socio-Political Roots of Authoritarianism*, New York: Praeger, 1983.

27. For a negative view, see Callahan, op. cit.

28. Taylor, (1998), op. cit.

29. Josef Silverstein, "The Evolution and Salience of Burma's National Political Culture", in Rotberg, op. cit.

30. Writing generically, Ingelhart asks why doesn't the military take over more often given their coercive power? The answer lies in alternative strong cultural norms. Ingelhart, op. cit., p. 55.

31. Under military regulations, anyone with a foreign passport, married to a foreigner, or whose children are married to a foreigner or hold foreign allegiance, such as passports, cannot hold certain government positions. General Khin Nyunt publicly disowned his son who had married a Singaporean airline stewardess.

32. Required paramilitary training for males in 2002/3 was explained to some of those trainees that they were the "holding operation" against American

intervention until the Chinese came to their aid. Personal interview, Rangoon. Whether the planned move of various ministries to Pyinmana in central Myanmar is a result of this attitude is impossible to verify.

33. At that time, the military was against making Buddhism the state religion because they realized that some of the minorities, such as the Karen, Kachin, and Chin, in all of whose respective populations substantial portions were Christian, would object and they feared rebellion. There is an extensive literature on the political role of Buddhism in Burma.

34. Aung San Suu Kyi, "In Quest of Democracy", in *Freedom from Fear and Other Writings*, London: Viking, 1991, pp. 167–79. The duties are: Liberality, morality, self-sacrifice, generosity, integrity, kindness, austerity, non-anger, non-violence, forbearance.

35. Donald Eugene Smith, *Religion and Politics in Burma*, Princeton: Princeton University Press, 1965, p. viii.

36. General Than Shwe is said to feel that the Arakan-Bangladesh frontier is the most unstable area for Myanmar, and he has paid special attention to increasing Burmese security in that region. Historically, there is justification for this view, for Burmese incursions in this area prompted the first Anglo-Burmese War of 1824–26.

37. David Brown, *The State and Ethnic Politics in Southeast Asia*, London: Routledge, 1994.

38. Personal interviews, Myanmar, August 2004. The formation of the minority training institute in Sagaing Division, now transformed into a university under the SLORC/SPDC, trains minorities to integrate into Burman society. Policies have varied. See Kyaw Yin Hlaing, "The Politics of Language Policy in Myanmar: Imagining Togetherness, Practicing Difference?" (unpublished manuscript), and Mary P. Callahan, "Language Policy in Modern Burma", in Michael E. Brown and Sumit Ganguly, eds. *Fighting Words. Language Policy and Ethnic Relations in Asia*, Cambridge: MIT Press, 2003, pp. 143–76.

39. The term is from Gustaaf Houtman, *Mental Culture in Burmese Crisis Politics. Aung San Suu Kyi and the National League for Democracy*. Monograph Series no. 33, Tokyo University of Foreign Studies, Institute for the Study of Languages and Cultures of Asia and Africa, 1999.

40. Who ultimately was responsible for authorizing that destruction is in dispute. In August 1988, Dr Maung Maung, who was then president, offered to rebuild the building.

41. North Korea has more than double the number of troops, but the military is still controlled by a civilian, Kim Jong Il, and the Korean Workers Party.

42. There is some anecdotal evidence that such extractions have caused some urban migration to avoid such problems. Personal interviews, Rangoon, 2004.

43. See, for example, the keynote address by General Khin Nyunt in the volume

Seminar on Understanding Myanmar. Yangon: Institute of Strategic and International Studies, 27–28 January 2004. Also personal interview, July 2003. Also, the Minister of Information's 23 October 2005 extensive statement to counter the Havel and Tuttu report of 19 September 2005.

44. This issue was raised by this writer in the Council on Foreign Relations debate on Burma in 2003, but was rejected by the chair. See *Burma: Time for a Change*, New York: Council on Foreign Relations, 2003, and this writer's dissent.
45. Aung San Suu Kyi, op. cit., p. 173.
46. The revealing Burmese study on this subject is by Ardeth Maung Thawnghmung, *Behind the Teak Curtain. Authoritarianism, Agricultural Policies and Political Legitimacy in Rural Burma/Myanmar*, New York: Kegan Paul, 2004.
47. The role of the headman was transformed under colonial rule from that of the highest village authority to the lowest government position, thus undercutting his status. See Furnivall, *Colonial Policy and Practice*, Cambridge: Cambridge University Press, 1947.
48. If one calculates that there are 400,000 military and a family size of about five, then some two million people (four per cent) of the population have some access to the military's coffers. If one adds the upper reaches of the civil service and their families, then perhaps a total of some 10 per cent of the population relate to subsidized supplies to some degree. The extended family outreach would, of course, be far greater. There is an obvious and important difference within the military between the officer and enlisted class and the benefits that accrue to each.
49. Spiro, Melford E. *Buddhism and Society. A Great Tradition and its Burmese Vicissitudes*. New York: Harper & Row, 1970, p. 439.
50. See David I. Steinberg, "Myanmar and the requirements of Mobilization and Orthodoxy; The Union Solidarity and Development Association", in *Burma Debate*, February 1997.
51. One question of internal military legitimacy was whether Khin Nyunt, with all of his power, had it because he never commanded troops in the field.
52. If some of the leadership have vested interests in continuing the ceasefires because they have been granted economic concessions, the rank and file of some minorities may have different views.
53. Zunetta Liddell, "International Policies Toward Burma: Western Governments, NGOs and Multilateral Institutions".
54. Paulo Sergio Pinheiro, Special Rapporteur, "Situation of Human Rights in Myanmar". United Nations, Fall 2005.
55. In Rangoon there have been rumors that some in the military have said to people that if the military, as presently planned, retains only 25 per cent of the seats in the parliament as reserved for active-duty officers, this is far better

than the present situation where the populace has no say in the governance, as under the new system they could elect 75 per cent of their representatives.

56. Donald G. McCloud, *System and Process in Southeast Asia*, Boulder: Westview Press, 1996, p. 73.

57. See David I. Steinberg, unpublished paper, on democratization in North Korea and Burma, Department of State, Bureau for Intelligence and Research, November 2004.

58. Personal interview, Rangoon.

59. Paul Collier and Anke Hoeffler, "Oil Democracies". Unpublished paper, Department of Economics, University of Oxford.

60. One might keep in mind the uprising in Hungary in 1956, when the United States encouraged Eastern Europe to break away from the Soviet Union and then did nothing to help, or 1919 when Woodrow Wilson's Fourteen Points, stipulating the self determination of nations, led to the Korean uprising (1 March 1919, still celebrated as a national holiday) for independence and resulted in brutal repression by the Japanese colonial powers as the United States ignored the tragedy that it induced, having effectively given Korea over to the Japanese in return for a free hand in the Philippines under the secret Taft-Katsura Agreement of 1905.

References

Alagappa, Muthiah. *Political Legitimacy in Southeast Asia*. Palo Alto: Stanford University Press, 1995.

Anderson, Benedict O'G. "The Concept of Power in Javanese Culture", in *Culture and Politics in Indonesia*, edited by Clair Holt. Ithaca: Cornell University Press, 1972.

––––––. *Imagined Communities: Reflection on the Origins and Spread of Nationalism*. London: Verso, 1991.

Ardeth Maung Thawnghmung. *Behind the Teak Curtain. Authoritarianism, Agricultural Policies and Political Legitimacy in Rural Burma/Myanmar*. New York: Kegan Paul, 2004.

Aung San Suu Kyi. "In Quest of Democracy", in *Freedom from Fear and Other Writings*. London: Viking, 1991.

Aung-Thwin, Michael. "1948 and Burma's Myth of Independence", in *The Future of Burma in Perspective*, edited by Josef Silverstein. Athens, Ohio: Center for International Studies, 1974, pp. 19–34.

Aung-Thwin, Michael. *Pagan. The Origins of Modern Burma*. Honolulu: University of Hawaii Press, 1985.

Brown, David. *The State and Ethnic Politics in Southeast Asia*. London: Routledge, 1994.

Burma: Time for a Change. New York: Council on Foreign Relations, 2003.

Callahan, Mary P. "Language Policy in Modern Burma", in *Fighting Words. Language Policy and Ethnic Relations in Asia*, edited by Michael E. Brown and Sumit Ganguly. Cambridge: MIT Press, 2003, pp. 143–76.

Collier, Paul and Hoeffler, Anke. "Oil Democracies". Unpublished paper, Department of Economics, University of Oxford, n.d.

Furnivall, J.S. *Colonial Policy and Practice*. Cambridge: Cambridge University Press, 1947.

Geertz, Clifford, ed. *Old Societies and New States. The Quest for Modernity in Asia and Africa*. London: The Free Press of Glencoe. 1962.

Harrison, Lawrence E., ed. *Culture Matters. How Values Shape Human* Progress. New York: Basic Books, 2000.

Heine-Geldern. "Conceptions of State and Kingship in Southeast Asia", in *Southeast Asia: The Politics of National Integration* edited by John T. McAlister, Jr. New York: Random House, 1973, pp. 90–101.

Houtman, Gustaaf. *Mental Culture in Burmese Crisis Politics. Aung San Suu Kyi and the National League for Democracy*. Monograph Series no. 33, Tokyo University of Foreign Studies, Institute for the Study of Languages and Cultures of Asia and Africa, 1999.

Inglehart, Ronald. *Modernization and Postmodernization. Culture, Economic, and Political Change in 43 Societies*. Princeton: Princeton University Press, 1997.

International Crisis Group. "Myanmar Backgrounder: Ethnic Minority Politics". *Brussels: Report 52*, 7 May 2003.

Kane, John. *The Politics of Moral Capital*. Cambridge: Cambridge University Press, 2001.

Kyaw Yin Hlaing. "The Politics of Language Policy in Myanmar: Imagining Togetherness, Practicing Difference?" Unpublished manuscript, n.d.

Liddell, Zunetta. "International Policies Toward Burma: Western Governments, NGOs and Miltilateral Institutions." Unpublished manuscript, n.d.

Maung Maung Gyi. *Burmese Political Values. The Socio-Political Roots of Authoritarianism*. New York: Praeger, 1983.

McCloud, Donald G. *System and Process in Southeast Asia*. Boulder: Westview Press. 1996.

Nash, Manning. *The Golden Road to Modernity: Village Life in Contemporary Burma*. New York: John Wiley & Sons, 1965.

Nevill, *The Brothel Boy and Other Parables of Law*. London: Oxford University Press 1992.

Pinheiro, Paulo Sergio. "Situation of Human Rights in Myanmar". United Nations, Fall 2005.

Silverstein, Josef. "The Evolution and Salience of Burma's National Political Culture", in *Prospects for a Democratic Future*, edited by Rotberg, Robert I. Washington, D.C.: Brookings Institution Press, 1998.

Smith, Donald Eugene. *Religion and Politics in Burma*. Princeton: Princeton University Press, 1965.

Spiro, Melford E. *Buddhism and Society. A Great Tradition and its Burmese Vicissitudes*. New York: Harper & Row, 1970.

Steinberg, David I. "Myanmar and the Requirements of Mobilization and Orthodoxy: The Union Solidarity and Development Association", in *Burma Debate*, February 1997.

———. "On Social Mobility, the Military and Democratization: Contrasting Evolutions in Korea and Burma". *Southeast Asian Review of Asian Studies* XXVII (2005).

———. "Burma: The Roots of the Economic Malaise", in *Myanmar: Beyond Politics to Societal Imperatives*, edited by Robert Taylor, Kyaw Yin Hlaing, and Tin Maung Maung Than. Singapore: Institute of Southeast Asia Studies, 2005, pp. 86–116.

Taylor, R.H., ed., *The Politics of Elections in Southeast Asia*. Washington, D.C.: Woodrow Wilson Center Press, 1996.

———. "Elections in Burma/Myanmar: For Whom and Why?", in *The Politics of Elections in Southeast Asia*, edited by R.H. Taylor. Washington, D.C.: Woodrow Wilson Center Press, 1996.

———. "Political Values and Political Conflict in Burma", in *Burma. Prospects for a Democratic Future*, edited by Robert I. Rotberg, Washington, D.C.: Brookings Institution Press, 1998.

Trager, Frank N. "Democratic and Authoritarian Rule in a Not So Newly Independent Burma", in *The Future of Burma in Perspective*, edited by Josef Silverstein Silverstein. Athens, Ohio: Center for International Studies, 1974, pp. 65–79.

Weatherford, M. Stephen. "Mapping the Ties that Bind: Legitimacy, Representation, and Alienation". *The Western Political Quarterly* 44, no. 2 (June 1991).

7

Associational Life in Myanmar:
Past and Present

Kyaw Yin Hlaing

Traditionally, Myanmar was considered a country with lively and vibrant associational life. Most existing studies of politics and society in colonial and parliamentary Myanmar are filled with the history of social and religious organizations and their role in the socio-political developments of the country. However, since the military-led Revolutionary Council issued the 1964 National Security Act, scholars and journalists alike have stopped taking associational life in Myanmar seriously. While viewing the associations created by the Burma Socialist Programme Party government and the SLORC/SPDC as instruments used by the government to control society, most journalists and scholars discounted the importance of social and religious associations in Myanmar politics and society. As a result, there was no in-depth study of associational life in general during the socialist period. Recently, however, there have been some studies of social movement organizations that emerged during the Four-Eights Democratic Movement and some political and social welfare organizations that emerged during the late 1990s. These studies, however, place more emphasis on illustrating the extent of civil society space in the country rather than the general state of associational life.

As Robert Putnam and many others have argued, it is not just civil society organizations but all forms of associations that impact on socio-political and economic developments of a country. Some associations can "instil their members habit of cooperation, solidarity, and public spiritedness". In addition, associations can serve as a starting place for people to engage in social, political and economic collective actions.

This is not to suggest that all associations are good for society. An association can be used for the interest of an individual person, of a small group of people or of a large community. There are many illiberal and authoritarian associations that served mainly the interest of some authoritarian or exploitative individuals or groups. It is also worth noting that associations, once created, can be exploited not just by their creators but by others as well.

One's understanding of the state of civil society in a country depends largely on how he or she defines civil society. Although a number of recent studies treated some emerging organizations in Myanmar as civil society organizations, many political activists still questioned their status as civil society organizations at conferences and meetings on Myanmar politics. However, it is an undeniable fact that there have always been a plethora of associations throughout the colonial and post-colonial period. Although their impact on swift political change in the country is currently limited, I have shown elsewhere that many existing social and religious associations and organizations have great potential to become social movement organizations. Contrary to what some scholars and journalists have suggested, many social movement organizations that emerged during the Four-Eights Democratic Movement did not come into being from scratch. Rather, many of them came out of some existing social organizations. When the political opportunity structure opened, movement activists appropriated existing associations and organizations and turned them into social movement organizations. Therefore, regardless of the fact that they do not have any immediate major impact on politics at the present time, it is very important to understand the way the existing social and religious organizations emerged, how they functioned and how they interacted with the government. As in other societies, some associations in Myanmar serve the interest of governments more, some the interest of some small groups of people, and some associations worked for the unity and general welfare of the entire society whereas some others undermined the unity among various social and religious groups.

Although Myanmar has been an independent country for more than fifty years, there has yet to be a comprehensive study of the history of associational life in Myanmar. The purpose of this chapter is to help fill the gap in the studies of state-society relations in Myanmar by tracing the state of associational life in colonial, parliamentary, socialist and SLORC/SPDC Myanmar and by subsequently examining their role in politics and society.

The State of Associational Life in Pre-Colonial and Colonial Myanmar

Although formal organizations emerged only during the colonial period, associational life was not alien to Myanmar society. Community organizations that functioned more or less like neighbourhood organizations in Western countries have existed in almost every village in pre-colonial Myanmar. However, in pre-colonial days, these community organizations appeared to have functioned more like informal institutions than formal ones. It was in the colonial days that Myanmar people began to form formal associations and organizations that had societal influence beyond a small community. Thanks to Western education introduced by the British and the advent of print-capitalism in Myanmar, Myanmar people came to learn how formal organizations and associations could be formed and how people in other parts of the world, especially in Western countries, tried to achieve their social and political objectives by forming associations. Myanmar people also got a chance to personally witness the ways modern, formal associations were run when Christian missionaries and European, Indian and Chinese business people formed religious, social and business associations soon after they arrived in Myanmar.

The colonial government did not try to stop the formation of any associations. Even when some organizations engaged in anti-government (nationalist) activities, colonial officials arrested the members who engaged in such activities rather than disband the organizations. Therefore, there was a mushroom growth of modern, formal associations representing indigenous people in the first half of the twentieth century. It shows that Myanmar people did make good use of the knowledge of modern, formal associations rendered to them by colonialism. In general, the organizations formed by Myanmar people during the colonial days can be divided into eight groups — students unions, trade unions, religious organizations, political parties and organizations, ethnic associations, social welfare organizations, business organizations, professional associations, community (neighbourhood) organizations, and native place organizations.[1]

Probably because they represented the two modern institutions — universities and factories — brought into Myanmar by the colonial experience, student and labour unions were two of the most modern civil society organizations during the colonial period. Not only were they formal organizations, but their leaders were also popularly elected by their respective members. Although the size of the communities they represented was relatively small, students' and trade unions turned out to be politically influential organizations. Since the Rangoon University College student union staged one of the very first modern social movements in colonial Myanmar in 1920, student unions organized protests against the colonial government whenever the latter adopted policies which they thought would negatively affect indigenous people. Throughout the colonial period, student unions also served as training ground for nationalist leaders and future politicians. Many leading politicians of independent Myanmar started their political career as leading members of student unions.

Like student unions, labour unions were one of the organizations that learned to use the strike as a means of pressuring factory owners to make desired changes in factory operations. The first labour association was formed by Indian and Burmese workers from the railway department under the name of Amalgamated Society of Railways Servants of India and Burma in 1897.[2] Since most people working in the railways department were Indian, the association was dominated by Indians. However, active labour associations did not come into existence in Myanmar until World War I broke out in 1914. The first labour movement on Myanmar soil took place sometime in the year 1916 and 1917 when American oil drillers launched a strike over the management of the drilling department. Although the strike ended in vain in two days, Myanmar workers learned how to form labour unions and how to engage in labour movements from then.[3] The first full-fledged labour union with Burmese workers was formed in Yenangyaung in 1921 under the name of the Oilfield Labour Union.[4] Although there emerged some labour movements led by Myanmar workers in the 1920s, a major unified labour union emerged only when the leading nationalist organization, Do-Bama Asiayone, started organizing labour in 1935.[5] In general, labour unions usually focused on the welfare of their respective members. However, when communism became popular among young nationalist leaders, labour became an important political entity. As a result, starting in the mid-1930s, labour unions were led not by workers but by nationalist and political leaders and the labour movement became a part of the nationalist movement. When the *Htaung-ton-yar-pyi* (Thirteen Hundred) Revolution ocurred as the biggest peaceful anti-colonial government demonstration, it was initiated by a labour union from Chauk, a small central Myanmar city with a large oil field and refinery. Many student, nationalist and political leaders joined the demonstration. Since then onwards, many more labour unions emerged. There were 25 registered unions in 1946. The number increased to 33 in 1947 and to 56 in 1948.[6]

Religious groups were also very active in colonial Myanmar. There existed Christian, Muslim and Buddhist organizations. The Christian and Muslim organizations usually engaged in missionary and other religious activities and stayed out of politics. Buddhist organizations, on the other hand, needed to be distinguished as politically conscious and non-political organizations. As Buddhism declined under British rule, a large number of devoted Buddhist monks and laymen came to form several Buddhist associations to rekindle their religion. Some religious organizations engaged in raising funds to support monks who were pursuing Buddhist studies, taking action against undisciplined monks, renovating and guarding religious temples and holding religious festivals. There were also some Buddhist organizations which resorted to political means in trying to rekindle declining Buddhism. These politically conscious religious organizations engaged in anti-(colonial) government activities because they felt that Buddhist *sasana* could not flourish without the patronage of a Buddhist ruler.[7] Many politically conscious religious organizations were deeply involved in the anti-colonial movement. The *Yahanpyo* Aphwe (All Burma Young Monk Association), the biggest politically conscious *sangha* organization, was even seen as a leading anti-colonial political organization. While working with nationalist organizations for the independence of the country, these politically conscious religious organizations successfully pressured the colonial government to ban shoe-wearing in Buddhist temples, mobilized the public to boycott imported goods, raised funds for nationalist organizations, and guarded religious temples. It is worth noting that some religious organizations gravitate between political and non-political inclinations back and forth. For instance, the Young Men's Buddhist Association — an association formed by Western educated youth who were inspired by the Young Men's Christian Association — were involved in several political activities in the 1920s but came to focus mainly on religious activities in the 1940s.

Learning lessons from India and other colonies, several educated and well-to-do Myanmar community leaders formed nationalist-cum-social organizations. The General Council of Burmese Associations (GCBA) was one such prominent organization. Under the leadership of the GCBA were several *winthanu athin* (nationalist associations) in various parts of the country.[8] These organizations switched between being nationalist organizations and political parties back and forth. The GCBA and affiliated *winthanu athin* sometimes mobilized ordinary people to launch a protest against some government policies. During elections, *winthanu athins* campaigned for the political parties they supported. However, these *winthanu athin* and the GCBA were often not united. Different factions in the groups vied for control of the organizations. Sometimes, the split was caused by differences within the leadership over some policy issues. Until the emergence of the Do-Bama Asiayone, most nationalist organizations mixed political and nationalist goals. Leaders of Do-Bama Asiayone, however, placed more emphasis on independence and considered power politics only one of the means they might adopt to achieve independence for the country. There were also several political parties and some spin-off organizations from the political parties. Since Burmese politics during the colonial era was very personal, political parties and their spin-off organizations were often the instruments which their leaders used to amass political power. For instance, Ba Maw used both the Sinyatha Party [Proletariat Party] and its spin-off organization, the sweat army, in trying to mobilize public support for himself and his followers. Such organizations continued to exist even after the country attained independence.

Ethnic organizations were also politically active in colonial Myanmar. There were Karen, Kachin, Shan, Mon, Kayah, Rakhine and Burman ethnic associations and they were all involved in political and social activities. These organizations played a major role in the development of modern nationalism and ethnic consciousness among their respective ethnic communities. In response to the fact that colonialism created several new welfare issues which traditional welfare practices could not cope with, several indigenous communities in various parts of the country came to reorganize their loosely organized informal community organizations as formal community organizations. In addition, copying Indian and Chinese native place organizations, indigenous people who moved from their native places to big cities, especially Mandalay and Rangoon, where jobs were abundant, also came to form similar organizations. Community and native place organizations usually served an intermediary function among their members.[9]

There were also some social welfare organizations that performed a mediating function between the state and their respective members. Although a few of these organizations were organized by nationalist leaders as a part of their attempt to mobilize the public, most of them were initiated by politically conscious citizens who often were negatively affected by some government policies. For instance, a group of indigenous lawyers, private school teachers and businessmen formed the *a-khun-htan-a-thin* [the Tax-payers Association] in Mandalay in response to the government's imposition of unfair taxes on them and the members of the community of which they were a part.[10] The exact number of such social welfare organizations is not currently available. However, a former nationalist leader estimated that there were no less than a hundred *a-khun-htan-a-thin*-like social welfare organizations in colonial Myanmar.[11] These social welfare organizations proved to be effective intermediaries between the state and the people they represented. For instance, the Mandalay *a-khun-htan-a-thin* successfully pressured the government to repeal the imposition of tax on shops opened in pagodas and on small business people who walked around the city and sold some local delicacies, and to reduce the salary of parliamentarians from 500 kyat to 250 kyat.[12] Although they were formal organizations, many social welfare associations functioned more like traditional organizations. Members of these traditional, formal organizations did not have to elect the leadership. They were usually formed and run by some capable people and their effectiveness as intermediaries between the state and their members depended upon the capability and well-connectedness of those leaders. Many such organizations were said to have stopped functioning when their capable leaders passed away or retired from the organizations owing to ill health or some other personal reasons.[13] There were also some *ad hoc* organizations which were formed to tackle certain problems. Such organizations ceased to exist once the problems were solved.[14]

Business association was another new phenomenon created by colonialism. As mentioned earlier, British and Indian businesses formed business organizations right after they started their business operations in Myanmar. Since foreign business organizations did not accept indigenous business people as members, the latter had to form their own organizations. The activities engaged in by foreign and indigenous business people included educating their members on the nature of the world market and pressuring the government to allocate more loans to the businesses of their members. By 1940, there were more than ten big indigenous and foreign business organizations. These big business organizations became politically important when the colonial government allowed them to send representatives to the Legislative Assembly. There also emerged more than a hundred local indigenous business and market organizations which were formed to coordinate business activities in their respective local areas and to serve as intermediaries between the local state officials and their members. These local indigenous organizations also organized strikes when local officials raised taxes imposed on them.[15] There were also some business organizations which served only as institutions that helped their members solve many business problems on their own. The Mandalay Traders, Brokers and Industrialists Association, for instance, served as a place where business people in Mandalay got together to decide commodity prices. It also served as a mediator when members had disagreements over business transactions.[16] But it did not serve as an intermediary between the state and its members. Since most of their members were Buddhists, local business and market organizations also organized religious ceremonies.[17]

There were also some professional organizations in colonial Myanmar. The most prominent ones included the Pensioners' Association and the Journalists' Association. Both professional organizations usually served merely as a gathering place for their respective members. Although some members of these organizations were involved in political activities on their own, these two professional organizations did not participate in any political movements.

All in all, with the exception of the suppression of the political activities organized by nationalist organizations, the colonial government did not try to prevent the emergence of social, religious and political organizations. As a result, there was vibrant associational life in colonial Myanmar. It was due to many of these organizations that Myanmar people became politically conscious, thereby leading to the independence of the country.

The State of Civil Society Organizations in Parliamentary Myanmar

Myanmar saw the emergence of numerous new associations and organizations in the wake of the attainment of independence from the British in 1948. It was in part because the relatively open parliamentary system bequeathed by the British allowed the public to form both political and non-political organizations freely and in part because the first prime minister of independent Myanmar, U Nu, encouraged the people, especially business people, to work together by forming social and business associations.[18] The problem with the state of civil society in parliamentary Myanmar was that the borderline between civil and political societies was very ambiguous. In order to counter the communist penetration of the society, the Anti-Fascist People's Freedom League (AFPFL) (the ruling party of independent Myanmar between 1948 and 1958) formed the All Burma Peasants' Organization (APBO), the Federation of Trades Organization (Burma) (FTOB), the Trade Union Congress (Burma)

(TUCB), the Youth League, and the All Burma Women's Organization. Although local peasant and business organizations and trade unions were not required to join AFPFL-sponsored social organizations, the ruling party lured them to join its affiliated social organizations. Politicians also used these associations as their power bases. Although members of these organizations did not enjoy political autonomy, their membership in ruling-party affiliated social organizations allowed them to have access to senior government officials and state-controlled resources.[19] Politicians distributed the resources they controlled to members of their respective power-base organizations. When opposition party members criticized the government in a parliamentary session for giving agricultural loans mainly to the members of the AFPFL-affiliated APBO, the then Minister of Agriculture, Bo Khin Maung Galay, bluntly responded, "Mr Chairman, let me respond bravely. We distributed agricultural loans only to the members of the ABPO that supported the AFPFL."[20] A retired worker who used to work for Mandalay University during the parliamentary days also noted that he often sought the assistance of local politicians whenever he was bullied by the bureaucrats from the university. His association with the AFPFL-affiliated trade union gave him chances to get to know prominent politicians.[21] As a result, it became a norm that if one wanted to have access to state largesse, one should join either the ruling party or its affiliated social organizations. The author also heard similar stories from five other former factory workers and four former politicians.

Therefore, most of several hundreds new small business and industrial organizations and labour unions that emerged in the first fifteen years after independence had themselves affiliated to the social organizations of the ruling party. Only a few labour unions and peasant organizations affiliated themselves with the left-wing opposition party, the National United Front. A retired politician estimated that about 95 per cent of labour unions and small business organizations were affiliated to the TUCB and FTOB respectively.[22] It is worth noting that in the parliamentary period, one saw more small business and industrial organizations than labour, youth, peasant and women organizations. This development was because although youths, workers, peasants and women could join their respective ruling party-affiliated social organizations individually, industrialists and businessmen could only join the FTOB as groups. It is also worth nothing that all major business organizations, both foreign and indigenous, were not affiliated to the AFPFL. This was mainly because the FTOB only accepted small business organizations formed by indigenous business people as members.

This does not mean that all big business associations acted like independent organizations. The independence of indigenous business people was compromised by the fact that most members of indigenous business organizations either joined the business or industrial associations that were affiliated with the ruling party. For instance, the Council of Burma Industries made a leading member of the AFPFL, Kyaw Nyein, its patron.[23] Only the associations of foreign business people were found to have acted like autonomous organizations. This, however, was not because they wanted to be autonomous. An Indian businessman noted that "if we could affiliate our associations with the ruling party, we would do it but it would be a political suicide for Burmese politicians. They would not want our associations to be affiliated to their party."[24] The business associations that were formed to resolve coordination problems between business people rather than to serve as intermediary between the state and the business community also acted quite freely and more like independent civil society organizations.[25] The Brokers' and Traders' Association in Mandalay was a good example.

All religious organizations, Buddhist and non-Buddhist, were found to have been more independent of the state than labour, peasant and small business organizations. Because the government was then dominated by Buddhist locals, non-Buddhist religious organizations kept a low profile and focused their attention mainly on providing religious services to followers of their respective religions. Buddhist organizations, however, could undertake the promotion of Buddhism more freely and effectively than they did in the colonial days. They even managed to pressure the government to make Buddhism the state religion for a brief period. As in the colonial period, non-political religious organizations continued to stay out of power politics. However, politically conscious religious organizations participated in political activities more actively than they did during the colonial period. They helped the political parties which promised to bring about desired political, social and religious changes to win the election. In general, most politically conscious religious organizations sided with the ruling party. However, such organizations did not simply serve the interest of the state. They protested against the state if they did not find the state's policies, especially religious ones, agreeable. For instance, the Presiding Monk Association and the *Yahanpyo Aphwe* [All Burma Young Monk Association] which was often identified as branches of the AFPFL, protested to the government when Prime Minister U Nu introduced the teaching of Islam and Christianity in secondary schools. There were also cases where some powerful leaders of *sangha* organizations controlled local governments from behind the scene. For instance, in the late 1950s, the leader of the *Yahanpyo Aphwe*, U Kuthala, was as powerful as the regional military commander.[26] He administered all Buddhist temples in Mandalay the way he wanted. He also had local authorities arrest the monks and laymen who tried to block him from doing things his way. Monks who did not get along with leading members of the *sangha* organizations which were very close to leading members of the ruling party formed their own *sangha* organization and sided with opposition parties. For instance, the *Yahannge Aphwe* (which also means Young Monk Association) which supported left-wing opposition groups, was formed by monks who did not get along with the members of the *Yahanpyo Aphwe*. The monasteries dominated by members of the *Yahannge Aphwe* helped the left-wing political parties and let them use their monasteries for refuge or to hold meetings.

All student unions in parliamentary Myanmar proved to be more autonomous of the government than most politically conscious *sangha* groups. It was not that student unions stayed out of power politics. All three major student organizations that competed for the control of student unions were affiliated to various political groups that were competing for political power. While the Democratic Student Organization represented the AFPFL, the *Tat-Oo* [Front] and the *Tat-Oo-Thit* [New Front] served as agents for the main opposition party, National United Front, and the major underground party, the Burma Communist Party respectively.[27] Probably because students were more sympathetic to underdogs, left-wing student organizations always managed to win union elections. Student unions, therefore, did not function like representatives of the government on university campuses. Although they always stood up for students whenever there was a dispute between a student body and the university administration, in dealing with the government, student unions often acted more like an opposition party than an independent organization. The criticism of student unions against government policies always reflected the views of the opposition parties. A former chairman of the Mandalay university student union revealed that "when a student union was dominated by the *Tat-Oo-Thit,* the union would deal with the government according to the guidelines of the underground Communist Party. At the same time, when a student union was dominated by the *Tat-Oo*, it would deal with the government in the way the National United Front would."[28]

Unlike other indigenous organizations, professional, native and community organizations remained totally independent of the state and power politics even after independence. Just like in the case of the non-Buddhist religious organizations, foreign race-based organizations also stayed out of power politics and worked only for the welfare of their respective members. However, many indigenous minority organizations became political as minority leaders started demanding autonomous status for their respective states a few years after independence. In fact, indigenous minority organizations became politically more active after independence. Such indigenous minority organizations were typically found in major cities and at universities.

In 1958, personal rivalry in the leadership of the ruling AFPFL resulted in the split of the AFPFL as the AFPFL (Clean) and the AFPFL (Stable). With the help of the left-wing opposition party, National United Front, the AFPFL (Clean) continued to control the government and the AFPFL (Stable) became a leading opposition in the parliament. The split was not confined to the party alone. All social organizations also split into two. Naturally, the business, labour and peasant organizations that sided with the opposition AFPFL (Stable) lost their access to state largesse. The government controlled by the AFPFL (Clean) also punished the supporters of the AFPFL (Stable) by withdrawing business permits which were already granted to them at the time of the party split. For instance, AFPFL (Permanent) leader Kyaw Nyein granted 60 million Kyat to members of his power-base organization, the Council of Burma Industries, a few months before the AFPFL split. After the split, however, leader of the AFPFL (Clean) Prime Minister U Nu recalled all the loans Kyaw Nyein had granted to his supporters.[29] In late 1960, most ruling party-affiliated social organizations ceased to be constituent organizations of the ruling party, as U Nu ordered all members of his party which was then renamed the Union Party, to resign from all social organizations if they wished to remain members of the party.[30] Apparently, U Nu reasoned that the existence of constituent social organizations contributed to factional politics in his party. In the meantime, many business people and labour leaders who suffered from the spillover effects of the AFPFL split began to talk about forming a truly independent business organization.[31] If these business and labour leaders had had a chance to reform their organizations, Myanmar could have come to possess a large number of mature and independent civil society organizations. However, this development was prevented by a coup staged by the military in 1962.

In sum, although many organizations were affiliated to political parties, there was vibrant associational life in parliamentary Myanmar. Many organizations matured during the period, and it is very likely that many would have emerged as effective civil society organizations if the country had not been taken over by the military.

The State of Civil Society in Socialist Myanmar

In 1962, the military took control of the country and launched a *khit-pyone-taw-hlan-ye* [social revolution] by establishing the Burma Socialist Programme Party (BSPP) and by adopting the Burmese Way to Socialism. In so doing, the military-dominated socialist government, also known as the BSPP government, tried to transform the social, political and economic systems of the country. In that process, the BSPP government issued the 1964 National Security Act that outlawed all existing political organizations and forbade the formation of new political organizations without getting permission from the government.[32] The law allowed only the government's Burma Socialist Programme Party and its affiliated organizations to exist. Furthermore, that the law did not define political organizations not only entrusted the government with discretionary power to go after any organizations it wanted to, but also discouraged the general public from being members of politically controversial organizations. Right after the National Unity Act was issued, the government literally outlawed all organizations that had the potential to mount challenges to it.[33] The government also arrested some outspoken leaders of outlawed political organizations including monks and dynamited the historic Yangon University student union building in order to make sure that their organizations did perish. Although the law did not outlaw business organizations, the anti-capitalist campaigns carried out by the BSPP government drove many foreign business people out of the country and made the existence of private business organizations irrelevant to the new political and economic environment. Furthermore, the government also created the Workers' Asiayone [the Workers' Organizing Committee], the Peasant Asiayone [the Peasants' Organizing Committee], the Lanzin Youth Organization, the War Veteran Organization, the Literary Workers' Association, and the Actors, Artists and Performers' Association, claiming that they were more formal channels for the public to make their needs and problems known to the higher levels of the government.[34]

Just like in most other socialist and communist countries, state-sponsored organizations did not represent the interests of the social sectors whose names they bore. They were merely corporatist organizations that the government used as instruments to contain the demands of the public and to keep watch over potential saboteurs of the party.[35] The constitution of all of these organizations clearly stated that their members would participate in the construction of a socialist society under the tutelage of the Burma Socialist Programme Party. Therefore, the social organizations formed by the BSPP government were by no means qualified to be civil society organizations. They were supposed to serve as watchdogs for the government. The Literary Workers' Organization not only absorbed the formerly independent Journalists' Organization and Writers' Association but also required its members to write stories and articles in support of the party and its policies. Furthermore, members of the Literary Workers' Organization were obliged to report to the government whenever they found that some of their fellow writers were defaming the party in print.[36] The same responsibilities were imposed on members of other organizations as well. Members of the Lanzin Youth Organization were instructed by their respective township Lanzin Youth committee to keep an eye on the activities of suspicious youths. Although the law did not forbid the formation of non-political peasant, youth, worker, writer, journalist, and artist organizations, both the government and its watchdog organizations did not tolerate the existence any non-state organizations that rivalled state-sponsored organizations. Whenever some journalists, writers and artists tried to form independent organizations, the government, with the help of members of state-sponsored social organizations and other state agents, managed to outlaw them by finding fault in the way they functioned. For instance, in the mid-1970s, a group of writers and journalists in Mandalay formed an independent literary group known as the Saturday Literary Discussion Group. The government's Literary Workers' Association looked at it as a rival group and kept a "fault-finding" eye on its activities. When members of the Saturday Literary Discussion Group had a discussion on the literary work of a left-wing nationalist leader, a senior member of the government's Literary Workers' Association successfully had the Saturday Literary Discussion Group banned by the government on the charge of spreading communist literature.[37]

However, it is worth nothing that the BSPP affiliated societal groups were not totally useless for its members. Several workers and peasants could make use of those organizations to receive assistance from party-state officials in dealing with their bosses. In fact, in several state-owned factories, workers were more powerful than managers and engineers until the labour protest broke out in 1976. Until the mid-1970s, workers at government-owned factories were in a privileged position. If their managers refused to give them what they wanted, they could just go to the party office and inform the cadre who was in charge of labour affairs.[38] The cadre would then order the managers to give the workers what they wanted. However, after the labour protest in 1976, the Party Central Executive Committee decided to discipline the workers by putting managers and engineers in charge of the Workers' Asiayone in their respective factories.[39] Until then, managers and engineers were merely ordinary members of the Asiayone and workers were leaders of the Asiayone in the factories. As a result, workers could not use the Workers' Asiayone for their interests as much as they used to be able to. Several individual workers, however, continued to be able to use the Asiayone as a channel to present their grievances to the party state. A former worker-cum-party cadre noted that,

> It is not that the Asiayone did not do anything for us anymore. We still got a chance to meet local and regional party bosses at Asiayone meetings. Otherwise, we wouldn't be able to meet senior party-state officials. Some of us managed to present the difficulties we were going through to senior party state officials at those meetings. We often did that privately. I am not suggesting that senior officials would always help us solve our problems. They sometimes did intervene when we successfully convinced them that we were being mistreated by our bosses.[40]

In a similar vein, peasants also got a chance to get to know senior party state officials at the meetings of the Peasants' Asiayone and used the connection when they needed the assistance of senior party state officials. A peasant-cum-party cadre noted,

> The Peasants' Asiayone did not do much for us but they were not totally useless either. When the Mandalay Regional Party confiscated our farm land in the early 1980s, it did not initially give us any compensation. Regional party officials just said, the state owned all farm land in the country, it could take away pieces of farm land at any time it wanted to. I then made an appointment with the senior official from the Regional Party Unit who was in charge of peasant affairs and explained to him that since we make a living on our farm land, we would lose our means of living if we lost our farmlands. Therefore, the

party should give financial compensation which we would need to start new businesses. The party official I talked to initially said he could not do anything but after I explained to him, said he would consult with other senior party officials on the matter. We all then got 2500 kyat for every acre of farm land we lost.[41]

As mentioned earlier, in spite of the repressive measures taken by the socialist government against societal groups, many organizations remained intact and some politically sensitive organizations also managed to live on by keeping a low profile. The organizations that the BSPP government tried to put an end to included political parties and their affiliated organizations such as student unions, business organizations and politically conscious *sangha* organizations. Although all political parties and their affiliated organizations, peasant organizations, and trade and student unions ceased to exist, the Union of Burma Chamber of Commerce and Industry, the Mandalay Traders, Brokers and Industralist Association, hundreds of market associations and the biggest politically conscious *sangha* organization, *Yahanpyo Apwe* [All Burma Young Monk Association], continued to exist throughout the socialist period.[42] Due to government surveillance, members of the *Yahanpyo Aphwe*, however, stopped participating in political activities and devoted most of their time to the administration of Mandalay Hill (a hill with several religious temples and Buddha statues). The Union of Burma Chamber of Commerce and Industry (UBCCI) continued to exist because some of its leading members kept the office open throughout the socialist period. The Mandalay traders, brokers and industrialists association managed to escape the BSPP government's anti-capitalist campaigns by making itself look like a religious organization under the new name, the Traders, Brokers and Industrialists [*kahtina*] Association.[43] Under the guise of the religious association, the Mandalay Traders, Brokers, and Industrialists [*kahtina*] Association functioned in the way it did during the pre-socialist days. The BSPP government was fully aware of the continued existence of the UBCCI and the tricks played by the Mandalay Traders, Brokers and Industrialists Association. BSPP government officials condoned the existence of the UBCCI and the Mandalay Traders, Brokers and Industrialists Association because they did not think that they could pose any threat to the government. These two business organizations, for their part, not only assumed a non-threatening posture but also tried to keep amicable relations with local authorities either by bribing them or making donations to state functions.[44]

The organizations that remained completely intact included non-political religious organizations including the YMBA, native-place organizations, community organizations, and race-based organizations. Apart from community organizations, all other organizations had the potential for social influence beyond a ward or village temple. The government also allowed the formation of new religious and native-place organizations provided that they all registered with the Home Ministry. A retired journalist estimated that the number of native-place organizations in Yangon and Mandalay doubled during the socialist period. Although the government tried to put some party cadres into the board of trustees of some big temples which served as venues for political activities and some race-based organizations, especially the associations of ethnic minorities with insurgent groups under surveillance, it allowed religious and social organizations to engage in non-political activities freely.

There also emerged a good number of informal organizations during the socialist period. These organizations took the form of informal organizations mainly because the government would not allow them to exist legally. Such informal organizations were usually formed by students and writers. Members of these groups regularly but informally got together at a place and discussed the subjects of their common interest. Politics was a subject most of these groups were interested in. Some groups also required their members to read political literature, especially those banned by the government, before they came to regular discussion sessions. Some of these groups, especially student groups, also celebrated the anniversaries of some political events by secretly disseminating pamphlets with political messages on university campuses and by writing graffiti of anti-government slogans on the walls of classrooms. "In those days [during the socialist period]," notes a former Lanzin youth leader, "you were sure to receive pamphlets with anti-government messages around July 7. Anti-government students usually did it to [commemorate] the anniversary of the government's demolition of the student union building on the Yangon university campus. Whenever July 7 was drawing near, university authorities asked students like me [Lanzin youth leaders] to keep an eye on suspicious students."[45] In 1974, some members of informal student groups managed to form a somewhat formal student organization and organized a big protest against the government when the government refused to hold a state funeral ceremony for deceased former UN Secretary General U Thant. However, students went informal again when the government brutally cracked down on the protests. In 1985, an informal student group even managed to mark the tenth anniversary of the U Thant affair protest by publishing pictures, cartoons and articles with coded anti-government messages in the Yangon University's annual magazine. There was no way of knowing the exact number of such informal political organizations operating in socialist Myanmar. However, a former member of an informal student reading group estimated that there existed no less than forty informal students and writers' organizations in various parts of the country in the 1980s.[46] As shown elsewhere in this chapter, it was these informal networks that played crucial roles in the Four-Eights democratic movement that brought down the socialist government.[47]

In sum, the social organizations created by the state to use as social control tools also served as access routes for ordinary people to party-state officials. At the same time, not all non-political organizations were unaffected by the BSPP government's National Security Act. Some political and business organizations also managed to survive by assuming a non-political and non-threatening posture or by turning themselves into informal organizations. Although the membership of community organizations were confined to the people living in the community, that of many religious, native-place and race-based organizations was open to people from the whole city and, in some cases, the whole country.

The State of Civil Society during the SLORC/SPDC Period

The current military government, initially known as the State Law and Order Restoration Council (SLORC), now known as the State Peace and Development Council (SPDC), took control of the country by cracking down on the Four Eights' democratic movement. Immediately upon seizing power, the junta followed its predecessor's suit and sought to restrict civil society space. It gave two options to the pro-democratic movements: these organizations were either to disband or convert themselves into political parties. Also, those desirous of forming non-political social welfare organizations were required to register their organizations with the Ministry of Home Affairs. In order to restrict the movement of the Myanmar people, the junta issued a decree that assemblies of more than six people were illegal. The government also arrested a large number of people, including student leaders, in order to hamper the development of any anti-government movement. Fearing arrest, a mass exodus of several hundred students to Thailand occurred. Students who had fled to the border areas formed overseas pro-democracy organizations. Among these are the National Coalition Government of the Union of Burma (NCGUB), the National Council of Union of Burma (NCUB), the All Burma Students' Democratic Front (ABSDF), the Free Burma Coalition (FBC), the Burma Strategic Group, the NLD (Liberated Area or NLD-LA), the All Burma Federation of Students Unions (ABFSU), the Association to Assist Political Prisoners (AAPP), the Forum for Democracy in Burma (FDB), Federation of Trade Unions of Burma (FTUB), and the Vigorous Student Warriors. All these organizations actively engaged in various anti-government activities in several foreign countries such as Thailand, EU member states and the United States. Regardless of government suppression, some small student organizations had the tenacity to remain alive even in 1996.

In addition to taking harsh actions against social movement organizations, the junta also created several new organizations such as the Union of Myanmar Chamber of Commerce and Industry (UMCCI), the Rice Millers' and Merchants' Association, the Association of Fishery Product Traders, the Maternal and Child Care Association, and the Union Solidarity and Development Association (USDA). The junta manipulated the way these associations functioned by making its supporters their leaders and used them merely as tools for controlling society. For instance, the USDA — an association led by senior government officials — and the Maternal and Child Care Association — an organization led by wives of senior government officials — were used to mobilize supporters and to monitor the activities of opponents of the regime. Various business organizations were equally used to contain the demands of the business community and to raise funds for state activities and to co-opt existing independent business organizations like the Mandalay Traders, Brokers and Industrialists Association. The junta also tried to control the pre-existing artists', literary and musicians' organizations by replacing their executive committees with the people it trusted and used them to recruit volunteers for its legitimating activities.

Like during the socialist period, government organized non-governmental organizations (GONGOs) continued to serve as a channel through which individual people could meet senior government officials. More than ten business people informed me that although the business associations could not do much for them, they joined them because they wanted to establish connections with senior government officials. Some business people also joined the USDA to get to know government officials. A government official also informed me that his boss stopped giving him a hard time after he joined the USDA.[48] In some local areas, community leaders also reportedly used the USDA as a channel to obtaining state-controlled resources for their own communities. A community leader from a township in Shan state was quoted as saying that he and his colleagues used the USDA in trying to convince the local senior officials to build a school in their neighbourhood.[49]

Some business associations have recently tried to become like a properly institutionalized association that could really work for the interests of their members. For instance, the Myanmar Federation of Fisheries (MFF) ran their organization so well that the minister of livestock and fisheries spent time once a week at the headquarters of the federation. The members could openly discuss their problems with the minister and other officials from the ministry. According to a local analyst, the minister and other senior officials helped MFF members solve many of their problems. Following the footstep of the MFF, the minister of commerce has started having regular meetings with members of the UMCCI to discuss problems prevalent in the economy.[50]

Although the military government tried to restrict the parameters of legal, autonomous associational space, it did not do away with associational space in its entirety. Non-political civil society organizations are still able to find room to manoeuvre their activities. A large number of neighbourhood organizations remain and have in fact continued to function. Although some of them did convert into social movement organizations during the 1988 movement, they immediately receded into their former guises and engaged in mainly non-political social activities at the conclusion of the movement. In conjunction with these neighbourhood organizations, numerous native-place and ethnic organizations as well social welfare organizations emerged in various parts of the country. The reason behind the widespread formation of various social welfare organizations in many major cities was born out of necessity. After 1988, the government opened up the economy and with that, the cost of living escalated, especially the cost of medical care and funerals. In fact, the cost of medical care and funerals increased by almost 300 to 400 per cent. The rental of funeral cars from the city municipal office in many areas is a daunting experience because it is often a bureaucratic and unhelpful process that could yield negative results, due to the limited number of cars and difficulty in renting cars from the city municipal office.

After witnessing the difficulties of the ordinary people, some community leaders, Buddhist monks, retirees and businesspeople came together to form social welfare organizations. The first such organizations appeared in Yangon and Mandalay. These organizations were so successful at achieving their aims that many such organizations sprang up in many other parts of the country. There are two premises for the actions of these organizations: Helping the poor who cannot afford medical help and helping those who could neither afford nor hire a hearse. Although government hospitals still existed to cater to the needs of their patients, the newly implemented system, whereby a patient has to purchase his own medicine, plaster, alcohol and so on, was a disservice to the people. Not only did patients have to purchase their own medication and other related items, the ruling made it explicit that hospitals would only provide space for patients. People from these social welfare organizations in Yangon and Mandalay therefore sought to alleviate the plight of the poor. For instance, the secretary of Mandalay's Byamaso Foundation goes to the hospitals in the city every morning to ascertain the medical needs of the poor patients. After obtaining all the information, he would return to his office and consult his treasurer so as to withdraw funds to buy medication, which would then be distributed to the needy patients.[51] The Byamaso Foundation also sought to rent funeral cars to people. After the military took over the country, it took control of the cemeteries in the city and opened new cemeteries in far-flung areas 30–40 miles (50–60 kilometres) from the cities thus unnecessarily raising the bereaved family's funeral expenses. Since most people could neither afford to travel such a distance nor rent a hearse from the city municipal office, the Byamaso Foundation rented funeral cars to people regardless of religious background for a nominal fee. Thus the locally-funded Foundations can be said to have done a lot for the people.[52]

Although it was a non-political association, the Byamaso Foundation initially encountered some harassment from the local government officials. Because the Byamaso Foundation was more popular than the government's Maternal and Child Care Association which provided similar services to the public, the Mandalay regional commander and his wife, patrons of the Mandalay branch of the Maternal and Child Care Association, tried to control it by offering some financial assistance and by trying to put some government officials on the executive committees of the association. The leaders of the Byamaso Foundation refused to accept both financial assistance and the people the regional commander tried to plant into their association. The associations which refused to comply with the demands of local authorities often ran the risk of being harassed by local state agents. Although the government rarely inspected the accounts of non-controversial independent social organizations, the Byamaso Foundation, for a while, found its accounts being checked by government accountants every once in a while. Members of the Byamaso Foundation had to try to stay away from any activities that were even remotely political, in order to keep themselves and their organization out of trouble.[53]

In tandem with these foundations were other private organizations that sought to help children of poor families and allow them to continue schooling. Such formal and informal organizations give poor children scholarships. A well-known formal one is the Tun Foundation. The Tun Foundation has a bank and all the profits from this bank are converted into scholarships for children from poor families. Informal groups are where individual people try to accomplish their objectives through their own personal network. Thus, it is common that those who can afford it would give loans to people in rural areas. These loans are often interest-free or carry a nominal interest rate. As part of the poverty alleviation activities, some business people use their own informal networks to help the poor whenever they can. These informal networks, which function in both Lower and Upper Myanmar, frequently extend their aid to the rural areas. As such, there are instances where some retirees and business people raised funds in their respective communities and redistribute the funds to needy people from certain rural areas. These civil society actors also donated books and computers to Buddhist monastic schools. Likewise, they also try to develop technology and machines to help villagers perform their tasks more efficiently. There are more than fifteen such organizations functioning in Myanmar.

Since the government's expansion of legal associational space in the mid-1990s, both international and domestic NGOs have also been allowed to work on social development programmes. These various NGOs are given the latitude to operate freely so long as they do not challenge the government in any way and steer clear of all political activities. Some organizations like Eco-dev, which comprises formers employees of the forestry department, are engaged primarily in environmental programmes. Additionally, more than thirty international NGOs have been actively engaged in poverty alleviation and educating people about HIV/AIDS. Many of these NGOs have schemes whereby villagers are given agricultural training and shown how to increase their crop yield and produce. Likewise, domestic civil society organizations could function alongside the NGOs because they had funding from foreign organizations.

MATTA, YMCA and other Christian organizations have been participating in HIV/AIDS and other poverty alleviation programmes along with the international organizations. Although these domestic social organizations usually work independently, there were occasions when they cooperated with international NGOs.

In a similar vein, as Ja Nan has explained in her chapter, the emergence of peace and minority cultural organizations in many minority areas can also be attributed to the government's expansion of legal civil society space. Founded and established by a handful of both Christian and Buddhist religious leaders, these peace and minority cultural organizations seek to serve as intermediaries between the government and the minority insurgent groups. Parallel to all these organizations are a set of organizations that were not registered with government agencies but were not considered illegal. The ground on which such organizations tread is indeed a grey area, for though the government is aware of their existence, they are not hassled as long as they do not challenge the government. One such organization is the Kachin Consultative Assembly (KCA). Another such informal organization is the Karen Development Committee (KDC). As Alan Saw Oo has discussed in his chapter, the KDC was formed by well-educated and respected Karen community leaders. Operated from Insein in Yangon, the KDC has engaged in several social welfare and educational activities for Karen nationals.

To be sure, not all associations flourished under SLORC/SPDC rule. Because the junta consistently tried to keep students and the *sangha* out of politics, there was a significant decline in student-initiated study groups and active *sangha* organizations. In the first three years of SLORC/SPDC rule, some twenty informal student organizations remained active. They organized some sporadic anti-government protests in Yangon and Mandalay. The junta had learned from the past, however, and accordingly took harsh actions toward members of informal groups. In terms of suppression, the government always took pre-emptive action against student organizations. Students who tried to organize anti-government activities in the early 1990s were given long prison terms. In order to undermine the student movement, the junta closed down universities and colleges for three years after it took control of the country. Even after schools were re-opened, the government shut them down again whenever student groups tried to organize protests. In the early 1990s, while rewarding the students who collaborated with the government with business licences, the government fired the government servant-parents of student activists.

The government also established more universities with the intention of distancing students from one another. Due to frequent closure of universities and colleges, there were many students waiting to enter tertiary education when the universities were re-opened. In order to accommodate all the waiting students, the government shortened the semester and the duration of studies. Thus, instead of obtaining a degree in four years, it can now be done in three. The government also ensured that most students passed their examinations very easily. Cheating was condoned in examinations and students who failed in the examinations were allowed to take supplementary examinations. Fewer and fewer students came to value the university degrees. The rising cost of living also prevented students from being a part of any activities that could get their families into trouble. The cost of a university education in the pre-SLORC/SPDC days was about 12,000 kyats a year. Now, a student needs 30,000 to 50,000 kyats a month to sustain him/herself. Most of the money goes to travelling expenses since most students were re-assigned to universities in far-flung areas. On top of that, it is now much harder to get jobs. Moreover, many students stayed out of political movements because they did not want to create additional problems for their families. Under such circumstances, students came to spend less time on university campuses and have less interest in participating in political movements. Students who wished to be involved in political movements either had to join the main opposition party, the National League for Democracy, or fled to the Thai-Myanmar border and joined the ABSDF. Although this author managed to find some twenty reading groups at the beginning of the early 1990s, he could not find a single formal reading group in Myanmar in 2002.

The junta also tried to deal with activist monks very severely by arresting many monks after they seized control of the country. Those that continued to organize anti-government protests were also arrested and either sent to labour camps or were shot. In the early 1990s, on the grounds that the government had shot a monk to death, the Buddhist monks in Mandalay launched a boycott against the SLORC/SPDC whereby they refused to perform religious rites for government officials. The situation was dire to the point that the chairman of the Military Council had to go to Mandalay to beg the apology of the monks. According to Buddhist law, the monks had to lift the boycott once their offender apologized. After the apology was made and the boycott lifted, the junta proceeded to arrest the leaders of the boycott and sent them to labour camps. In an attempt to keep the activities of monks in check, the government also issued a decree that barred monks from forming independent *sangha* organizations and required monks to have identification cards.

The government did not just try to suppress monks. In a bid to persuade the monks to its side, the junta also created many new titles and made big donations in gifts and kind to leading monks at various monasteries. Very often, government officials would present leading monks with luxury cars and other expensive products. Those monks who got along with the government received many benefits for themselves and their monasteries. In addition, the government also tried to co-opt the anti-government Buddhist monks through *saya-dajaga* [teacher-disciple] relations. So keen were the government officials at securing the blessing and influence of the monks that they tried to help the monks without being asked. Regardless of the junta's increased persuasion campaign, the majority of the monks remained critical of the government. However, due to the high cost of participating in anti-government activities, most Buddhist monks stopped participating in open anti-government protests since the late 1990s. However, several Buddhist monasteries continued to provide shelter to political activists and remained critical of the government.

All in all, regardless of the junta's anti-civil society measures, Myanmar does have somewhat vibrant civic and social organizations. As long as they do not directly challenge the government or its rule, non-political organizations are allowed to function quite freely. Although these associations can turn themselves into politically conscious civil society groups when the political opportunity structure permitted, they are not currently in a position to challenge the government. The government does not tolerate any organizations that are openly involved in political activities aimed at bringing it down.

Conclusion

Since exerting control over the population is a part of the state formation process, every government in Myanmar tried to control the population through co-optation, neutralization, and suppression. Not all governments, however, placed equal emphasis on all three means. Some resorted to repression more frequently than others. The colonial and parliamentary governments allowed social, religious and political organizations to operate as long as these organizations did not take any subversive actions against them. The socialist and current military governments, on the other hand, were more proactive than their colonial and parliamentary counterparts. While trying to co-opt the general public through government organized non-governmental organizations (GONGO), they passed several rules and regulations that allowed them to take repressive action against hostile societal groups freely. However, this chapter has shown that regardless of the nature of the political system, social, religious and political organizations always played an important role in the society. Some politically conscious people tried to organize themselves into informal organizations and turn themselves into formal social movement organizations, often by appropriating existing non-political civil society organizations, when the political opportunities obtain. Although GONGOs created by all post-colonial governments were supposed to serve the interests of their respective patron governments, they also served as channels which ordinary people could use in trying to gain access to senior officials and state-controlled resources.

Notes

1. One might argue that nationalist organizations should also be considered civil society organizations for the way they engaged in political activities was quite similar to the way pro-democracy civil society organizations engaged in democratic activities. However, I decided not to categorize them as civil society organizations, since most nationalist organizations turned themselves into political parties a few years after they were formed.
2. Thakin Lwin, *Myanmar Nyainggyan a-lut-tha-ma-lut-sha-mu-tha-myaing* [History of Labour Movement in Myanmar] Yangon: Bagan Book, 1968, p. 181.
3. Myo Tun Lin, *Labour Movement in Myanmar* (M.A. thesis, Institute of Economics, Yangon), p. 15.
4. Ibid.
5. the Burma Socialist Programme Party, *Myanmar a-lut-tha-ma-lut-sha-mu* [Labour Movement in Myanmar] Yangon: the Burma Socialist Programme Party Headquarters, 1972, pp. 198–99.
6. Thakin Lwin, p. 175.
7. D.E. Smith, *Religion and Politics in Burma*, Princeton: Princeton University Press, 1965, p. 54.
8. Robert Taylor, *The State in Burma*, Honolulu: University of Hawaii Press, 1987, p. 185.
9. Interviews, members of ten various native-place organizations, December 2001.
10. Suu Hngyat, *A-nay-shok-man-da-lay* [The Slow Walking Mandalay] Yangon: Win Media, 2001, p. 36.
11. Interview, a former nationalist leader, December 2001.

12. Suu Hngyat, *A-nay-shok-man-da-lay*, p. 37.
13. Interview, a journalist, December 2001.
14. Ibid.
15. Suu Hngyat, *A-nay-shok-man-da-lay*, pp. 37–38.
16. Interview, a businessman, December 2001.
17. Suu Hngyat, *A-nay-shok-man-da-lay*, pp. 47, 53–54.
18. Hugh Tinker, *The Union of Burma*, 2nd ed., London: Oxford University Press, 1959, pp. 66.
19. Kyaw Yin Hlaing, "The Politics of State-Business Relations in Post-Colonial Burma", Ph.D. dissertation, Cornell University, 2001, pp. 87–88.
20. Aung Than, *Hse-chuk-hnit-naing-gyan-ye-a-thway-a-kyone* [The Sixteen Year Political Experience], pp. 100–01.
21. Interview, a retired worker, July 1999.
22. Interview, a retired politician, December 2001.
23. Kyaw Yin Hlaing, "The Politics of State-Business Relations in Post-Colonial Burma", p. 111.
24. Interview, October 1998.
25. Interview, a businessman, December 2001.
26. Interivew, a former student leader, December 2001.
27. Min Kyaw, *Kyundaw nainggya ye bawa* [My Political Life], unpublished manuscript, pp. 4–5.
28. Interview, December 2003.
29. Kyaw Yin Hlaing, "The Politics of State-Business Relations in Post-Colonial Burma", p. 89.
30. Ibid., p. 93.
31. Ibid., pp. 116–17.
32. U Ba Kyaing, *A-htoo-nin-a-htwe-htwe-u-pa-de-pund-gyoke* [A Compilation of Special and General Laws] Yangon: 1983, Yi Yi Swe Sarpay, pp. 176–77.
33. Interview, a former BSPP government official, December 2001.
34. Kyaw Yin Hlaing, "The Politics of State-Business Relations in Post-Colonial Myanmar", p. 141.
35. Ibid.
36. Ibid.
37. Interview, a writer, January 2002.
38. Interview, a member of the Worker Asiayone, June 2004.
39. Interview, a party cadre, June 2004.
40. Ibid.
41. Interview, a party cadre, July 1999.
42. Interview, a retired politician, January 2002.
43. Interview, a senior member of the UBCCI, March 1998; Interview, a senior member of the Traders, Brokers and Industrialists Association, September 1998; Suu Hngyat, *A-nay-shok-man-da-lay*, p. 57.
44. Interview, a former BSPP government official, January 2002.

45. Interview, a former Lanzin Youth leader, December 2001.
46. Interview, a former member of a [now defunct] informal student reading group, September 1998. To be sure, such informal political student and student organizations were not unique to Socialist Burma. There existed several similar informal discussion groups both in the colonial and the parliamentary periods. However, in the pre-BSPP days, members of most infomal organizations were gradually absorbed into either political or civil society organizations. In the socialist period, members of informal political organizations had to remain infomal when they decided to join either communist or other insurgent groups. It is worth noting that members of most informal political organizations did not join insurgent groups. Most of them just stopped going to the meetings once they felt that they no longer wanted to be a part of them.
47. Kyaw Yin Hlaing, "Burma: Civil Society Skirting the Regime", in *Civil Society and Political Change in Asia*, edited by Muthiah Alagappa, Stanford: Standford University Press 2004, pp. 389–418.
48. Interview, July 2005.
49. Interview, December 2005.
50. Interviews, September 2005.
51. Interview, May 2003.
52. Ibid.
53. Ibid.

References

Aung Than. *Hse-chuk-hnit-naing-gyan-ye-a-thway-a-kyone [the Sixteen Year Political Experience]* n.d., n.p.
Kyaw Yin Hlaing. *The Politics of State-Business Relations in Post-Colonial Burma*. Ph.D. dissertation, Cornell University, May 2001.
———. "Burma: Civil Society Skirting the Regime", in *Civil Society and Political Change in Asia*, edited by Muthiah Alagappa. Stanford: Standford University Press, 2004, pp. 389–418.
Min Kyaw. *Kyundaw nainggya ye bawa [My political life]*, Unpublished manuscript. n.d.
Myo Tun Lin. *Labour Movement in Myanmar* (M.A. thesis, Institute of Economics, Yangon).
Smith, D.E. *Religion and Politics in Burma*. Princeton: Princeton University Press, 1965.
Suu Hngyat. *A-nay-shok-man-da-lay [The Slow Walking Mandalay]*. Yangon: Win Media, 2001.
Taylor, Robert. *The State in Burma*. Honolulu: University of Hawaii Press, 1987.

Thakin Lwin. *Myanmar Nyainggyan a-lut-tha-ma-lut-sha-mu-tha-myaing* [*History of Labour Movement in Myanmar*]. Yangon: Bagan Book, 1968.

The Burma Socialist Programme Party. *Myanmar a-lut-tha-ma-lut-sha-mu* [*Labour Movement in Myanmar*]. Yangon: the Burma Socialist Programme Party Headquarters, 1972.

Tinker, Hugh. *The Union of Burma*, 2nd ed. London: Oxford University Press, 1959.

U Ba Kyaing. *A-htoo-nin-a-htwe-htwe-u-pa-de-pund-gyoke* [*A Compilation of Special and General Laws*]. Yangon: Yi Ti Swe Sarpay, 1983.

8

Mapping the Contours of Human Security Challenges in Myanmar

Tin Maung Maung Than

Secure states do not necessarily mean secure [inhabitants and] citizens[1]

THE THREE MAIN NATIONAL CAUSES[2]
Non-disintegration of the Union
Non-disintegration of the national solidarity
Perpetuation of national sovereignty
FOUR POLITICAL OBJECTIVES[3]
Stability of the state, community peace and tranquility, prevalence of law and order
National reconsolidation
Emergence of a new enduring state constitution
Building of a new modern developed nation in accordance with the new state constitution
PEOPLE'S DESIRE[4]
Oppose those relying on external elements, acting as stooges, holding negative views
Oppose those trying to jeopardize stability of the State and progress of the nation
Oppose foreign nations interfering in internal affairs of the State
Crush all internal and external destructive elements as the common enemy

Introduction

Since the military took power in Myanmar on 18 September 1988, most of the academic literature and almost all of the news and commentaries on Myanmar politics and security have been focused on three broad themes:

Human rights and democracy issues revolving around the democracy icon Daw Aung San Suu Kyi,[5] the narcotics issue associated with the infamous "Golden Triangle" and ethnic issues viewed as a dichotomous relationship between the majority Bamar and the minority ethnic nationalities. With such a fixation on these seemingly intractable problems, equally significant issues relevant to the physical and spiritual well-being of Myanmar's inhabitants — both citizens and non-citizens alike — remain relatively obscured and unarticulated. This chapter is an attempt to address those issues from a human security perspective in order to highlight the vulnerabilities of the people of Myanmar to threats which are perhaps more insidious and no less deserving of policy sensitivity and response than those posed by armed conflict, erosion of national sovereignty and loss of territorial integrity. The aim is to identify a "convergence of the development and security agendas".[6]

The Concept of Human Security

Until a decade ago, the term "security" had generally been associated with the concept of the nation-state (oftentimes conflated with the regime in power) and its survival in the international system of sovereign states. In other words, the state was identified as the exclusive referent for security. Territorial integrity and sovereignty were the core values of the state that were defended at all costs. The principal threat against these core values had been the use of military force and the preferred approach to counter such a threat was either through self-reliance or some form of alliance with other states that shared some common interest in the fight against the aggressor. There was no consideration for the human inhabitants of the nation-state in this conception of security.[7]

On the other hand, human security is based on the "idea that the individual or community must be at least one of the referent points in answering the eternal questions of security for whom, of what, and by what means", and it is a contested concept.[8] There is no consensus even among the proponents on the exact definition as well as on its operational aspects.[9] It has been on the margins of international relations theory for the decade or so since its inception straddling the domains of human development and non-traditional security concerns.[10] It has been dismissed as "analytically problematic, morally risky, unsustainable, counter-productive and 'so vague that it verges on the meaningless' "[11] by many international relations theorists of the realist persuasion who regard state-centric "national security" as the more relevant and viable concept in theorizing the world of sovereign states.[12] Nevertheless, proponents of human security contend that it "reflects real-world developments that cannot be captured by the narrow and military-focused notion of national security alone".[13] As such, the concept is important "for providing a language and a rationale for raising the concerns of the majority of humanity on the diplomatic and scholarly international relations agenda" thereby allowing the "protection of the vulnerable via the reduction of risk".[14] Especially, "it underscores how the state, as it endeavoured in the past to address 'needs' was in fact marginalizing or oppressing many groups, thus creating 'fear'."[15] Moreover, in the context of foreign policy, "the human security agenda satisfies the utilitarian impulses of policymakers, appeals to their moral instincts, and in doing so, provides a framework for improving the mess" in "much of contemporary world politics".[16] The contention is that "human security is not an epiphenomenona, but rather part of an embryonic global trend in the way that states define and pursue their security needs".[17] After all, a country's well being is judged by the general satisfaction of its citizens on a number of issue areas.

According to one of the earliest proponents of the human security approach, there appears to be two strands of conceptualization in delineating the definitional scope of human security. The "broad or "holistic" concept stemming from the UNDP *Human Development Report 1994* (hereafter referred to as HDR1994) which emphasized equally the ideas of "freedom from fear" and freedom from want" and a narrower limited variant "somewhat labeled 'the freedom-from-fear' approach", focusing only on situations of "extreme vulnerability, usually in the context of intrastate war".[18] The latter has often been labelled the "middle powers' approach" exemplified by the so-called "Canadian School" of human security.[19]

According to the HDR1994, the progenitor of the holistic strand, human security has two main aspects:

> [F]irst, safety from such chronic threats as hunger, disease and repression.
> And second, it means protection from sudden and hurtful disruptions in
> the patterns of daily life — whether in homes, in jobs or in communities.[20]

On the other hand, human security is not synonymous with "human development" which is a "broader concept" that envisages a process of "widening the range of people's choices". In fact, human security is meant to ensure that "people can exercise" those very "choices safely and freely — and that they can be relatively confident that the opportunities they have today are not totally lost tomorrow."[21] In other words, "human security was said to be a necessary but not sufficient precondition for human development."[22] Seven "main categories" were listed in the HDR1994 as "threats to human security":[23]

- Economic security
- Food security
- Health security
- Environmental security
- Personal security
- Community security
- Political security.

The culmination of this holistic approach is embodied in the report of the Commission on Human Security (CHS),[24] entitled *Human Security Now* (2003), which elaborated on the concept as:

> The aim of human security is to protect the vital core of all human rights in ways that enhance human freedoms and human fulfillment. ... [it] means protecting fundamental freedoms ... that are the essence of life ... protecting people from critical (severs) and pervasive (widespread) threats and situations ... using processes that built on people's strengths and aspirations ... creating political, social, environmental, economic, military and cultural systems that together give people the building blocks of survival, livelihood and dignity.[25]

Unlike the HDR1994, the CHS report did not supply an "itemized list of what makes up human security". Instead, it left the consideration of what is deemed to be "vital" — in terms of being "the essence of life" and "crucially important" — to the people (under threat) themselves, noting that such notions vary "across individuals and societies".[26] However, the chapters of the CHS report indicated that human security "may include economic downturn, financial crisis, health epidemics, terrorism, crime and internal conflict, war, post-conflict instability and poverty that kills and angers."[27]

The second strand that narrowly defines human security in terms of protecting "individuals and communities in situations of violent conflict" emphasizes "extreme vulnerability, usually in the context of intrastate war".[28] A striking example of this approach is the annual *Human Security Report*, published since 1994 by the Human Security Centre at the Liu Institute of Global Issues, University of British Columbia, in which the threat to human security was narrowly defined as "the relatively conventional one of political and criminal violence."[29] Probably, the most prominent exposition of this approach was the report entitled *Responsibility to Protect* (R2P) published in December 2001 by the International Commission on Intervention and State Sovereignty (ICISS) which framed "the issue of intervention and sovereignty in terms of the responsibility [of the state] to protect" its citizens from "threats to life, health, livelihood, personal safety and human dignity"which were regarded as "fundamental components of human security". As such, it echoed the concerns of the HDR1994 though the R2P put the onus on the state to which the vulnerable belong. However, the more controversial part of the R2P is its insistence that "states that are either unable or unwilling to discharge their responsibility" be subject to external intervention. By moving from a broad conception of threats and indivisibility [of human security] to a specific focus on two types of threats that might warrant outside *military* intervention", *viz.*, "large-scale loss of life and ethnic cleansing", the Canadian-backed R2P apparently made an "innovative" point in the discourse on human security.[30] This last point that entails provision of "the just cause threshold as well as precautionary principles, right authority, and operational principles" has probably caused more anxiety and misapprehension than any other exposition of human security among security establishments of many developing countries.[31]

Meanwhile, four common characteristics may be identified among the various interpretations and conceptualizations of human security. They are: The individual is treated as the "referent object of security"; "human security recognizes a wide range of potential threats" having regarded the "notion of security in broad terms"; the "interdependent nature of security" is accepted; and it is "essentially proactive" in the sense that it allows "preventive measures" to be taken in a threat situation to forestall a crisis.[32]

For the purpose of this chapter the broad conceptual approach is taken as a basis for examining the issue of human security in Myanmar. For that matter, six of the seven-component threat framework proposed by the HDR1994 will be utilized,[33] drawing upon publicly available empirical data. The aim is to provide an analytical framework to inform national and regional development strategies so as to bring about peace and prosperity to all the citizens of Myanmar. However, to put the human security dimension in a proper context a brief exposition of Myanmar's overwhelmingly state-centred national security perspective is in order at this juncture.

Myanmar's National Security Perspective

The Myanmar language word for the term security is *Lon-choan-yei*. Its connotation implies a sense of safety through an enveloping impermeability. For various reasons associated with Myanmar's historical experience with colonialism, World War II, the civil war (in the first decade of independence) and the Cold War, as well as the multi-ethnic nature of its polity (see Appendix 1), successive Myanmar governments have always adopted a state-centric national security policy approach with much emphasis on national sovereignty, territorial integrity and national unity (of all ethnic nationalities), concomitant with the tendency to conflate national security with regime security.[34] Apparently, the ruling elites (be they parliamentarians or military commanders), like their counterparts in many Asian, states have always "felt that states were the best (and perhaps only) providers of security and ... ferociously guarded the principles of absolute sovereignty and non-interference in domestic affairs."[35] It follows that the "state, usually referred to as *naing-ngan-daw* (literally, royal state) has been the primary referent for 'national' security" and a reification of the state.[36] Moreover, the conceptualization and scope of national security in Myanmar since its independence in 1948, "have essentially been determined by a small elite [dominated by the military] who, for all practical purposes, seem to be insulated from societal" concerns.[37] All along, Myanmar's security outlook has been preoccupied with domestic threats, the most serious being intra-state war characterized by violent challenges from a variety of ethnic and ideological insurgencies that weighed heavily on the military dimension. External aggression has never been a credible threat though some neighbours did have overt ideological links and covert logistical links with internal insurgencies.[38]

Ruled by the military junta known as the State Peace and Development Council (SPDC), present-day Myanmar is a rare example of the "national security state" with "preference for order and conformity over pluralism and diversity"[39] as exemplified by the slogans entitled "three main national causes", "political objectives" and "people's desire" (see above) which highlight the military regime's emphatic discourse on state-centric national security. Nevertheless, there are many prevailing and potential threats to the people of Myanmar other than those under the ambit of the national security agenda and which may be viewed as human security concerns. These will be delineated in the sections below.

Human Security Concerns for Myanmar

As mentioned before, the seven-point HDR1994 framework can be applied to identify and examine serious threats to vulnerable sections of Myanmar society that need serious attention from policymakers and the ruling elite.

Threats to Economic Security

Economic security means "assuring every individual a minimum requisite income" and poverty may be considered as a major threat to it.[40] However, abject poverty is not evident in Myanmar and the threat is mainly in the form of rising inflation, stagnant wages and lack of job opportunities. Despite impressive increases in agriculture production, irrigation schemes, dams, and other economic infrastructure in the last dozen years and the government's claim of some 8 per cent real GDP (gross domestic product) growth in the last eight years, the per capita GDP in US dollar terms at market exchange rate (around Kyats 900 to a dollar) was only around US$180 in fiscal year 2003.[41] From this figure, one can make an educated guess that a large proportion of Myanmar's 54 million people must have fallen under the United Nations' minimal norm of one U.S. dollar a day. According to one estimate, some "15 million people were living below minimum subsistence level" in late 1990s while "another 5 million" were "precariously just above it".[42] This is partly due to the huge loss in value of the inconvertible Myanmar currency (Kyat or K) with the free market rate of the Kyat to the U.S. dollar ballooning thirty times in less than two decades. In fact, the ratio of the free market exchange rate (Kyats to U.S. dollar) to the official exchange rate (pegged to the IMF special drawing rights SDR at around Kyats 6.42 per dollar) hit an all time high of over two hundred times as the exchange rate sank to Kyats 1365 per dollar at the end of September 2005.[43]

There was double-digit price inflation annually in percentage terms for most of the last dozen years with the average consumer price index (CPI) for the entire country quadrupling between 1997 and 2003. The CPI for Yangon city increased from 100 in the base year 1986 to over 2,000 in January 2000. Consequently, household expenditures (especially in urban areas) escalated. For example, average monthly household expenditure in Yangon city increased from around K2,000 in 1989 to over 37,000 in 2001 with over 68 per cent of that spent on food and beverages alone.[44] Retail prices of commodities increased by 20–30 per cent in the first nine months of 2005. The average spot price of one *tical* (0.525 troy ounce) of 24K gold, another indicator of inflation, surpassed the K300,000 mark in September 2005 compared to K14,200 in September 1989.[45] Meanwhile, wages in the public sector could not keep up with inflation; e.g., a university lecturer earning K800–1,000 in 1989 saw the salary increasing to about K8,000–9,000 in 2001 and to less than 15,000 by 2005. Even private sector wages, which are generally higher than the public sector, have fallen behind inflation of commodity prices. With top quality rice costing around K250 per kilogram and whole chicken selling close to K1,900 per kilogram in Yangon city (end of September 2005 prices), the typical salary of a mid-level manager (with a postgraduate degree) in the private sector which lies in the K50,000–60,000 range does not go very far in terms of purchasing power.[46]

The persistence of cross-border labour migration on a large scale is taken as an indication of a substantial problem in the lack of economic security in some regions and certain sections of society since the late 1980s.[47] The bulk of Myanmar's economic migrants could be found in the labour force of Western and Southern Thailand with most of them lacking proper travel documents. Recent estimates of the Myanmar migrant population, many working under harsh conditions (low pay, no rights or representation, long hours, poor work safety, and vulnerable to extortion and harassment by security personnel) in Thailand ranged from 800,000 to 1 million persons. In fact, 1.28 million foreign workers registered with Thai authorities in July 2004, of which over 814,000 applied for work permits. Out of 814,247 successful applicants who were issued work permits between 1 July and 15 December 2004, 610,106 turned out to be Myanmar nationals.[48] Moreover, thousands of Myanmar migrants entered Malaysia through southern Thailand and ended up working illegally.[49] Since most of them had left Myanmar illegally, they had no recourse to legal protection and ran the risk of being prosecuted once they got back to their home country.

Anecdotal evidence suggests that there are also tens of thousands Myanmar nationals, who though having left the country with proper travel documents (obtained at great expense) ended up working illegally in Japan, Thailand, Malaysia and even Singapore.[50]

One vulnerable section of Myanmar's population emerged, ironically, with the success of eradicating poppy cultivation in the Shan states. Hundreds of thousands of cultivators belonging to several hill tribes lost their only livelihood despite government and local leadership's efforts to implement crop substitution schemes that were hampered by unfavourable market conditions and ecological constraints.[51]

Threats to Food Security

Food security can be understood in terms of guaranteed "physical and economic access to basic food".[52] Myanmar is reputed to be a country with abundance of food and its overall agriculture output has steadily increased over the last twenty-five years.[53] Nonetheless, there have been some indications of the likelihood of localized pockets of communities facing acute and even chronic shortage of food that warrants the attention of policymakers and state managers. This seems to be mainly due to conflict situations, administrative constraints and structural (economic) conditions.[54] Threats to food security affect health security (see below) as well and the World Food Programme (WFP) claimed that some 15 per cent of the population faced "food insecurity", while "one out of three young children are chronically malnourished". The WFP had been assisting around 760,000 people "including malnourished children, refugees from neighbouring Bangladesh and former opium farmers".[55] There is also a distinct possibility that internally displaced persons (IDP see the section on threats to community security below) are easily vulnerable to food insecurity.

Threats to Health Security

Health security guarantees "a minimum protection from disease and unhealthy lifestyles".[56] In this respect, there has been substantial improvement in Myanmar's public health infrastructure during the last dozen years. Marked increases in the number of public healthcare personnel at all levels as well as public health facilities are evident in government statistics. To cite a few illustrative examples of quantitative improvements between 1988 and 2005: the number of doctors rose from 3,185 to 6,338; nurses from 4,515 to 10,003, midwives from 8,019 to 9,572; other health care staff from 3,882 to 5,998; hospitals from 631 to 819; health units (rural, maternal & child care, regional, and school) from 1,829 to 1,964; traditional medicine (TM) hospitals from 2 to 14; TM dispensaries from 89 to 237; tertiary medical educational facilities from 4 to 14; and training schools from 26 to 43.[57] Meanwhile, life expectancy at birth for rural males increased by 4.6 years to 60.8 and by 2.9 years to 63.3 for females whereas for the urban population the corresponding increments were 2.5 years to 61.5 for males and 2.4 years to 65.6 for females.[58] Myanmar doctors had also successfully carried out kidney transplants, open-heart surgery, limb-reattachments, Siamese-twins separations and other advanced medical practices.[59] Moreover, immunization and nutrition action programmes had also been expanded and improved.[60]

However, there had been some worries by outside observers that public health in Myanmar exhibited serious deficiencies.[61] In fact, there have been three worrying trends in the health sector and the prevalence of several high morbidity and communicable diseases that warrants redress to forestall serious threats against health security. The first trend is the low and stagnating level of public health spending as a share of GDP which has been further aggravated by the falling purchasing power of the local currency *vis-a-vis* imported medical supplies and equipment. The second trend is the escalating cost of private healthcare coupled with the expanding gap between the supply of subsidized care provided by the public health agencies and the services demanded by the patients (the first trend is likely to be responsible for this predicament in public healthcare). The third trend is the lack of substantial improvement in mortality rates despite the best efforts by public health authorities. Moreover, HIV/AIDS, Tuberculosis, Malaria, and Hepatitis B & C may be identified as major illnesses threatening health security in Myanmar.

As Table 8.1 illustrates, the public expenditure for health had stagnated at a very low level of around 0.2-0.3 per cent (even when compared to 1 per cent in 1984/85 fiscal year under one-party socialist rule) in recent years, except for 2002. The World Health Organization (WHO) had also estimated that, in "international dollars" (estimated in terms of purchasing power parity or PPP), Myanmar's per capita public expenditure on health was US$2 and US$6 respectively for 1998 and 2002.

The corresponding per capita total (public plus private) expenditure was only US$20 and US$30 respectively.[62] The Asian Development Bank (ADB), in its check list of Millennium Development Goals (MDG) in the GMS (Greater Mekong Sub-region) placed Myanmar in the "low access" range (Vietnam was accorded "medium access" and Thailand "good access",

TABLE 8.1
Government Expenditure on Health as Share of GDP

Year	1998	1999	2000	2001	2002
Per cent	0.19	0.2	0.3	0.26	0.41

Source: World Health Organization (WHO) online country data on Myanmar at <http://www3.who.int/php/whosis_images/>

top among the four groupings) with regard to the MDG indicator showing the percentage of population with sustainable access to affordable essential drugs in 1999.[63] The financial resources available for the public health sector appear woefully inadequate, given these unfavourable trends in both relative and absolute purchasing power terms.

According to WHO estimates, Myanmar's average private expenditure on health, as a share of total expenditure (in local currency terms), had been over 80 per cent in recent years (for example, 89.4 per cent in 1998 and 81.5 per cent in 2002). Similarly, the corresponding average "out-of-pocket expenditure" as a share of total private expenditure remained very high at over 95 per cent (for example, 99.7 per cent for both 1998 and 2002).[64] The latter set of figures could be attributed to the virtual absence of health care insurance in Myanmar. This is also worrying because of the rising cost of private health care services in the last decade. Although the state has been providing "free" healthcare since independence in 1948, it has never been able to provide enough resources to satisfy public demand. Under the market-oriented economic system implemented during the last fifteen years, public health facilities had introduced full-fee paying facilities for well-to-do patients and a system of "sharing costs for health", whereby those who can afford cross-subsidize the needy. Moreover, donations in cash and kind are also solicited from charitable individuals as well as commercial enterprises and private entrepreneurs.

However, as can be seen from Table 8.2, the attendance at government hospitals in the period from 1990 to 2002 had fallen and then stagnated despite the fact that there had been a steady increase of the population as well as the number of available hospitals. This seems to suggest that, barring a drastic improvement in public overall healthiness (an unlikely event), some patients either felt that the services provided, though relatively cheap, were not to their satisfaction or, worse, they could not even afford to seek public health services, not to mention private ones.

The opening up of the economy since 1989 had resulted in the mushrooming of private health care service providers in the form of specialist- and poly-clinics, diagnostic laboratories and medical centres with facilities for in-house patient care.[65] At the same time, anecdotal evidence suggests that the gap between lower and middle class incomes in terms of affordibility for private health care costs associated with consultation, clinical investigations, childbirth, surgery, and hospitalization had widened.[66] Many low-income families are known to have resorted to self-medication with home remedies or widely available patent medicine

TABLE 8.2
Government Hospital Attendance (in thousands)

Fiscal Year	1985/86	1990/91	1995/96	1996/97	1997/98	1998/99	1999/2000	2000/01	2001/02	2002/03
In-patients	1,055	1,043	870	889	875	904	869	832	908	939
Out-patients	9,456	6,284	3,150	2,808	2,350	2,124	2,127	2,119	2,426	2,382

Source: *Statistical Yearbook 2003* (Yangon: Central Statistical Organization, 2003)

and the relatively cheaper TM products; most of which are of inferior quality and unregulated.[67]

As for the third trend, the "mortality stratum" classification of the World Health Organization (WHO), Myanmar appeared under the group described as "Southeast Asia with high child and high adult mortality".[68] According to WHO country statistics, "under-five mortality in terms of probability of dying by five years of age " (per thousand) for Myanmar (estimated for 2003) averaged 117 for males and 93 for females while the corresponding "adult mortality in terms of probability of dying between 15 and 60 years of age" was 337 for males and 222 for females.[69] As revealed in Table 8.3, the stagnating trends of the maternal and infant mortality rates (per 1,000 live births) in both rural and urban Myanmar had not seen any improvement between 1990 and 2002. Thus, women and children would remain vulnerable to mortal threats at the crucial point of childbirth until and unless a dedicated policy focus is established and relevant resources are brought together in a concerted effort to address this issue.

In the early years of the fight against HVI/AIDS, Myanmar authorities seemed to have taken the view that it was a lifestyle disease that would remain within the small high-risk section of the polity comprising homosexuals (usually frowned upon and somewhat circumscribed by social norms) and intravenous drug users. The official stand then appeared to be that, given Myanmar's conservative and puritanical religious (mainly Buddhist) and cultural values, mores and practices, and the fact that prostitution had been illegal, it could be tackled mainly by the state alone, on a self-reliant basis, as a clinical problem. The associated risk of rampant transmission into the rest of society was initially regarded as not so significant as to warrant a concerted campaign on a broad front involving societal actors as well.[70] However, towards the beginning of the twenty-first century, cognizant of global and regional concerns over the HIV/AIDS pandemic and increasing evidence of HIV/AIDS transmission through heterosexual relations, the authorities seemed to have realized the extent and severity of the problem with its economic and social ramifications.[71] Hence they quickly decided to address the issue holistically with external assistance.[72] On the other hand, in the absence of comprehensive survey data estimates of the extent of HIV incidence in Myanmar is a contested figure. At the lower end is the official figure of 6,727 AIDS cases and an estimated 46,968 HIV infections up to March 2003 with 2,843 deaths reported.[73] However, it was also

TABLE 8.3
Maternal and Infant Mortality Rates (per 1,000 live births)

Year	1985	1990	1995	1996	1997	1998	1999	2000	2001	2002(p)
Maternal (rural)	2.1	1.9	1.8	1.9	1.7	1.8	2.8	1.9	1.8	1.9
Maternal (urban)	1.2	1.0	1.0	1.0	1.0	1.0	1.8	1.1	1.0	1.1
Infant (rural)	47.0	48.8	49.7	49.8	48.6	48.7	62.5	50.2	50.1	50.7
Infant (urban)	47.2	47.0	47.3	47.5	47.1	47.2	55.1	48.5	48.3	48.4

Notes: (p) is for provisional estimate; the data for 1999 was from the National Mortality Survey 1999 but the anomaly of the sudden spikes in that year remains unexplained.

Source: *Statistical Yearbook 2003* (Yangon: Central Statistical Organization, 2003)

revealed that for Myanmar the estimated number of "persons living with HIV/AIDS (PLWHA)" in 2004 was 338,911.[74] This figure is comparable to the estimate by the UN Joint Programme on HIV/AIDS (UNAIDS) which gave the number of adults infected with HIV by the end of 2003 at around 320,000 or some 1.3 per cent of the corresponding cohort.[75] Much higher is the WHO estimate (2001) of some 510,000 HIV infections, amounting to nearly 2 per cent of the age cohort of 15–49 years.[76] On the other hand, "published reports are all in agreement that the prevalence of HIV is increasing, with both infection rates and reported AIDS cases."[77] It appears that "[e]ven under the most optimistic scenario it seems unrealistic to expect that Myanmar will escape significant social and economic disruption related to the spread of HIV/AIDS" and as such this disease poses a clear and present danger to Myanmar's health security.[78] Moreover, because of cross-border migration, Myanmar's HIV/AIDS issue also has transnational and even regional implications in human security terms.[79]

Tuberculosis, a curable disease, has been the bane of low-income Myanmar patients who cannot afford the cost of the required prolonged treatment. Realizing the nature of the problem, Myanmar health authorities adopted the DOTS (directly observed treatment short course) strategy in 1997, in line with the WHO recommendations. Covering some 300 out of 324 townships, the strategy had, by 2002, achieved an 82 per cent cure rate for new cases and a 70 per cent detection rate. It was reported that over 100,000 TB patients were under treatment with drugs provided by the Geneva-based Global Drug Facility (GDF). With external assistance to procure medicine and enhance detection, the TB menace appears to be on the verge of being effectively addressed as illustrated in Table 8.3, where the specific death rate appeared to have slightly improved after 1998. However, a sustained effort to significantly reduce the threat may require more resources (both domestic and external) than what had been available up to the present.[80]

Malaria is endemic in Myanmar with high seasonal incidence in the remote and border regions[81] and urban areas have also been affected, probably through human carriers.[82] Government sources stated that 750,000 cases were reported in 2003 and 2,000 new cases occurred daily costing over K6 million per day for treatment alone.[83] As shown in Table 8.4, specific death rates has not improved in recent years and had even exhibited a slightly rising trend since 1990 despite government efforts to eradicate malaria with the help of limited foreign humanitarian assistance.[84]

TABLE 8.4
Specific Death Rates for Tuberculosis and Malaria
(Urban, per 100,000 people)

Year	1985	1990	1995	1996	1997	1998	1999	2000	2001	2002
Tuberculosis	33.1	32.6	33.2	33.4	33.4	33.2	26.5	27.4	27.1	26.7
Malaria	20.0	20.0	22.2	22.2	22.2	28.4	27.5	28.7	29.8	30.8

Source: *Statistical Yearbook 2003* (Yangon: Central Statistical Organization, 2003)

In the last couple of years, Myanmar health authorities as well as the international health community had realized the debilitating impact of the three major illnesses identified as HIV/AIDS, tuberculosis (TB) and malaria that have been serious sources of morbidity and which impose a heavy burden on state and society. Consequently, the health authorities are focusing on these three communicable diseases as a target group and have solicited substantial external assistance (to the tune of several million U.S. dollars a year) to address them.[85] Still, it appears that it is a long way to go before one could reduce these threats to a manageable level. In this respect, the termination of the Global Fund (to fight AIDS, tuberculosis and malaria) grants on 18 August 2005, after disbursing less than US$12 million out of a total US$98.4 million scheduled over a 5-year period (2005–2010), was a serious setback for Myanmar's campaign against these three diseases. The main reason cited by the Global Fund were the government imposition of new restrictive rules and procedures on "travel and clearance" and "review of procurement of medical and other supplies" that "would effectively prevent the implementation of performance-based and time-bound programs in the country". These allegations were strongly denied by the authorities concerned who promised to carry out the task with whatever resources available.[86]

Hepatitis B and C are silent killers whose level of incidence in Myanmar is yet to be ascertained. Wild estimates of 10 per cent incidence bandied about in recent years are highly dubious but anecdotal evidence and an unscientific sampling amongst the current author's friends and relatives suggest that both taken in conjunction are a serious health problem for urban dwellers, to say the least. Aflatoxin in food, less than robust screening in blood transfusions, slack and inadequate sanitizing procedures in dental and medical clinics (compounded by Myanmar patients' widespread preference for intravenous medication and injections), and lack of health screening are probably the main causes of concern in this case.

Finally, there is the looming ultimate health security threat in the form of the Avian Flu viral pandemic for which Myanmar health authorities have been preparing with what little resources they can muster but obviously need a lot more help from external sources.[87]

Threats to Environmental Security

Environmental security entails "protecting people from the short- and long-term ravages of nature, man-made threats in nature, and deterioration of the natural environment".[88] The main threat to environmental security seems to be the problem of deforestation, mainly due to (mostly illegal) commercial logging and human encroachment for cultivation and firewood. Despite the government's insistence that the amount of Myanmar's forest cover has not changed for the last decade or so and that nearly 5,000 square kilometres of reforestation had been accomplished[89] other sources indicated that the average deforestation rate between 1990 and 1995 was an estimated 1.4 per cent.[90] The Asian Development Bank reported that Myanmar's forest cover had declined from 60.2 per cent in 1990 to 52.3 per cent in 2000.[91] Even after logging concessions (mainly to Thai businessmen and Yunnan merchants) have been scaled down and regulatory measures against clear-cutting and enforcement against illegal logging were beefed up in the late 1990s, conservation-focused non-governmental organizations (NGOs) still insisted that the denuding of Myanmar's forests continued unabated.[92] In fact, Myanmar's forestry minister had revealed in January 2006 that annually, more than 100,000 tonnes of timber were "illegally extracted from Kachin and Shan states in Northern Myanmar and smuggled into China" and "stopping" this "would not only have economic benefits but also help conserve the environment".[93]

Another issue is the environmental impact of large dams being built as mega projects for hydro-power generation or for multi-purpose usage of the stored water. It is doubtful whether several of these projects in the Thanlwin (Salween) river and offshoots of the Ayeyarwady (Irrawaddy) river had undergone robust environmental impact studies, especially regarding their negative impact upon some ethnic communities affected by them.[94]

Threats to Personal Security

Personal security may be broadly defined as "protecting people from physical violence, whether from the state, from external states, from violent individuals and sub-state actors".[95] Myanmar's national security imperatives have, unfortunately, led to policies and measures that threatened the personal security of some individuals belonging to certain sections of society. Moreover, relative economic deprivation and the lure of higher income in neighbouring countries (push and pull factors) have also led to cross-border migration (majority of migrants are illegal) in which the personal security of the migrant is threatened by the exploitative practices of the employer and local law enforcement authorities (of which many are corrupt) in the host country (see section on economic security above). The manifestation of all these threats can be found in contentious issues related to allegations of forced labour (including porters), child labour, child soldiers, rape as a tool of war, land mines, internally displaced persons (IDP), refugees, stateless persons, and human trafficking.[96]

Myanmar authorities have, all along, denied that serious problems existed for most of the afore-mentioned issues. For others, such as forced labour, child soldiers and human trafficking, the government, while acknowledging the problem, contended that the scope of the problem was rather small and/or were due to local breaches of regulations and standing orders. Meanwhile, relevant high-level ministerial committees were formed and administrative measures (for investigation, deterrence and punitive action) were instituted in recent years. The government had also conceded to some demands by concerned organizations such as the International Labour Organization (ILO) and had allowed representation from ILO and the International Red Cross (IRC) to facilitate dialogue and independent investigation. Nevertheless, many NGOs, such as Human Rights Watch, Amnesty International, anti-government organizations, ethnic rebel groups, democratic lobbies and some Western governments as well as international bodies such as the ILO and the United Nations Commission on Human Rights (UNCHR) have been insisting that such threats are ongoing and the government has done very little in substance to address them.[97]

Threats to Community Security

Community security requires protection of a group of people "from loss of traditional relationships and values and from sectarian and ethnic violence".[98] In Myanmar, threats to community security can be found in some of the less integrated communities. Occasionally, the relatively large Muslim community in the Rakhine state and smaller ones scattered all over the country faced violent reactions from the Buddhist majority, if and when perceived or real tensions over race and religion boiled over, notwithstanding the government's constant efforts to maintain law and order and communal peace and religious harmony.[99] It is believed that there are hundreds of thousands of stateless persons among the Muslim population in Myanmar's Western Rakhine state. Calling themselves "Rohingya", many of these families migrated from Bangladesh over the last 150 years and claimed to have been persecuted and often fled *en masse* into Bangladesh to be repatriated repeatedly. Up to early 2005, some 20,000 Muslim refugees from Myanmar still remained in refugee camps in Bangladesh. The Myanmar Government does not recognize Rohingya as an ethnic group and seems to regard them as aliens rather than natives.[100] Malaysia has offered political asylum to about 10,000 such persons. Similarly, expatriate dissidents and foreign religious organizations as well as the United States have alleged that Christians in Myanmar were subjected to coerced conversions, constraints on religious freedom and social discrimination (see Annex 8.2 for religious composition in Myanmar).[101]

Another community facing potential and real threats to security comprises several ethnic groups in the former war zones of Northern and Eastern Myanmar. These post-conflict societies, though still subject to occasional conflict due to the presence of pockets of Shan (Shan State Army South or Shan United Revolutionary Army), Kayin (Karen National Liberation Army) and Kayah (armed wing of the Kayah National Progressive Party) rebel groups in their vicinity, are trying to rebuild and rehabilitate their communities shattered by decades of violent conflict with the government as well as intra-group and intra-ethnic conflicts. The problems associated with this category of vulnerable communities seeking a peace dividend warrants a separate study on its own and is therefore dealt with in a separate section below.

Peace and Reconstruction: Ethnic Groups in Myanmar

If peace is simply taken as the absence of war, it can be said that peace prevails in the borderlands of Myanmar both in the east bordering Thailand and in the west across from Bangladesh. This is the official government view. It follows from this assertion that reconstruction has also being going on in earnest since the first ceasefire arrangement was concluded with ethnic Wa troops of the now defunct Burma Communist Party (BCP) in 1989. The military government claimed that it had spent some 65 billion Kyats and US$550 million up to the end of January 2005[102] (over US$10 billion equivalent in official exchange rate or around US$65 million if the average prevailing free market exchange rate for end of 2005 is used) on the multi-sector (mainly for education, health and infrastructure projects) border-areas development (BAD) scheme (see Annex 8.3 for enumeration of physical infrastrucutre). This reconstruction effort extends over 18 regions in Myanmar's western, northern and eastern border regions (in all seven states and two divisions, covering over 83,000 square miles (nearly 32 per cent of the country's area) and encompassing some 5.3 million inhabitants in 68 townships (out of 324 townships in the country).[103] The programme's coverage seems quite significant given that some 46 per cent of the non-Bamar ethnic population reportedly reside in these areas (for the demographics of ethnic nationalities, see Annex 8.2).[104]

On the other hand, "peace goes beyond ending belligerency to creating a new state of affairs that can be defined in positive terms" and there has only been a partial transformation in that respect.[105] Moreover, both these notions about peace and reconstruction propounded by the military managers of the Myanmar state and their ramifications are problematic as they are challenged by detractors of the military regime that include, *inter alia*, human rights advocacy groups, dissident groups representing a variety of ethnic communities, opposition activists, NGOs, some Western governments and even agencies of the United Nations. It also belies the fact that most of the IDPs in Myanmar are located in these areas and a considerable number of refugees and illegal immigrants in countries with borders contiguous to Myanmar are from the very same areas. Furthermore, complaints about religious persecution, widespread rape, forced labour, arbitrary arrests, and extra-judicial killings continue despite the seeming peace (see the section on personal security above).

At the national level, issues of peace and reconstruction are determined by the ruling military elite, who sets the terms and define the parameters from a state security perspective. They profess to uphold "national interests" and have instituted a top down approach. In their national project of bringing peace to the border lands, as part of the larger project to establish "national unity", as well as in reconstructing the war-ravaged areas, these state managers, who are military commanders, have set the rules of the game and have drawn up an "inclusion list" in terms of "who gets what". To them, everything is black and white and there is no room for grey areas. Their overarching quest for the elusive "national unity" places the state above communities, families and individuals. Culture, language and identity of those duly affected are supposed to reflect the dominant Bamar (Burman) paradigm.[106] On the other hand, the regime's many peace agreements with armed ethnic groups could be seen as the first stage of a multi-stage peace and reconciliation process leading towards the elusive goal of unity among the ethnic groups of Myanmar.[107] It is imperative that the subsequent stages be followed through in a manner consistent with the human security paradigm.

Not surprisingly, the picture from the ground is rather more complex and fraught with uncertainties. Following the peace agreements between the government and the leaders of the armed groups it is not uncommon to find "frustration, disillusionment, misunderstandings about what has and what has not been agreed to", among the rank and file and there is little change in the "underlying structural conditions" of the conflict.[108] Different individuals, families and communities reap differential benefits or suffer differential losses from the state project for peace and reconstruction. Many belabour under the dual authority of the central state authorities as well as the local rebel elite-turned "national race leaders". Predatory taxation and pillage by insurgent groups in the past are replaced by rent-seeking and business monopolization by, more or less, the same groups led by state-endorsed "leaders of national races", the latter resorting to garner patronage from the military leadership instead of fighting the military government.

Moreover, internal tensions within the ceasefire groups continue to threaten peace and security within their own communities. The major ceasefire groups like the Kachin and Mon, though more politically sophisticated than the others (altogether seventeen groups had been acknowledged by the government) appeared to be suffering from internal rifts (mainly due to corruption and jostling for power in anticipation of the new political order) and problems of leadership succession as their leaders, who were involved in original peace deals, had passed away. For instance, there was a short-lived coup, in mid-September 2005, against the NDA-K (New Democratic Army-Kachin, an armed group that entered into ceasefire in December 1989 and comprising ethnic Kachins also known as Red Shan, from the defunct Maoist Burma Communist Party or BCP War Zone 101) chairman (who was away in Yangon) in which his headquarters was taken over by those loyal to the general secretary. The coup collapsed in two weeks' time due to a counter-coup by troops loyal to the chairman, backed by government authority. In November, the splinter group from the KIA (Kachin Independence Army which is the military arm of the ceasefire group Kachin Independence Organization or KIO) that broke away in 2004 after being accused of attempting to stage a coup, further split when some refused to follow their leader Colonel Lasang Aung Wa when he moved to a new area designated as their quasi-autonomous territory by the government (*Irrawaddy*, online news, 15 November 2005, available at <www.irrawaddy.org>).

Among the armed groups that had made peace with the junta the "peace dividend" and the extent of reconstruction are also varied. Those with powerful armies and/or occupying strategic zones at the border or those who "came into the legal fold" earlier, got better deals for the elites as well as the community as a whole. Some stragglers and marginal players in the national security calculus have to be contented with less generous terms and smaller budgets for reconstruction. There are also those, like the Karenni (Kayah) who found themselves at the end of what was perceived as a raw deal and went back to armed conflict. Some like the Mons found the price of peace rather steep in terms of creeping attenuation of local authority and forgone opportunities for commercial gains, which they believed had retarded the pace of reconstruction through communal efforts.[109]

For those ethnic groups who had missed the boat in reaching ceasefire arrangements with the junta, there is neither peace nor reconstruction. In fact, of the two major groups who are till fighting (as at October 2005), the Shan and the Kayin, the government refuses to extend any peace overture to the Shan faction known as Shan State Army South (SSA, the name preferred by the group) or Shan United Revolutionary Army (SURA, the name used by the junta) while peace talks had been intermittent with the Karen National Union (KNU), the political arm of the Kayins who had fought the government for over five decades.

There is also a regional dimension in Myanmar's effort to establish peace and embark upon reconstruction in its borderlands. In particular, Thailand found that its decades-old practice of having ethnic armed groups as a buffer to its west was no longer tenable. In the second half of the 1990s, the Myanmar military increasingly made its presence felt at the border, a rather unsettling situation for the Thai military and Border Patrol Police. Contested areas along the poorly demarcated border assume heightened significance and the potential for military confrontation between the two neighbours increased and in fact materialized in 2001 and 2002. Peace does not stop the flood of drugs flowing into Thailand as traffickers shifted from opium/heroin to the more lucrative and logistically conducive "Yaba" or methamphetamine. It became a serious national security issue for Thailand and remains a source of tension between the two states. Decades-old problems of refugees and illegal migrants/workers also came out into the open and further complicated bilateral relations. Reconstruction of physical infrastructure and movement of people on the Myanmar side have also been viewed with suspicion by some quarters in the Thai military and political establishment.[110] Despite substantial progress made in Thai-Myanmar relations under Thaksin's leadership through the establishment of a number of economic cooperation schemes and diplomatic support of Myanmar's seven-point road map, centuries-old historical baggage and very different political cultures of the two regimes still inhibit the realization of the full potential for these two countries to reap the peace dividend through closer cooperation.[111]

All in all, one can argue that though state-centric "national security" has been greatly enhanced by the peace agreements in Myanmar, the "human security" of those inhabiting the border lands of Myanmar is yet to be assured. The latter has lagged behind the former and it is imperative that the state managers acknowledge the existence of the gap between the two and strive to narrow it through inclusive and participatory approaches that take alternative views into consideration. Only then, can effective reconstruction be implemented with the wholehearted cooperation of the polity concerned. In this respect the international community should lend support to enhancing human security not only in the border regions but in the heartland of Myanmar as well. For a start, international humanitarian assistance in the health and education sectors as well as poverty alleviation programmes (see Annex 8.4) should be launched as a coordinated effort with enough safeguards to ensure that the target communities benefit directly from the aid.[112] Local NGOs (non-governmental organizations) and some INGOs (international NGOs) already in Myanmar could become channels for such assistance. However, just pumping money into problem areas is not the answer and care must be taken to first build up the absorptive capacity of both the local partners and the target community. Inevitably, the relevant government agencies and GONGOs (government organized NGOs) must be given some role in the process without actually letting them take control of the entire process.[113]

The Way Ahead

It is evident from the afore-mentioned exposition that various threats to human security are present in Myanmar.[114] Some of the sources of human insecurity "results directly from existing power structures which determine who enjoys the entitlement to security and who does not".[115] Nevertheless, the most relevant issues in Myanmar's human security agenda need not be incompatible with the existing power structure and the future configuration envisaged by the junta if framed in a non-zero sum non-confrontational approach. One example is the developmental approach undertaken by the BAD programme and its apparent contribution to peace-building in border areas in general and quasi-autonomous zones allocated to ceasefire groups in particular.[116] The human security agenda is, however, yet to be incorporated in Myanmar's national security perspective and despite the current military leaders proclivity for establishing a strong centralized unitary state, "resisting external interference, and embracing nineteenth-century conceptions of hard-shell sovereignty",[117] all is not lost for human security advocates hoping to introduce a people-centred approach in Myanmar. Notwithstanding the illiberal political regime being formulated by the current ruling elite, there is no doubt that they are all committed to the state-building project — albeit on their own interpretation of state-nation-society relationship. If the human security agenda can resonate with the developmental impulses of the military leaders, it may be possible to build on such a convergence and in turn build a cooperative paradigm informed by the possibility to concomitantly undertake nation-building by incorporating a human security component. Presumably, such an approach would not be seen as a challenge to the state and regime but rather, enhance the currently ongoing state-building exercise by attracting more resources from within society as well as the international community. In fact, "human security is achievable only in synergistic collaboration across social, institutional, and sectoral boundaries."[118] It is up to the advocates of the human security approach to fashion such a paradigm so that the ruling elite could find no reason at all to resist and reject it. On the other hand, it is imperative that all "participants" in this endeavour take a very long-term view of future benefits as "a human security agenda almost by definition requires consistency and patience".[119]

Annex 8.1

Officially Designated Ethnic groups
(Major Groups) in Myanmar

Major group	Percentage share of population	
	1983 (Census)	2003 (estimate)
Kachin (12 sub-nationalities)	1.4	1.4
Kayah (9 sub-nationalities)	0.4	0.5
Kayin (11 sub-nationalities)	6.2	6.4
Chin (53 sub-nationalities)	2.2	2.1
Bamar (9 sub-nationalities)	69.0	67.9
Mon (no sub-nationality)	2.4	2.7
Rakhine (7 sub-nationalities)	4.5	4.2
Shan (33 sub-nationalities)	8.5	9.4
Others (unspecified & foreign races)	5.4	5.4

Sources: Government of Burma (1986); *Lokethar Pyithu Neizin* (daily), 26 September 1990; and Hla Min, "Political Situation in the Union of Myanmar and Its Role in the Region" (Yangon: Ministry of Defence, April 2004).

Racial Composition of Myanmar's Ethnic States
(per cent; based on 1983 Census)

	Chin State	Kachin State	Kayin State	Kayah Sate	Mon State	Rakhine State*	Shan State
Bamar	0.8 (0.8)	29.3 (29.1)	14.1 (14.1)	17.5 (20.6)	37.2 (37.2)	0.7 (0.7)	11.1 (11.4)
Chin	94.6 (92.9)	–	–	–	–	3.2 (3.1)	–
Kachin	–	38.1 (n.a.)	–	–	–	–	3.8 (n.a.)
Kayin	–	–	57.1 (50.9)	6.4 (5.4)	15.7 (12.7)	–	–
Kayah	–	–	–	55.9 (54.1)	–	–	1.2 (–)
Mon	–	–	17.1 (17.7)	–	38.2 (38.2)	–	–
Rakhine	4.4 (3.7)	–	–	–	–	67.8 (64.3)	–
Shan	–	24.2 (23.4)	3.0 (2.9)	16.6 (8.5)	–	–	76.4 (35.2)

Notes: – denotes less than 1 per cent or negligible; n.a. denotes not available; * Bangladeshis comprised 24.3 per cent according to the 1983 Census. The figures in parentheses are estimates based on more recent data published in 2003 in which only the Jinghpaw sub-group of the Kachin was enumerated. The share for Shan also dropped drastically because only the Shan dialect sub-group of the overall Shan ethnic group comprising 33 sub-group was tallied. The figures do not add up to 100 due to the presence of non-indigenous races in all states.
Source: Government of Burma Census, various issues; and Hla Min op. cit.

Annex 8.2

Major Faiths in Myanmar (1983 Census)

Faith	per cent share
Buddhist	89.4
Christian	4.9
Muslim	3.9
Hindu	0.5
Animist & Others	1.3

Source: Government of Burma (1986)

Religious Composition of Myanmar's Ethnic States (per cent; 1983 Census)

	Chin State	Kachin State	Kayin State	Kayah State	Mon State	Rakhine State	Shan State
Animist	14.2	2.9	0.2	12.5	0.1	1.2	6.5
Buddhist	10.8	57.8	83.7	46.2	92.2	69.7	83.9
Christian	72.7	36.4	9.4	39.7	0.5	0.4	8.0
Muslim	0.1	1.5	5.2	1.2	6.0	28.5	1.2

Note: The figures do not add up to 100 due to the presence of those with other faiths such as Hindus.
Source: Government of Burma 1987, various issues.

Annex 8.3

Selected Infrastructure Developments
under the BAD Programme (up to end-2005)

Description	Unit
Earth road (miles)	3,181
Gravel road (miles)	1,995
Asphalt road (miles)	351
Bridges (big/small/suspension)	55/725/26
Schools (primary/middle/high)	852/90/92
Hospitals	79
Clinic	105
Rural health centre	58
Rural health cntre (branch)	140
Agriculture office/Farm	31/117
Dam (incl. under construction)/Canal	46/5
Tractor depot	11
Livestock farm/Veterinary office	19/41
Post office	52
Telephone station	85
Telegraph office	44
TV repeating station	106
Generator	262

Source: "Border Areas Witness Sustained Progress", *New Light of Myanmar*, 23–27 December 2005.

Annex 8.4

Selected Target Areas for Enhancing Human Security in Myanmar

Health
- Enhanced pre- and post-natal care for mother and child
- Provision of nutritional needs for children under five years old
- Control of disease vectors for malaria and dengue fever
- Affordable generic drugs for chronic and acute ailments
- Health education and holistic approach to tackle HIV/AIDS, TB, and Hepatitis
- Comprehensive surveillance system for viral pandemic outbreaks with rapid feedback and adequate quarantine/treatment facilities
- Counselling for victims of psychological trauma in post-conflict situations

Economy
- Targeted poverty alleviation programme for most vulnerable sections of society
- Viable alternative income generation for opium farmers
- Female work opportunities in both urban and rural areas
- Means of livelihood for resettled IDP, refugees and demobilized rank and file of armed ethnic groups
- Extensive introduction of micro-financing schemes for small businesses

Environment
- Environmental impact analysis for all major development projects

Peace-building and personal security
- Reconciliation of bottom-up and top-down approaches in resource allocation for reconstruction and development
- Incorporation of psychological and cultural dimensions in regional development planning
- Opportunities to address grievances at the grassroots and accountability and transparency in local governance
- Mechanisms to supplement hierarchical (authority) structures for addressing grassroots grievances
- Systematic de-mining and neutralization of explosive material in conflict zones

Notes

1. Words in parentheses are the author's addition to the original phrase taken from Paul M. Evans, "Human Security and East Asia: In the Beginning", *Journal of East Asian Studies* 4, no. 2 (2004), p. 265.
2. The paramount national resolutions affirmed by the ruling military junta.
3. One of the three sets of national objectives stipulated by the ruling military junta; the other two sets are concerned with economic and social goals.
4. Slogan carried daily by government newspapers for the last few years.
5. This issue gained much prominence after Daw Aung San Suu Kyi was awarded the Noble Peace Prize in 1991 following the military government's refusal to hand over power to her party, the National League for Democracy (NLD), which convincingly won the elections of May 1990.
6. See Caroline Thomas, *Global Governance, Development and Human Security: The Challenge of Poverty and Inequality*, London: Pluto Press, 2000, p. 3.
7. For an elaboration on the concept of state security, see, for example, Muthiah Alagappa, "Rethinking Security: A Critical Review and Appraisal", in *Asian Security Practice: Material and Ideational Influences*, edited by Muthiah Alagappa, Stanford: Stanford University Press, 1998, pp. 27–64.
8. Evans, op. cit., p. 263.
9. See, for example, "Special Section: What is Human Security", *Security Dialogue* 35, no. 3 (2004): 345–71. For a noteworthy attempt to define human security in such a way that it can be operationalized, see Gary King and Christopher J.L. Murray, "Rethinking Human Security", *Political Science Quarterly* 116, no. 4 (2001–02): 585–610. The article advocates a more rigorous single definition of human security based on the concept of "generalized poverty" whereby an individual dips below a "pre-defined threshold in any of the component areas of well-being". (ibid., p. 594). An interesting perspective on human security in relation to economic growth can be found in S. Mansoob Murshed, "Human Security from the Standpoint of an Economist", paper presented at the World Bank, Annual Bank Conference on Development Economics, Amsterdam, 23–24 May 2005, mimeographed.
10. See, for example, UNDP, *Human Development Report 1994*, New York: United Nations Development Programme, 1994, pp. 22–40; and Andrew Tan and Kenneth Boutin, eds., *Non-Traditional Security Issues in Southeast Asia*, Singapore: Select Books, 2001.
11. Evan, op. cit., p. 264.
12. See, for example, Pauline Kerr, *The Evolving Dialectic between State-Centric and Human-Centric Security*, Department of International Relations, Working Paper 2003/2, Canberra: Research School of Pacific and Asian Studies, 2003 for a discussion on the two different approaches and attempts at reconciling them.

13. Amitav Acharya, "A Holistic Paradigm", *Security Dialogue* 35, no. 3 (2004): 355.
14. See Caroline Thomas, "A Bridge between the Interconnected Challenges Confronting the World", ibid., pp. 353–54.
15. See Pierre P. Lizee, "Human Security in Vietnam, Laos, and Cambodia", *Contemporary Southeast Asia* 24, no. 3 (2002), p. 513.
16. Pauline Kerr, William T. Tow and Marianne Hanson, "The Utility of the Human Security Agenda for Policy-makers", *Asian Journal of Political Science* 11, no. 2 (2003): 89, 109. The human security agenda, has been endorsed by the UN Secretary General Kofi Annan and the World Bank President James Wolfensohn and was also incorporated in the security discourse of the UN Security Council as well as the "security policies" of Australia, Canada, Japan and Thailand. (see ibid., p. 91; and Thomas, *Global Governance*, op. cit., p. 3)
17. Kerr et al., p. 91.
18. Evans, op. cit., pp. 266–67. There is evidently a Japanese-sponsored third variant which is actually an off-shoot of the broad approach that emerged in the wake of the Asian financial crisis of 1997/98 and which entails good governance and provision of social safety nets for the vulnerable sector (see Don Hubert, "An Idea that Works in Practice", *Security Dialogue* 35, no. 3 (2004): 351; and also, *The Asian Crisis and Human Security: An Intellectual Dialogue on Building Asia's Tomorrow Tokyo 1998*, Tokyo and Singapore: JCIE and ISEAS, 1999; and *Cross-Sectoral Partnership in Enhancing Human Security: Third Intellectual Dialogue on Building Asia's Tomorrow, Bangkok June 2000*, Tokyo and Singapore: JCIE and ISEAS, 2002).
19. For a comparison of the two approaches to human security, see Kanti Bajpai, *Human Security: Concept and Measurement*, Kroc Institute Occasional Paper no. 19 (August 2000).
20. UNDP op. cit., p. 23.
21. Ibid.
22. See Taylor Owen, "Human Security — Conflict, Critique and Consensus: Colloquium Remarks and a Proposal for a Threshold-Based Definition", *Security Dialogue* 35, no. 3 (2004): 381.
23. UNDP, op. cit., pp. 24–25.
24. "The Commission on Human Security was established in January 2001 through the initiative of the Government of Japan and in response to the UN Secretary-General's call at the 2000 Millennium Summit for a world 'free of want' and 'free of fear' The Commission consisted of twelve prominent international figures, including Mrs Sadako Ogata (former UN High Commissioner for Refugees) and Professor Amartya Sen (1998 Nobel Economics Prize Laureate). <www.humansecurity-chs.org>.
25. Modified from quote in Evans, op. cit., p. 266.
26. Ibid. It has been contended that the CHR "muddled the waters further" by

using the phrase "'vital core of all human lives' and then declining to specify the content of this phrase" (Roland Paris, "Still an Inscrutable Concept", *Security Dialogue* 35, no. 3 (2004): 371).

27. See Sabina Alkire, "A Vital Core that Must be Treated with the Same Gravitas as Traditional Security Threats", ibid., p. 360.

28. See Evans, op. cit., p. 267.

29. See Andrew Mack, "The Concept of Human Security", in *Promoting Security: But How and For Whom?*, edited by Michael Brzoska and Peter J. Croll, Bonn: BICC, 2004, p. 49.

30. Evans, op. cit., pp. 268–69. In response to a "challenge from the UN Secretary-General, Canada's Prime Minister Jean Chrétien announced the establishment of the International Commission on Intervention and State Sovereignty during the United Nations Millennium Summit in September 2000". The ICISS was "launched by then Canadian Foreign Minister Lloyd Axworthy on 14 September 2000, with a mandate to promote a comprehensive debate on the relationship between intervention and sovereignty, with a view to fostering global political consensus on how to move from polemics towards action within the international system... it was hoped that ICISS would be able to find new ways of reconciling the seemingly irreconcilable notions of intervention and state sovereignty." <www.iciss.ca/progress-en.asp>.

31. See, for example, Evans, op. cit., pp. 271–74.

32. See David Capie and Paul Evans, *The Asia-Pacific Security Lexicon*, Singapore: Institute of Southeast Asian Studies, 2002, pp. 140–41.

33. The political security issue will not be discussed as Myanmar is currently under direct military rule and the junta has yet to conclude the new constitution-formulating process.

34. This section draws heavily from Tin Maung Maung Than, "Myanmar: Preoccupation with Regime Survival, National Unity, and Stability" in Alagappa op. cit., pp. 390-416. See, also, Mary P Callahan, *Making Enemies: War and State Building in Burma*, Ithaca; Cornell University Press, 2003 for the historical roots of Myanmar's state security concerns.

35. See Evans, op. cit., p. 269.

36. See Tin Maung Maung Than, op. cit., p. 394.

37. Ibid., p.391.

38. The Chinese Communist Party had supported the Burma Communist Party rebellion for nearly three decades until Deng Xiaoping put a stop to it (see Maung Aung Myoe, "The Counterinsurgency in Myanmar: The Government's Response to the Burma Communist Party", PhD dissertation, Australian National University, Canberra, 1999). Thailand used ethnic rebel groups straddling its border with Myanmar as a buffer for decades until the late 1990s.providing opportunities for soliciting logistical support and using the

Thai side of the border as a safe haven (see idem., *Neither Friend nor Foe, Myanmar's Relationship with Thailand Since 1988: A View from Yangon*, Singapore: Institute of Defence and Strategic Studies, 2002, chapter 2.

39. See Tin Maung Maung Than, op. cit., p. 416.

40. See Dan Henk, "Human Security: Relevance and Implications", *Parameters* (Summer 2005), p. 93.

41. See "TABLE 2.2 "Gross Domestic Product per capita" on the ASEAN web site at <http://www.aseansec.org/macroeconomic/aq_gdp22.htm>.

42. Cited in Robert Taylor and Morten Pedersen, "Supporting Burma's/Myanmar Reconciliation Process; Challenges and Opportunities" Independent Report for the European Commission, Brussels, January 2005, p. 13.

43. See, for example, <http://www.irrawaddy.org>, home page (accessed on 14 October 2005).

44. See *Statistical Yearbook 2002*, Yangon: Central Statistical Organization, 2002, p. 439.

45. See *Selected Monthly Economic Indicators*, Yangon: Central Statistical Organization, November-December 1990, p. 16 and "Burmese Currency Crash Continues", online news, 30 September 2005 at http://www.irrawaddy.org.

46. Private communications. The six- to ten-fold pay rise, in April 2006, for public service personnel had temporarily rectified the low pay problem.

47. Both pull and push factors seem to be operative in this case. The push factors are mainly unemployment, low wages and poverty while the pull factors may be identified as a relatively higher income and better employment opportunities (however adverse the conditions may be) and the accessibility of migration channels facilitated by a thriving network of intermediaries (informal social networks capitalizing on kinship, friendship and community ties as well as an organized migration industry that includes brokers and traffickers).

48. See, Jerrold W. Huguet and Sureeporn Punpuing, *International Migration in Thailand* Report to the International Organization for Migration (IOM), Bangkok, angkok: IOM, 2005. See, also, Dennis Arnold, *The Situation of Burmese Migrant Workers in Mae Sot Thailand*, Southeast Asia Research Centre Working Paper Series, no. 71, City University of Hong Kong (September 2004),and Marwaan Macan-Markar, "Thailand, in Need of Workers, Eases up on Migrants", *Inter Press Service*, 17 August 2004. For illustrative examples of the plight of Myanmar migrants in Thailand, see, Hanna Ingber, "Even Legal Migrants Face Problems", *Irrawaddy*, 1 June 2005, reproduced in *BurmaNet News* (1 June 2005); Amnesty International, "Thailand: The Plight of Burmese Migrant Workers", Report (June 2005); and "Burmese Caught in a Vicious Circle", *The Nation*, 15 January 2005, reproduced in the internet newsgroup *BurmaNet News*, 15–18 January 2005.

Given that over 168,000 Myanmar nationals were arrested in Thailand in 2003 for immigration offences the number of unregistered (hence no work permit) Myanmar workers in Thailand could run into hundreds of thousands ("Thailand Arrested 280,000 Illegals, Mostly from Myanmar in 2003", *AFP*, 3 January 2004, reproduced in *BurmaNet News*, 3–5 January 2004).

49. Malaysian authorities revealed that 4,071 Myanmar illegal immigrants were deported to Thailand in 2001. See "8,345 Illegal Aliens Deported", *New Straits Times (Malaysia)*, 15 February 2002, posted in the online newsgroup <soc.culture.burma> (17 February 2002).

50. Japan is the choice destination due to the highest possible earnings in hard currency terms. The front-end cost of such an attempt to enter those countries can range from some 3 million Kyats for Japan to several hundred thousands Kyats for other countries.

51. See, for example, ""Myanmar Drug War Impoverishes Former Opium Growers — WFP", *Reuters*, 14 September 2004, reproduced in *BurmaNet News*, 14 September 2004.

52. See Henk, op. cit., p. 93.

53. See, for example, "Myanmar Top Leader Stresses Ensuring Food Security in Future", Xinhua News Agency, 16 November 2004, reproduced in *BurmaNet News* (16 November 2004). For recent official data on agriculture output, see Thiha Aung, "Hailing the 58th Anniversary Union Day: Let Us March to New Golden Land of Unity and Amity Without Fail", *The New Light of Myanmar* (hereafter *NLM*), 12 February 2005 (online edition at <www.Myanmar.com/nlm/article?Feb12.htm>).

54. See, for example, *inter alia*, Peaceway Foundation, "The Right to Food Denied: The Current Situation of Food Security in Burma" (2004) online version downloaded from the site <www.burmaissues.org/En/ Right%20to%20Food/righttofooddenied.php> on 12 August 2004; and Asian Legal Resource Centre — ALRC, "Statement on Food Scarcity in Myanmar", 30 March 2004 received by Commission on Human Rights, reproduced in *BurmaNet News*, 31 March 2004. All these could be dismissed as anti-government propaganda but they seem to indicate the plausibility of such threats under certain local conditions.

55. See Aung Lwin Oo, "UN Warns of Humanitarian Crisis in Burma" *Irrawaddy*, 5 August 2005 reproduced in *BurmaNet News*, 5 August 2005; and Darren Schuettler, "Myanmar to Lift Food Aid Tax, Barriers Remain-WFP" *Reuters*, 5 August 2005, reproduced in ibid. Crop-substitution of poppy for buckwheat was initiated around 1997 in the Kokang region with Japanese aid but was found to be economically unviable without Japanese subsidies. At around 2,500 acres in 2004, it could cover only a small portion of the area formerly devoted to poppy plantation (see Myo Lwin, "Japan to give WFP $500,00 for Rice, Buckwheat Biscuits Project", *Myanmar Times*, 4–11 April 2005, p. 5).

56. See Henk, op. cit., p. 93.
57. See Thiha Aung, op. cit. However, most of the health professionals are situated in and around Yangon (the capital of Myanmar) and big cities.
58. Ibid. On the other hand, according to the World Health Organization (WHO), in 2003, Myanmar's average "life expectancy at birth" was 56 for males and 63 for females as compared to 67 and 73 respectively for Thailand, 65 and 68 respectively for Indonesia, and 63 (for both male and female) for Bangladesh (see <http://www3.who.int/whosis/country/compare.cfm?=MMR&indicator= ....>)
59. See, for example, "Kidney Transplant Performed for 11th Time", the *NLM*, 18 July 2005.
60. See, for example, Sandar Linn and Thein Linn, "Update Begins for National Food, Nutrition Action Plan", *Myanmar Times*, 4–10 April 2005, p. 6; and Sandar Linn, "Infant Immunisation Program Targets Hepatitis B Infections", *Myanmar Times*, 23–29 May 2005, p. 4.
61. See, for example, Jessica Curtis, "Poor Sanitation a Killer of Burma's Children: UNICEF", *Mizzima News*, 28 Febraury 2006, reproduced in *BurmaNet News*, 28 Febraury 2006; and Alfred Oehlers, "Public Health in Burma: Anatomy of Crisis", *Journal of Contemporary Asia* 35, no. 2 (2005): 195–206.
62. See <http://www3.who.int/php/whosis_images/...>. In comparison, the per capita total health expenditure in international dollars (in 2002) for Thailand was 321, Indonesia was 110, and Bangladesh was 54 (see <http://www3.who.int/whosis/country/compare.cfm?=MMR&indicator=....>)
63. See *The GMS Beyond Borders: Regional Cooperation Strategy and Program 2004–2008*, Manila: Asian Development Bank, 2004, p. 66.
64. See <http://www3.who.int/php/whosis_images/...>.
65. Those in the last category virtually function as private hospitals but their legal status is still not quite that of a full-fledged hospital, as the government had not officially sanctioned them to be classified as a licensed hospital. Nevertheless, the "Yellow Pages" published by the Yangon City Development Committee (YCDC the municipal authority of the capital city) listed twelve such "centres" under the heading "HOSPITALS (PRIVATE)" (see, YCDC, *Yangon Directory* 2005, p. 1056).
66. Current (2005) outpatient consultation fees range from K200 to K2,000 per visit exclusive of treatment and medication; clinical investigation can cost anywhere up to tens of thousands kyats; normal child-birth may cost up to K300,000, major surgery costs run over K1,000,000. Perhaps, a few dozen specialists in Yangon (population of over five million), probably rake in millions of Kyats per month.
67. See, for example, Rachel M. Safman, "Assessing the Impact of HIV and Other Health Issues on Myanmar's Development", in *Myanmar: Beyond Politics to Social Imperatives*, edited by Kyaw Yin Hlaing, Robert Taylor

and Tin Maung Maung Than, Singapore: Institute of Southeast Asian Studies, 2005), pp. 119–22; and "Myanmar Officials Seize Millions of Fake Drugs", *Drug Week*, 3 February 2004, reproduced in *BurmaNet News*, 3 February 2004.

68. WHO, op. cit., p. 157.
69. See <http://wwww3.who.int/whosis/country/indicators.cfm?country=mmr>.
70. The likely sources of heterosexual transmissions are soldiers, truckers, mimers, border traders and migrant workers.
71. See, for example, Ajay Tandon, "Macroeconomic Impact of HIV/AIDS in the Asian and Paqciifc Region", ERD Working Paper no. 75, Manila: Asian Development Bank, November 2005.
72. See, for example, "Thailand Donates Condoms, Medicine to Myanmar", *Associated Press*, 22 September 2004, reproduced in *BurmaNet News*, 22 September 2004; Vanessa Hua, "Burma Confronts Taboo, Educate Villagers about HIV Prevention", *The San Francisco Chronicle*, 14 May 2004, reproduced in *BurmaNet News*, 14 May 2005; Nwe Nwe Aye "100 pc Condom Use Campaign to be Expanded to More Townships" *Myanmar Times*, 26 July–1 August 2004, p. 4; and "HIV/AIDS Control Mass Activities Launched", *NLM*, 10 September 2005. For a succinct overview of the HIV/AIDS situation in contemporary Myanmar, see Safman, op. cit., pp. 122–39.
73. The same data set reported that 68 per cent of AIDS cases involved heterosexuals, 30 per cent were drug users and the rest attributed to mother-child transmissions (see "Myanmar Steps Up Fight Against 3 Communicable Diseases", *Xinhua News Agency*, 17 February 2004, reproduced in *BurmaNet News*, 14–17 February 2004.
74. Dr Min Thwe, "Women, Girls, HIV and AIDS", in *NL M*, 30 November 2004. (online edition at <www.myanmar.com/nlm/article/Nov30a.htm>).
75. See International Crisis Group (ICG), "Myanmar: Update on HIV/AIDS Policy", *Asia Briefing*, Yangon and Brussels, 16 December 2004, p. 2.
76. See Safman, op. cit., p. 123.
77. Ibid.
78. Ibid., p. 133. See, also, ICG, op. cit.
79. There had been many reports in the international mass media of rising incidence of HIV/AIDS in Yunnan, India and among migrant workers in the western provinces of Thailand. See, for example, Surajit Khaund, "The Opposite Side of Border Fence", *Mizzima News*, 18 November 2004, reproduced in *BurmaNet News*, 19 November 2004; and Jim Pollard, "Struggling to Stem Ranong's Tide of HIV", *The Nation*, 28 June 2005, reproduced in *BurmaNet News* (26–28 June 2004).
80. See, for example, "Int'l Aid Helps Myanmar Fights TB", *Xinhua News Agency*, 1 March 2005, reproduced in *BurmaNet News*, 1 March 2005.
81. See, for example., Nwe Nwe Aye, "German NGO Fights Scourge of Malaria

in Southern Wa Region", *The Myanmar Times*, 14–20 June 2004, reproduced in *BurmaNet News*, 15 June 2004.

82. It is possible that military personnel and those who work as truckers, traders and miners have been such carriers.

83. See Sandar Linn "Health Official Highlights the High Cost of Malaria", *The Myanmar Times*, 26 July–1 August 2004, p. 5. The fatality rate averaged around 0.4 per cent in the last few years (See "Malaria Epidemic Situation Remains Normal in Myanmar", *Xinhua News Agency*, 20 August 2004, reproduced in *BurmaNet News*, 20 August 2004).

84. This could be due to better reporting and wider statistical coverage. Nevertheless, it should be taken seriously. See, for example, note 74 above and "Japan Donates Over US$50,000 to Burma", *Democratic Voice of Burma*, 31 August 2005, reproduced in *BurmaNet News*, 1 September 2005.

85. In August 2004, the Myanmar Health Ministry, the UNDP and the Global Fund (to fight AIDS, Tuberculosis and Malaria) signed an agreement which promised to deliver US$98.5 million worth of assistance over five years (see "US 4.2 M Grant Agreement Signed for Fighting TB Component", *NLM*, 4 August 2004 (online at <http://mission.itu.ch/MISSIONS/Myanmar/04nlm/n040805.htm>).

86. For the Global Fund's perspective, see "Fact Sheet, Termination of Grants to Myanmar", 18 August 2005 at <http://www.theglobalfund.org/en/media_center/press/pr_050819_factsheet.pdf>. For Myanmar's official point of view, see the "Statement by Country Coordinating Mechanism Myanmar" dated 19 August 2003, published in the *NLM*, 23 August 2005. See, also, Clive Parker, "International Community Seeks to Overcome Global Fund Setback", *Irrawaddy*, 2 September 2005, reproduced in *BurmaNet News*, 3–6 September 2005. This unfortunate episode is a classic example of state security imperatives clashing with a human security initiative that was based on liberal notions of transparency and governance.

87. For critical views, see, for example, Ed Copley, "Myanmar — The World's Bird Flu Black Hole?", *Reuters*, 9 October 2005, reproduced in *BurmaNet News*, 12 October 2005; and Alan Sipress, "Experts Fear Burma is Ill-Equipped to Handle Bird Flu", *The Washington Post*, 15 January 2006, reproduced in *BurmaNet News*, 14–17 January 2006. For a more sympathetic outlook, see *Associated Press*, "Myanmar Says WHO Approved National Bird Flu Plan, but Found Lab Shortages", 25 January 2006, reproduced in *BurmaNet News*, 25 January 2006.

88. See Henk, op. cit., p. 93.

89. See, for example, Thiha Aung, op. cit. Government statistics maintained that forest cover has remained constant since the 1997/98 fiscal year though environmental NGOs (non-governmental organizations) claimed that continued illegal logging had further depleted the forests; see for example,

Global Witness, *A Conflict of Interest — The Uncertain Future of Burma's Forests*, (London: Global Witness, October 2003.

90. See Lee Poh Onn, "Deforestation in Myanmar and Indochina", in *Cross-Sectoral Partnership in Enhancing Human Security: Third Intellectual Dialogue on Building Asia's Tomorrow, Bangkok June 2000*, Tokyo and Singapore: JCIE and ISEAS, 2002, Table 2, p. 121.

91. *The GMS Beyond Borders*, op. cit., p. 62.

92. See, for example, a Global Witness briefing document which claimed that in fiscal year "2003–04, a minimum 1.3 million m³ RWE [round wood equivalent] of timber exports, almost tow-thirds of the total, were illegal" and "in 2003" illegal timber trade with China accounted for some "98%" of China's wood imports from Myanmar (Global Witness, *A Choice for China: Ending the Destruction of Burma's Northern Frontier Forests*, London: Global Witness, October 2005, p. 9).

93. See Ye Lwin, "Bid to End Illegal Timber Trade", *Myanmar Times*, 16–22 January 2006.

94. For an environmental-friendly approach on dams in general, see "Dams and Development: A New Framework for Decision-Making" The Report of the World Commission on Dams, 16 November 2000, available at <http://www.dams.org>. For Myanmar, see, for example, "Chinese Companies Building Hydropower Projects in Myanmar", *Xinhua*, 2 September 2005, reproduced in *BurmaNet News*, 2 September 2005. There are also negative consequences in the socio-cultural and economic domains caused by the displacement of affected communities from their 'ancestral' land (see, for example, Earth Rights International, "Flooding the Future: Hydropower and Cultural Survival in the Salween River Basin", 2005, available at <http://earthrights.org/burma/floodthefuture.shtml>, downloaded on 3 September 2005).

95. See Henk, op. cit., p. 93.

96. On the forced labour issue, see, for example, "Report of the Very High-Level Team", ILO Governing Body 292nd session, GB.292/7/3, Geneva, March 2005 and Earth Rights International, "Recent Trends in the Use of Forced Labor in Burma", 3 August 2005, at <http://www.earthrights.org/burma/fltrends.shtml>. For allegations on the rape issue, see, for example, Subhatra Bhumiprabhas, "Rights Group Document Further Abuse of Women by Burmese Junta", *The Nation*, 9 September 2004, reproduced in *BurmaNet News*, 9 September 2004. Myanmar had not acceded to the Mine Ban Treaty. See, for example, "Burma (Myanmar), Land Mine Monitor Report (2004)" available on <http://www.ichl.org/lm/2004/burma>; and Yeni, "Burma's Killing Fields", *Irrawaddy*, 15 September 2005, reproduced in *BurmaNet News*, 29 September 2005. For allegations on child soldiers, see, for example, "Myanmar" in *Child Soldiers Global Report 2004* Myanmar reportedly had

600,000 to one million IDPs at the turn of the century and sporadic displacements of thousands during military campaigns against the insurgents. See, for example, Global IDP, "Profile of Internal Displacement: Myanmar (Burma), 27 June 2005, at <http://www.idpproject.org>. It was reported that some 135,000 refugees (mostly ethnic minorities) were staying in nine camps in Thailand at the end of 2003 together with over 3,200 registered refugees in Bangkok (November 2004 figure). See, for example, Huguet and Punpuing op. cit. Human trafficking consists of trafficking for prostitution, work and child labour. Trafficking is closely associated with official corruption at local levels and immigration checkpoints. In Myanmar, the destination countries are Thailand (majority), Bangladesh and Malaysia (through Thailand). For a somewhat negative view, see, for example, Yeni, "Burma Among Asia's Worst Human Trafficking Violators", *Irrawaddy*, 6 June 2005, reproduced in *BurmaNet News*, 4–6 June 2005. For the Malaysian situation, see, for example, Ahmad Fairuz Othman, "Ring Smuggling in Foreigners", *New Straits Times (Malaysia)*, 13 May 2005, reproduced in *BurmaNet News*, 13 May 2005. For a recent summary of all such allegations, see "Report of the Special Rapporteur of the Commission on Human Rights on the Situation of Human Rights in Myanmar", 7 February 2006, E/CN.4/2006/34; report to the United Nations Commission on Human Rights, sixty-second session. Available at <http://www.ibiblio.org/obl/docs3/CHR2006-SRM.htm>.

97. For government responses, see, for example, Aung Kyi, Embassy of the Union of Myanmar, Washington, D.C., "Conditions in Myanmar", Letters to the Editor, *International Herald Tribune*, 21 June 2005, reproduced in *BurmaNet News*, 21 June 2005; the "Statement by H.E. U Nyunt Maung Shein, Permanent Representative of the Union of Myanmar at the Committee on the Application of Standards of the 93rd Session of the International Labour Conference", Geneva, 4 June 2005, available at <http://mission.itu.ch/ MISSIONS?Myanmar/statemnt/prstment/ILC_93_04062005.htm>; statement by the Myanmar Government on the report of the United Nations Committee on the Rights of Child, Information Sheet No. D3059 (I/L), 9 June 2004; and the announcement, dated 9 June 2005, by the Myanmar Ministry of Foreign Affairs regarding the "Fifth Annual Trafficking in Persons Report" issued by the U.S. State Department in June 2005, published in the *NLM*, 19 June 2005. Myanmar had also promulgated a tough law against human trafficking on 14 September 2005 (*NLM*, 15 September 2005).

98. See Henk, op. cit., p. 93.

99. For an example of allegations by dissident human rights advocates, see "Easy Targets: The Persecution of Muslims in Burma", a report published by the Karen Human Rights Group (May 2002) and available at <http://www.ibiblio.org/freeburma/humanrights/khrg/archive/khrg2002/khrg0202.pdf>.

100. For the rohingya side of the story, see, for example, Imtiaz Ahmed, "Globalization, Low-Intensity Conflict, & Protracted Statelessness/ Refugeehood: The Plight of the Rohingyas", *GSC Quarterly 13 (Summer/ Fall 2004)*, on-line version at <http://www.ssrc.org>. See, also, "Thousands of Myanmar Muslims Flee to Bangladesh" *Reuters*, 4 November 2004, reproduced in *BurmaNet News*, 4 November 2004.

101. See, for example, "Religious Persecution: A Campaign of Ethnocide against Chin Christians in Burma", published by the Chin Human Rights Organization, Ottawa, Canada, February 2004, available at <http:// www.chro.org/CHRO_images/ReligiousPersecution.pdf>; and "International Religious Freedom Report 2005", 8 November 2005, released by the Bureau of Democracy, Human Rights and Labour, available at <http://www.state.gov/ g/drl/rls/irf/2005/51506.htm>.

102. See "Measures already taken for the development of border areas" on the government's web page at <http://www.myanmar.gov.mm/ministry/ PBNRDA/b5.htm>.

103. Administratively Myanmar is divided into fourteen regions, comprising seven states (where non-Bamar ethnic nationalities are the majority) and seven divisions (where the majority of the inhabitants are Bamar).

104. However, it is not possible to predict whether it will produce "envy-free outcomes" which would ensure that each group of recipients "does not regard another player to be superior to what" the particular group has received (Mursshed, op. cit., p. 8). It has been argued that envy-free outcomes are important for durable peacemaking in post-conflict situations (ibid.).

105. Herbert C Kelman, "Transforming the Relationship between Former Enemies: A Social-Psychological Analysis", in *After the Peace: Resistance and Reconciliation*, edited by Robert L. Rothstein (Boulder Colo: Lynne Rienner, 1999), p. 197. Kelman identified four "essential components" of a "positive peace" as: "[m]utual acceptance and reconciliation"; a "sense of security and dignity for each" other among the former adversaries; a "pattern of cooperative interaction between" the protagonists; and "[I]nstitutionalization of a dynamic process of problem solving" (ibid.).

106. For a constructivist approach relating peacebuilding and human security by taking into consideration the psychological and cultural dimensions, a long-term view of post-conflict society from the bottom-up, local knowledge and indigenous institutions, see Earl Conteh-Morgan, "Peacebuilding and Human Security: A Constructivist Perspective", *International Journal of Peace Studies* 10, no. 1 (2005): 69–86.

107. For a theoretical delineation of possible stages in deepening the peace process, see, for example, Robert L. Rothstein, "Fragile Peace and Its Aftermath", in Rothstein, op. cit., pp. 242–43.

108. Ibid., p. 223.

109. "Looking Back in Sorrow: Mon Ceasefire with Burma Junta 10 Years on", DVB, 29 June 2005, online news at <http://english.dvb.no/print_news. php?id=5063>; Don Pathan, "UWSA Prepared to Assert Independence More Aggressively", *The Nation*, 18 July 2005, reproduced in *BurmaNet News*, 20 July 2005; and Nandar Chan, "SSA-N Soldiers Arrested in Border Town", *Irrawaddy*, 6 July 2005, reproduced in *BurmaNet News*, 6 July 2005.
110. See, for example, Maung Aung Myoe, *Neither Friend nor Foe*, op. cit.
111. See, for example, Thitinan Pongsudhirak, "A Win-Win Proposition for Thaksin", *Irrawaddy*, 17August 2005, reproduced in *BurmaNet News*, 17 August 2005.
112. Even those from the opposition camp had recognized the need for humanitarian assistance, see, for example, Yeni, "Burma's Former Student Leaders Call for Humanitarian Aid", *Irrawaddy*, 7 September 2005, reproduced in *BurmaNet News*, 7 September 2005.
113. For critical views on the international community's role in post-conflict peacebuilding, see, for example, Keith Krause and Oliver Jutersonke, "Peace, Security and Development in Post-Conflict Environments", *Security Dialogue* 36, no. 4 (2005): 447–62; and Beatrice Pouligny, "Civil Society and Post-Conflict Peacebuilding: Ambiguities of International Programmes Aimed at Building 'New' Societies", ibid., pp. 495–510. For Myanmar, see Kyaw Yin Hlaing, Robert H. Taylor and Tin Maung Maung Than, *Myanmar: Beyond Politics to Societal Imperatives*, Singapore: Institute of Southeast Asian Studies, 2005.
114. See, for example, Michael Casey, "Humanitarian Crisis Looming in Impoverished Myanmar: UN", *Associated Press*, 6 December 2005, reproduced in *BurmaNet News*, 6 December 2005.
115. Thomas, *Global Governance,* op. cit., p. 4.
116. However, it would help if the views of the relevant (ethnic) communities are seriously taken into consideration in identifying, prioritizing and implementing projects undertaken by the state in accordance with the overall BAD scheme. For a Norwegian exposition of a strategic framework from a developmental perspective on peacebuilding, see *Peacebuilding — A Developmental Perspective*, Oslo: Norwegian Ministry of Foreign Affairs, August 2004.
117. Evans, op. cit., p. 279.
118. Henk, op. cit., p. 103.
119. Ibid.

References

Acharya, Amitav. "A Holistic Paradigm", *Security Dialogue* 35, no. 3 (2004): 355–56.
Ahmad Fairuz Othman, "Ring Smuggling in Foreigners", *New Straits Times (Malaysia)*, 13 May 2005.

Alagappa, Muthiah."Rethinking Security: A Critical Review and Appraisal", in *Asian Security Practice: Material and Ideational Influences*, edited by Muthiah Alagappa, Stanford: Stanford University Press, 1998, pp. 27–64.

Alkire, Sabina. "A Vital Core that Must be Treated with the same Gravitas as Traditional Security Threats", *Security Dialogue* 35, no. 3 (2004): 359–60.

Amnesty International. "Thailand: The Plight of Burmese Migrant Workers", Report , June 2005.

Arnold, Dennis. *The Situation of Burmese Migrant Workers in Mae Sot Thailand*, Southeast Asia Research Centre Working Paper Series, no. 71, City University of Hong Kong, September 2004.

Asian Development Bank. *The GMS Beyond Borders: Regional Cooperation Strategy and Program 2004–2008*, Manila: Asian Development Bank, 2004.

Asian Legal Resource Centre — ALRC. "Statement on Food Scarcity in Myanmar", 30 March 2004.

Aung Kyi, Embassy of the Union of Myanmar, Washington, D.C. "Conditions in Myanmar", Letters to the Editor, *International Herald Tribune*, 21 June 2005.

Aung Lwin Oo. "UN Warns of Humanitarian Crisis in Burma" *Irrawaddy*, 5 August 2005.

Bajpai, Kanti. *Human Security: Concept and Measurement*, Kroc Institute Occasional Paper no. 19, August 2000.

Callahan, Mary P. *Making Enemies: War and State Building in Burma*. Ithaca; Cornell University Press, 2003.

Capie, David and Paul Evans. *The Asia-Pacific Security Lexicon*. Singapore: Institute of Southeast Asian Studies, 2002.

Casey, Michael. "Humanitarian Crisis Looming in Impoverished Myanmar: UN", *Associated Press*, 6 December 2005.

Chin Human Rights Organization. "Religious Persecution: A Campaign of Ethnocide against Chin Christians in Burma", Ottawa, Canada, February 2004.

Coalition to Stop the Use of Child Soldiers. "Myanmar" in *Child Soldiers Global Report 2004*, London, 2004.

Conteh-Morgan, Earl. "Peacebuilding and Human Security: A Constructivist Perspective" *International Journal of Peace Studies* 10, no. 1 (2005): 69–86.

Copley, Ed. "Myanmar — The World's Bird Flu Black Hole?", *Reuters*, 9 October 2005.

Curtis, Jessica. "Poor Sanitation a Killer of Burma's Children: UNICEF", *Mizzima News*, 28 Febraury 2006.

Evans, Paul M. "Human Security and East Asia: In the Beginning", *Journal of East Asian Studies* 4, no. 2 (2004): 263–84.

Global Fund. "Fact Sheet, Termination of Grants to Myanmar", 18 August 2005.

Global Witness. *A Conflict of Interest-The Uncertain Future of Burma's Forests*, London, October 2003.

———. *A Choice for China: Ending the Destruction of Burma's Northern Frontier Forests*, London, October 2005.

Government of Myanmar. "Statement by the Myanmar Government on the report of the United Nations Committee on the Rights of Child, Information Sheet No. D3059 (I/L), 9 June 2004.

———. "Statement by H.E. U Nyunt Maung Shein, Permanent Representative of the Union of Myanmar at the Committee on the Application of Standards of the 93rd Session of the International Labour Conference", Geneva, 4 June 2005.

Government of Norway. *Peacebuilding — A Developmental Perspective*. Oslo: Norwegian Ministry of Foreign Affairs, August 2004.

Government of United States. "International Religious Freedom Report 2005", 8 November 2005, released by the Bureau of Democracy, Human Rights and Labour.

Henk, Dan. "Human Security: Relevance and Implications", *Parameters* (Summer 2005): 91–106.

Hua, Vanessa. "Burma Confronts Taboo, Educate Villagers about HIV Prevention", *The San Francisco Chronicle*, 14 May 2004.

Hubert, Don. "An Idea that Works in Practice", *Security Dialogue* 35, no. 3 (2004): 351–52.

Huguet, Jerrold W. and Sureeporn Punpuing, *International Migration in Thailand* Report to the International Organization for Migration (IOM), Bangkok, 2005.

Imtiaz Ahmed, "Globalization, Low-Intensity Conflict, & Protracted Statelessness/ Refugeehood: The Plight of the Rohingyas", *GSC Quarterly* 13 (Summer/ Fall 2004).

Ingber, Hanna. "Even Legal Migrants Face Problems", *Irrawaddy*, 1 June 2005.

International Crisis Group (ICG). "Myanmar: Update on HIV/AIDS Policy", *Asia Briefing*, Yangon and Brussels, 16 December 2004.

International Labour Organization. "Report of the Very High-Level Team", ILO Governing Body 292nd session, GB.292/7/3, Geneva, March 2005.

Japan Center for International Exchange. *The Asian Crisis and Human Security: An Intellectual Dialogue on Building Asia's Tomorrow Tokyo 1998*. Tokyo and Singapore: JCIE and ISEAS, 1999.

———. *Cross-Sectoral Partnership in Enhancing Human Security: Third Intellectual Dialogue on Building Asia's Tomorrow, Bangkok June 2000*. Tokyo and Singapore: JCIE and ISEAS, 2002.

Karen Human Rights Group. "Easy Targets: The Persecution of Muslims in Burma", a report published by the Karen Human Rights Group, May 2002.

Kelman, Herbert C. "Transforming the Relationship between Former Enemies: A Social-Psychological Analysis", in *After the Peace: Resistance and Reconciliation*, edited by Robert L. Rothstein. Boulder Colo: Lynne Rienner, 1999, pp. 193–205.

Kerr, Pauline. *The Evolving Dialectic between State-Centric and Human-Centric Security*, Department of International Relations, Working Paper 2003/2, Canberra: Research School of Pacific and Asian Studies, 2003.

Kerr, Pauline, William T. Tow and Marianne Hanson, "The Utility of the Human Security Agenda for Policy-makers", *Asian Journal of Political Science* 11, no. 2 (2003): 89–114.

Khaund, Surajit. "The Opposite Side of Border Fence", *Mizzima News*, 18 November 2004.

King, Gary and Christopher J. L. Murray. "Rethinking Human Security", *Political Science Quarterly* 116, no. 4 (2001–02): 585–610.

Krause, Keith and Oliver Jutersonke, "Peace, Security and Development in Post-Conflict Environments", *Security Dialogue* 36, no. 4 (2005): 447–62.

Kyaw Yin Hlaing, Robert H. Taylor and Tin Maung Maung Than, *Myanmar: Beyond Politics to Societal Imperatives*. Singapore: Institute of Southeast Asian Studies, 2005.

Landmine Monitor. "Burma (Myanmar), Landmine Monitor Report 2004: Toward a Mine-Free World", Ottawa, 2004.

Lee Poh Onn. "Deforestation in Myanmar and Indochina", in *Cross-Sectoral Partnership in Enhancing Human Security: Third Intellectual Dialogue on Building Asia's Tomorrow, Bangkok June 2000*. Tokyo and Singapore: JCIE and ISEAS, 2002.

Lizee, Pierre P. "Human Security in Vietnam, Laos, and Cambodia", *Contemporary Southeast Asia* 24, no. 3 (2002): 509–27.

Macan-Markar, Marawn. "Thailand, in Need of Workers, Eases up on Migrants", *Inter Press Service*, 17 August 2004.

Mack, Andrew. "The Concept of Human Security", in *Promoting Security: But How and For Whom?*, brief 30, edited by Michael Brzoska and Peter J. Croll. Bonn: BICC, October 2004, pp. 47–50.

Maung Aung Myoe. "The Counterinsurgency in Myanmar: The Government's Response to the Burma Communist Party", Ph.D. dissertation, Australian National University, Canberra, 1999.

―――. *Neither Friend nor Foe, Myanmar's Relationship with Thailand Since 1988: A View from Yangon*. Singapore: Institute of Defence and Strategic Studies, 2002.

Min Thwe, Dr. "Women, Girls, HIV and AIDS", *New Light of Myanmar*, 30 November 2004.

Murshed, S. Mansoob. "Human Security from the Standpoint of an Economist", paper presented at the World Bank. Annual Bank Conference on Development Economics, Amsterdam, 23–24 May 2005, mimeographed.

Myanmar Ministry of Foreign Affairs. "Fifth Annual Trafficking in Persons Report" issued by the U.S. State Department in June 2005, *New Light of Myanmar*, 19 June 2005.

Myo Lwin, "Japan to Give WFP $500,00 for Rice, Buckwheat Biscuits Project", *Myanmar Times*, 4–11 April 2005, p. 5.

Nandar Chan, "SSA-N Soldiers Arrested in Border Town", *Irrawaddy*, 6 July 2005.

Nwe Nwe Aye, "German NGO Fights Scourge of Malaria in Southern Wa Region", *The Myanmar Times* 14–20 June 2004.

———. "100 pc Condom Use Campaign to be Expanded to More Townships", *Myanmar Times* 26 July–1 August 2004, p. 4.

Oehlers, Alfred. "Public Health in Burma: Anatomy of Crisis", *Journal of Contemporary Asia* 35, no. 2 (2005): 195–206.

Owen, Taylor. "Human Security — Conflict, Critique and Consensus: Colloquium Remarks and a Proposal for a Threshold-Based Definition", *Security Dialogue* 35, no. 3 (2004): 373–87.

Paris, Roland. "Still an Inscrutable Concept", *Security Dialogue* 35, no. 3 (2004): 370–71.

Parker, Clive. "International Community Seeks to Overcome Global Fund Setback", *Irrawaddy*, 2 September 2005.

Pathan, Don. "UWSA Prepared to Assert Independence More Aggressively", *The Nation*, 18 July 2005.

Peaceway Foundation. "The Right to Food Denied: The Current Situation of Food Security in Burma", 2004.

Pollard, Jim. "Struggling to Stem Ranong's Tide of HIV", *The Nation*, 28 June 2005.

Pouligny, Beatrice. "Civil Society and Post-Conflict Peacebuilding: Ambiguities of International Programmes Aimed at Building 'New' Societies", *Security Dialogue* 36, no. 4 (2005): 495–510.

Rothstein, Robert L. "Fragile Peace and Its Aftermath", in *After the Peace: Resistance and Reconciliation*, edited by Robert L. Rothstein. Boulder Colo: Lynne Rienner, 1999, pp. 223-47.

Safman, Rachel M. "Assessing the impact of HIV and Other Health Issues on Myanmar's Development", in *Myanmar: Beyond Politics to Social Imperatives*, edited by Kyaw Yin Hlaing, Robert Taylor and Tin Maung Maung Than, Singapore: Institute of Southeast Asian Studies, 2005, pp. 117–39.

Sandar Linn. "Infant Immunisation Program Targets Hepatitis B Infections", *Myanmar Times*, 23–29 May 2005, p. 4.

———. "Health Official Highlights the High Cost of Malaria", *Myanmar Times*, 26 July–1 August 2004, p. 5.

Sandar Linn and Thein Linn. "Update Begins for National Food, Nutrition Action Plan", *Myanmar Times*, 4–10 April 2005, p. 6.

Schuettler, Darren. "Myanmar to Lift Food Aid Tax, Barriers Remain-WFP" *Reuters*, 5 August 2005.

Sipress, Alan. "Experts Fear Burma is Ill-Equipped to Handle Bird Flu", *The Washington Post*, 15 January 2006.

Subhatra Bhumiprabhas. "Rights Group Document Further Abuse of Women by Burmese Junta", *The Nation*, 9 September 2004.

Tan, Andrew and Kenneth Boutin, eds. *Non-Traditional Security Issues in Southeast Asia*. Singapore: Select Books, 2001.

Tandon, Ajay. "Macroeconomic Impact of HIV/AIDS in the Asian and Paciifc Region", ERD Working Paper no. 75. Manila: Asian Development Bank, November 2005.

Taylor, Robert and Morten Pedersen. "Supporting Burma's/Myanmar Reconciliation Process; Challenges and Opportunities" Independent Report for the European Commission, Brussels, January 2005.

Thiha Aung. "Hailing the 58th Anniversary Union Day: Let Us March to New Golden Land of Unity and Amity Without Fail", *The New Light of Myanmar*, 12 February 2005.

Thitinan Pongsudhirak. "A Win-Win Proposition for Thaksin", *Irrawaddy*, 17 August 2005.

Thomas, Caroline. *Global Governance, Development and Human Security: The Challenge of Poverty and Inequality*, London: Pluto Press, 2000.

———. "A Bridge between the Interconnected Challenges Confronting the World", *Security Dialogue* 35, no. 3 (2004): 353–54.

Tin Maung Maung Than. "Myanmar: Preoccupation with Regime Survival, National Unity, and Stability", in *Asian Security Practice: Material an Ideational Influences*, edited by Muthiah Alagappa. Stanford: Stanford University Press, 1998, pp. 390–416.

United Nations Commission on Human Rights. "Report of the Special Rapporteur of the Commission on Human Rights on the Situation of Human Rights in Myanmar", 7 February 2006, E/CN.4/2006/34; report to the United Nations Commission on Human Rights, sixty-second session.

United Nations Development Programme. *Human Development Report 1994*. New York: United Nations Development Programme, 1994.

World Commission on Dams. "Dams and Development: A New Framework for Decision-Making". The Report of the World Commission on Dams, 16 November 2000.

Ye Lwin. "Bid to End Illegal Timber Trade", *Myanmar Times*, 16–22 January 2006.

Yeni, "Burma Among Asia's Worst Human Trafficking Violators", *Irrawaddy*, 6 June 2005.

———. "Burma's Former Student Leaders Call for Humanitarian Aid", *Irrawaddy*, 7 September 2005.

———. "Burma's Killing Fields", *Irrawaddy*, 15 September 2005.

9

Reflections on Confidence-building and Cooperation among Ethnic Groups in Myanmar: A Karen Case Study

Alan Saw U

Overview

The problems of Myanmar, especially the ethnic-related aspects, are deep-seated and quite complex. People both inside and outside the country often understand poorly the nature of Myanmar's intractable conflicts and their dynamics. Many people inside the country believe that the assumption of power by a democratically elected government will be quite sufficient to solve Myanmar's problems and that everything else will then easily follow. This is too simplistic an appraisal and ignores the country's historical experiences.

In the international community, few people are familiar with the long-standing conflicts between the successive central governments dominated by the majority ethnic group called the Bamars and the country's other minority ethnic groups. Even if they are aware of the conflicts, they tend to think that the only political solution is that the ruling military junta must relinquish power and hand it over to the political party that won the national election in 1990.

This chapter starts by reminding readers that each of the major cases of ethnic armed resistance started during Myanmar's previous period of parliamentary democracy, and that the ethnic issue has been, and continues to be, a central part of Myanmar's problematic political impasse. It reflects an inside view, outlining and analysing some of the landmarks along the

recent path of peace initiatives undertaken by the Karen National Union
— KNU, the Karen ethnic armed resistance group and the military junta
from 1994 up until now. This chapter advocates the consolidation of the
present ceasefire so that the Karen people will be able to contribute to
making Myanmar free from prolonged conflict.

Introduction

Myanmar is ethnically one of the most diverse countries in the world and
ever since gaining independence from the British in 1948, it has experienced
a complex set of conflicts between the central government and the ethnic
groups seeking either separate states or autonomous states within the
Union of Myanmar.

All the non-Burman ethnic groups consider themselves to be
discriminated against and marginalized by the central government, not
only politically and economically but also in terms of the deliberate
suppression of their social, language, cultural and religious rights. At the
heart of the discontents is the issue of lack of the right to teach and learn
their own ethnic languages.

The solution to the ethnic conflicts in Myanmar is without doubt one
of the major challenges facing the country today. It cannot therefore be
subordinated to or separated from the recognized need for political and
economic reform in the country.

At the international and regional levels, attention has focused on the
tension between the military junta and the political opposition over national
power, but the ethnic issues which represent a more intractable obstacle to
peace, development and democracy, seems to be neglected. The degree of
political and economic autonomy that should be conceded to ethnically
designated states needs to be taken into consideration too. The struggle
towards political transition to civilian rule and the endeavour for the
realization of the rights of all ethnic groups in Myanmar are inter-related
issues. Hence there is need for a two-track approach, namely, the need for
restoration of democracy and the need for realization of ethnic rights.

Background

Because of the armed insurrection of the Karens shortly after independence,
the Karen people in the country have been deprived of any legal form of
social-action oriented association, let alone political organization, that
would allow them to network for self-development and social progress.

Discrimination against the Karen populace has been so complete that the Karen people have in those years developed two distinctive characteristics, namely, a culture of silence and a culture of apathy.

In spite of the limitations and constraints, and diversities in dialects (Sgaw and Pwo), the Karen people are culturally linked under the umbrellas of Karen Christian churches and Karen Buddhist monasteries. The religious outreach activities of both the churches and monasteries entail social and welfare activities in their respective communities.

The assumption of direct power again by the military in 1988 resulted in the overthrow of the one-party socialist state. Repression of the rights of the ethnic communities continued, but alongside the post-1988 policy of free market economy in the form of military capitalism, there is emerging in the Karen community a significant development of social groupings which can be regarded as the emergence of community based, or civil society organizations. These emerging Karen civil society organizations have evolved in response to the need for the mediation and promotion of creative solutions to the armed conflict.

Response

Many Karen people in Myanmar have become very weary and fed up with the prolonged civil war and its consequences. They are of the opinion that it is imperative to get beyond their frustration, anger and helplessness and to direct their energies to mobilizing their cultural wisdom, religious knowledge and social understanding so as to constructively work towards a better future. Since the beginning of the 1990s, various Karen groups in Myanmar have been trying, in their own ways, to build confidence and strengthen capabilities of the various elements in the Karen community and to foster cooperation between them. The Karen leaders inside Myanmar have projected the idea of transferring the "armed struggle in the battlefield" to the "political struggle around the table". Likewise, among the circles of the armed resistance group, there has also emerged a desire to be a part of the political process within the country.

Action

1. Peace-making: Initiatives for Political Dialogue, Reconciliation and Ceasefire

During the early part of the 1990s, the position of the military junta was total defeat of all opposition by military might. To everybody's surprise, it later reversed its position, announcing a unilateral ceasefire in April 1992 and issuing a call for national reconciliation and peaceful settlement by negotiation. Then, in 1994, leaders from ethnic groups emerged trying to provide initiatives for reconciliation and acting as peace mediators between the military junta and the armed resistance groups. As a result of these efforts, various ceasefires have come into effect, bringing relief in some areas, reducing a lot of sufferings and helping to establish a sense of normalcy in conflict-affected areas.

The first effort from within the Karen community in Yangon to explore the possibility of a peace initiative occurred in August 1994 with a journey from Yangon to the headquarters of the KNU (Karen National Union) to meet with their top leaders. A second meeting with these leaders followed a month later in which a prominent Christian leader offered his services as an independent mediator, neither sanctioned by the military junta nor invited and approved by the KNU. However, he explained to them that his meetings with them were with the tacit knowledge, if not approval, of the Home Ministry of the military junta and his initiative was encouraged, if not approved, by both sides.

This Christian envoy, the then Archbishop Andrew U Mya Han of the Anglican Church in Myanmar, pleaded with Karen leaders to dedicate their efforts to the immediate "resolution of the Karen ethnic affairs" rather than shouldering the responsibility of ushering in "true democratic ideals and freedom for the whole country", which should be seen as a later process that would eventually emerge. The leaders of the Karen armed resistance responded positively to this suggestion, proposing that because of the deep-seated suspicion and distrust brought about by previous deceptions and broken promises, the necessary political dialogue could only occur satisfactorily between an encounter between the "opposition political alliance" and the military junta and that it must be held outside of Myanmar and with the assistance of an international mediator or observer. The military junta repeatedly rejected such an approach, insisting instead on separate ceasefire negotiations only with individual ethnic armed resistance groups, inside Myanmar and without international mediation, as their understanding of the situation is that ethnic politics is an internal or "family' affair.

Despite what could have been seen as a rebuff, a search began for a neutral venue and an independent observer so that at least preliminary talks could begin. Confidence-building initiatives also continued, with further goodwill visits to the KNU headquarters and a series of meetings with the military junta and the KNU to explore an appropriate formula for establishing a necessary level of mutual trust as a prerequisite for actual dialogue between the two. To the surprise of all, the KNU softened its position and made an unexpected unilateral concession by agreeing to have "bilateral talks", "within the country" on condition that prominent "Karen leaders within Myanmar" were willing and able to make available their services as mediators and independent observers. The KNU then sent an envoy with the task of identifying Karen leaders potentially worthy of acting as mediators and courageous to serve as "go betweens". As a result, a five-member Karen Peace Mediator Group came into being, recognized by both the military junta and the KNU. The concession made by the KNU in order to pursue a negotiated settlement with the military junta and the efforts of the peace brokers can be dismissed as seeking "peace at any price" by those idealists who are determined to achieve only "peace with justice". Peace with justice however, is not a product but a process, and this small initiative for reconciliation can be considered an important essential step, if not in itself an important achievement. It was an entry point.

Nonetheless it is clear, the series of shuttle mediation efforts carried out by the individual members and the Karen Peace Mediator Group as a whole, achieved a certain momentum with four confidence-building meetings between the military junta and the KNU between the years 1995 and 1997. Unfortunately, the talks broke down after the fourth round. The two sides saw the causes for the breakdown of the talks in their own terms, but the Karen mediators after consultation with the military junta noted a series of points:

- First, they noted that while the earlier talks had centred around peace, the later ones moved away from peace issues.
- Secondly, they noted that the military junta declared its willingness to enter into dialogue with the KNU again in the future and to recognize the Karen Mediator Group alone as a "go-between".
- Thirdly, the mediators stressed the need for the fostering of unity within the Karen community, giving priority to common Karen issues rather than others and refraining from any actions detrimental to achieving peace.

They urged that in the process of peace-making, it is imperative not to lose sight of the prevailing situation, and to focus on practical action and realistic steps that can be taken.

The KNU, however, claimed that the military junta had demanded that they unilaterally give up the armed struggle policy and return to the legal fold and start a development programme. They insisted that from their point of view there must be a political solution acceptable to both sides before a ceasefire could be agreed to. Naturally they blamed the military junta for the breakdown of the peace talks. In mid-2002, in order to try to revive the process, an informal roundtable forum of Karen leaders was convened under the patronage of one of the five-member Karen Peace Mediator Group. The outcome was an appeal to the leaders of the KNU requesting them to explore possible ways and means to resume the peace talks, through giving preference and priority to immediate and specific Karen issues and problems.

The KNU responded, emphasizing that they shared the longing for peace of all the Karen people and that the lack of peace was a direct reflection of the political situation. They urged the Karen leaders in Myanmar to press the military junta to establish genuine peace by effecting the necessary political change. In spite of their limitations, the five-member Karen Peace Mediator Group in their own ways, both as individuals and as a group, continued to explore the possibilities of resuming the peace talk through contacts with both sides as and when appropriate, through their own connections.

There was a strong feeling at that time among the Karen in Myanmar that if only Karen leaders of the armed resistance group and Karen inside Myanmar could grasp the moment, they might be able to engage politically with the military regime from "within the legal fold" while also addressing the urgent needs of Karen society. It was also realized by the Karen leaders in Myanmar that given the prevailing situation, Karen issues and problems that have been ongoing for the past half-a-century and more cannot be solved overnight. There is a need for a very thorough process and it might take another fifty years, but the ceasefire is seen as a prerequisite and the time for change is now.

The ensuing period of silence and stalemate in the ceasefire process for more than six years was a nightmare for the Karen people, who were looking forward to at least partial normalization of the national situation that would be achieved by a ceasefire between the KNU and the military regime. Then suddenly in late November 2003 the military regime extended its invitation through the Karen Peace Mediator Group to open dialogue without condition, the KNU readily responded positively. It was a surprise to all.

A five-member delegation from KNU was able to visit Yangon and other parts of Myanmar on a preliminary basis in early December 2003, and it was followed in January 2004 by a delegation to Yangon led by Vice-President Saw Bo Mya and a team of high ranking officials. In the talks, General Saw Bo Mya and General Khin Nyunt had frank and cordial discussions in which both sides expressed the view that efforts should be made for the realization of genuine peace between the two sides. At the same time, discussions were held for establishing a ceasefire and holding a political dialogue. Representatives of the two sides continued to hold talks over several days in mid-January 2004 and both sides agreed to establish a ceasefire, to discuss how to resolve problems of the internally displaced persons in the various affected areas, and to maintain contact in order to resolve problems arising during the interim period. Two more rounds of talks were held during the months of March and October, 2004 in Mawlamyine, Mon state and in Yangon. Unfortunately, the meeting in October 2004 was cut short due to internal differences within the military junta which resulted in the removal of the then Prime Minister, General Khin Nyunt, the architect of the various ceasefire deals.

Although the peace process was overwhelmed by the political crisis in the military junta, both sides claimed that the doors are open for the continuation of dialogue and the process for negotiated settlement. Consequently a meeting was held in March 2005 in Mawlamyine, Mon state. The KNU lamented that the military junta eroded the early potential of talks for problem-solving and that this had the effect of undermining the position of those in the KNU who were willing to work seriously to achieve a ceasefire and reinforced the position of KNU hardliners who did not consider a ceasefire necessary or attainable. In spite of the prevailing difficulties, the KNU expressed its satisfaction with the military junta's responses and willingness to have an informal discussion.

2. Peace-building: Through Initiatives for Development and Humanitarian Assistance

While a group of Karen in Myanmar were busy with the peace-making initiatives, another group, which in fact overlapped with the first, was busy with peace-building initiatives, attempting to identify Karen civil servants, businessmen and active Karen youth with a view to forming an advisory group for the development and progress of the Karen people. When the Karen National Congress for Democracy (KNCD), a Karen Political Party, was de-registered in 1990, there was a strong feeling within its leadership that there should at least be a Karen social organization that could serve as a vehicle for mobilizing and nurturing the Karens regardless of religious and ideological affiliations, and that such an organization should focus on the general welfare of the Karen community in Myanmar.

This view of fostering communal cohesion was reinforced by certain Christian social activists and resulted in the formation of a consortium group called the Karen Development Committee (KDC) in mid-June 1994. The KDC established as its aims, to mobilize and promote Karen people's participation in self-development and social progress. It set out five major objectives, namely:

- Promotion of Karen literature and culture
- Promotion of educational development and scholarships
- Promotion of livelihood and economic development
- Promotion of health and medical care
- Promotion of civil and social involvement.

For the purpose of legitimacy, the patronage of most of the members of the Karen Peace Mediator Group was mobilized, assigning members of the group to chair the five different sub-committees. The main activity of the KDC early in its life was a monthly encounter/forum of concerned Karen individuals for mutual sharing and consultation. This kind of forum resulted in the formation and registration of two companies, namely Kweh Ka Baw Company Limited (for delivery of healthcare services), and Klo Htoo Travels and Tours Company Limited. Only the Health Concerns sub-committee was able to carry out its envisaged activities to the fullest. Kwe Ka Baw Company Ltd was able to open Kwe Ka Baw Multi-purpose Hospital in Insein and there are now regional clinical and healthcare services in Taungoo, Dawai, Pathein, Paukaung, Phado, Okpo, Myaungmya, Hinthada and Myawaddy. The other four sub-committees, namely, Literature and Culture, Economic, Education, and Social, were slower to do anything tangible due to lack of funding support during the first ten years.

A youth wing of the KDC was organized and it developed into an independent Karen youth organization known as Rising Sun Group (RSG).

The youth group meets regularly once a month in various Buddhist monasteries. They also occasionally organize encounter meetings with other ethnic youth groups for mutual sharing of experiences. Likewise, a women's auxiliary wing was organized, now known as Karen Women's Action Group (KWAG), which meets from time to time to discuss women's issues.

The Education sub-committee, with the support of a network of groups related to the Literature and Culture sub-committee, jointly sponsored the very first nationwide Karen Forum on Development, again with the patronage of three members of the Karen Peace Mediator Group. The forum was held in Hpa-an, Karen State, from 2–6 April 2002. It was a gathering of 120 participants from twenty-eight local Karen civil society organizations including Christian clerics and Buddhist monks. At that nationwide Karen Development Forum, Professor Saw Tun Aung Chain in his keynote address, pointed out that because some Karen had chosen the path of armed resistance which had now been raging for over fifty years, the Karen people generally had suffered and were still subject to great privation and the Karen youth especially had lost many opportunities for education and development. He emphasized that it was time to look to the present and not cling to the past nor fantasize about the future. The Karen people, he said, were living in harmony and friendship with the other national races in many parts of the country, so they should understand that they could develop and flourish not in isolation but only in unity and cooperation with the other national races of Myanmar.

Arising from Professor Saw Tun Aung Chain's assessment, a number of individuals who were instrumental in formation of the KDC began sponsoring a series of meetings and workshops with a view to enlarging and transforming the KDC to develop into a broad-based organization representing various elements of the Karen community. Consequently, a constitution was drawn up and adopted at the KDC assembly meeting held on 27 March 2004. KDC aims to serve as a humanitarian and development assistance organization and is organized to provide services through five departments, namely, literature and culture, health, education, economic and social.

3. Peace Nurturing: Initiatives for Community Mediation and Conflict Resolution

Another initiative came from the leader of one of the groups which defected from KNU. In cooperation with a Hpa-an based Karen Buddhist abbot, a seminar was organized on "Peace in Karen State". This took place in December 1998 in Hpa-an, the capital of Karen state. The meeting was held at the state's Information and Public Relations Office. Both Christian clergy and Buddhist abbots were among the sixty participants present at that seminar.

A preparatory committee consisting of seven religious leaders and eleven laymen was formed and assigned to convene a nationwide consultation for the formation of a "Karen State Peace Committee". The preparatory committee convened a consultation on 1 February 1999 in the compound of the Anglican Church in Hpa-an, Karen state. The consultation was attended by Buddhist monks and Christian leaders from Karen state, Mon state, Tanintharyi division and Bago division, as well as a large group of Karen lay leaders. The consultation resulted in the formation of a nine-member "Karen State Peace Committee" (usually referred to as KPC) consisting of four Karen Buddhist monks and five Christian clerics. The KPC was empowered to co-opt additional members if needed and also to appoint a working group if necessary. The objectives of the KPC are:

- To work for peace-building through the leadership of the Karen religious leaders
- To work with other existing Karen civil society organizations for the emergence of peaceful Karen communities.

Given the situation, the KPC members have met only occasionally and on an informal basis. Some of the KPC members have established links with the Shalom/Peace Foundation through serving as members of Shalom-initiated Myanmar Ethnic Nationalities Mediators' Fellowship (MENMF), and also participating in training activities and seminars organized by Shalom on community mediation, reconciliation and conflict resolution.

Through the help and patronage of the KPC members, in March 2004, several Buddhist organizations and the Hpa-an Council of Churches formed a scholarship support group called Karen Educational Foundation (KEF). It aims to provide financial support not only to the deserving students at the primary and matriculation level, but also to bright Karen students to pursue higher studies both within the country and abroad. This scholarship programme is not limited to Karen youth in Karen state only but extends also to young Karens all over Myanmar.

Plans are currently underway for pooling and mobilizing resources from Karen individuals and organizations with a view to building up a capital fund for the Karen Educational Foundation.

4. Capacity-building: Initiatives in Education and Communication

Another initiative which emerged from the work of the Karen mediator group concerned the need to support, empower and link the individuals and groups or organizations responsible for the various community initiatives. Due to the differences in dialects (Sgaw, Pwo), lifestyles and livelihood (educated, not educated), religious affiliations (Buddhist, Christian) and political perspectives (pro-ceasefire, anti-ceasefire), the groups are quite diverse and had been carrying out their outreach activities without consultation and coordination. A think-tank group called Karen Development Network (KDN) was organized in January 2004 aimed at building up the capacity for institutional and organizational leadership, and to explore ways to extend education and communication activities in the community. It is a network group of Karen individuals who are respected by the Karen community and comprise prominent leaders and participants in various Karen civil society organizations. It is intended to serve as a mechanism for enhancing local initiatives through promoting "inter-community understanding" and fostering "inter-organization cooperation". Those involved are primarily Karen organizational and community leaders who are willing to share information related to their social activities in their respective communities. Some of the areas of concern that KDN has identified as needing or open to networking, cooperation and coordination are:

1. Peace-making and peace-building
2. Education and training efforts
3. Social reconstruction efforts (IDPs, resettlement, rehabilitation and social welfare services)
4. Healthcare, HIV/AIDS, and health education efforts
5. Awareness-building about current situation
6. Inter-faith engagement and inter-religious understanding
7. Conflict management
8. Media and information dissemination.

(1) Peace-making and Peace-building

Through the initiative of KDN, in March 2004 an intra-dialogue meeting took place among the prime movers of the various elements of the Karen community in the meeting hall of the Karen Baptist Theological Seminary, at Insein, Yangon. There were altogether sixty-four participants. Two keynote papers were presented, one by the Venerable Ashin Pyinya Thami (Taungalaya Sayadaw) who sent in his paper highlighting the need for Karen unity (but was unable to attend in person) and one by Professor Saw Tun Aung Chain who highlighted the need for a creative response to the challenges facing the Karen community.

Although this meeting was not conceived as a decision-making or programme-planning occasion, the consensus of the meeting was to support the holding of a national-level "Karen Peace Forum". This took place on 13–15 May 2004 in the Anglican Church Compound, in Hpa-an, Karen state. The Karen Peace Forum was attended by 139 participants representing various Karen civil society organizations (mainly literature and culture associations), including Karen political parties. It was organized by the Karen State Peace Committee (KPC) with the support of KDN. At that forum Professor Saw Tun Aung Chain, in his keynote address, urged all those present at the forum to work for reconciliation and peace and all the Karen civil society organizations to lend all their support to the KPC. The KNU was not able to send delegates but they did send a letter of felicitation stating its "commitment and determination to continue the efforts of political negotiation and settlement" based on the gentleman's agreement of ceasefire already made with the military junta on 16 January 2004.

Through the forum, the KPC was able to make its concerns known not only to the Karen public but also to the authorities of the military regime since personnel from intelligence and special branch were given the opportunity to be present throughout the forum. In addition to providing the authorities with all the papers related to the forum, the full CD-recorded documentation was also handed over to them. The positive result was that KPC was allowed by the authorities to send four delegates to the Karen unity seminar organized by the KNU on 20–21 June 2004 in Maesot, Thailand.

This positive outcome reinforced the conviction of KDN that not only is networking "possible", it is also essential, because of the need for mobilizing common commitment to working towards reconciliation and peace. KDN believes it is now evident that networking can help build more significant and more inclusive relationships among different elements of the Karen community and it can lead to new forms of cooperation not only among the like-minded but also others. Within a very short time, KDN has come to see its role not as a spokesperson for the networking bodies, but as a channel to provide a way for them in their efforts to "transcend the limitations of existing parameters and framework", to "think new thoughts", "dream new dreams" and "glimpse new visions".

Meanwhile, the networking partners seem to acknowledge that fora are needed to bring "differences of understanding" among the various groups into a mutually "committed dialogue" so that all may find their way to a clearer discernment and a more considered response to the prevailing situation. While initially engaging in networking for peace-making and peace- building, KDN has also explored the possibilities of networking in other areas of concerns especially education, capacity-building and communication.

(2) Education and Training

Many existing Karen civil society organizations, especially Christian churches and Buddhist monasteries, have been engaged in some way or other in education and training programmes for leadership development as a component of their social activities. Most of those programmes have tended to emphasize the individual spiritual and moral qualities that are needed by those who will assume leadership positions. Sincerity and commitment, however, are not sufficient for good leadership. There are many other qualities people need to be equipped with if they are to lead with effectiveness. Among those qualities is the ability to craft planning with a strategy. As such, KDN realizes that there is a need for training in "Strategy Planning Method" that draws lessons from the planning of military, political and commercial strategy. This reflects the proposition which says: "You must win the battle. Better still, before the battle, resolve the conflict! Better still, before the need arises, avoid the conflict."

This method has now been used by KDN in a series of training programmes for people who are in leadership positions in organizations in order to build up their capacity through providing them with exercises on "projecting the main aim as the maximum achievable in a limited time" and "weighing strong points and weak points for assessing the practicality of the main aim." As part of confidence-building among the younger generation of Karen Buddhist and Christian youth and also in sharpening their social analysis and perspectives, since 1999 a series of three-week Annual Karen Youth Exposure Trips has allowed annual groups of four Christian and four Buddhist youths to go to Thailand. The objectives of this programme are:

1. To provide an educational opportunity for those who want to be involved in social activity.
2. To provide an opportunity for youth to share their own different experiences and life.
3. To encourage the youth who want to initiate small-scale projects in their own community.
4. To promote the idea and concept of sustainable development.
5. To create awareness of spiritual development and preparing strong civil society for social change.

Another opportunity that has been made available to Karen youth has been to participate in different training and exposure functions of the Shalom/Peace Foundation and Metta Development Foundation. It is encouraging especially to see a couple of young Karen alumni of Metta Foundation ably and successfully leading Participatory Action Research (PAR) Trainings and Development Management Trainings (DMT). Arrangement is also being made with a view to send young Karen interns to work with Shalom/Peace Foundation as part of education and training outreach. Potential Karen leaders and scholars also manage from time to time to attend and participate in regional and international fora and training to further equip them for the future.

Another KDN initiative reflects the crucial need for the provision of affordable, high-quality and practical education and training. A twenty-module Australian-accredited course in Community Management was introduced in early January 2004. It is currently available using English distance education materials with periodic workshops in Yangon. Efforts have also begun to make the course available in Burmese and to extend its services to areas outside Yangon. Initially fifty students were enrolled in Yangon and now the first batch of eighteen students has completed the course and will graduate and be awarded a certificate fully accredited by an Australian institute of TAFE (Technical and Further Education). Preparations are already underway to expand this programme into other areas, namely: Pathein, Taungoo, Bago, Hpa-an, Mawlamyine, Mandalay and Lashio; enrolling up to sixty students per centre. Students from many ethnic groups have enrolled in the programme in Yangon, not just Karen and similarly the programme outside Yangon will be available to all, but the emphasis has been on offering it in places where it is accessible. Plans are underway to take the programme to other ethnic areas and from this year the accreditation will be provided by the Thailand-based Thai-German Institute.

(3) Social Reconstruction

Karen-related churches and monasteries are responding to the needs of the community in various ways. One way has been to provide help to the people affected by the disruption caused by armed conflict and facing life as internally displaced persons (IDPs). Essentially, internally displaced persons (IDPs), face different kinds of problems depending on where they are located, for example in the ethnic ceasefire areas, in areas of active conflict and in relocation sites arranged by the military junta.

Ceasefire areas are recognized as special regions with some autonomy for ethnic nationality authorities and as a secure place against the attack of the military junta, as per ceasefire agreement with the military junta. Active conflict areas are understood as areas where people are forced to hide from or at least not to expose themselves to government troops. Relocation sites are usually consolidated villages to which people have been ordered to move by the military junta after having been forcibly evicted from their home place, as their home places are considered support and supply bases for the armed ethnic resistance groups or tactically strategic.

A series of fora have been held mainly involving the leaders and staff of organizations responsible for the assistance programmes for the IDPs. The fora began with information-sharing and exchange of experiences of working with the IDPs in relocation sites. The focus has gradually shifted to improving and coordinating data in order to be able to develop an exchange of ideas with international agencies about more effective responses to this very serious problem. Through sharing and consultation with the international agencies, Karen community organizations will be able to take an advocacy role with regard to the provision of assistance on an expanded scale and formulating ideas for the reconstruction of conflict-affected areas.

(4) Awareness-building about the Current Situation

Another area of activity has been the fostering of a series of fora for members of Kayin political parties, conscientious leaders and young generation people (including some selected non-Karens as co-participants or resource persons) on issues of current concerns, for example, constitutional matters such as central authority *versus* local autonomy, and the impact of ceasefires. Due to the sensitivity of the situation, these kinds of educational and capacity-building services are referred to as programmes on civic education for promotion of citizens' responsibilities. KDN has also been approached by Chin community groups to help them start the same kind of programme.

(5) Media and Information Dissemination

As the media is tightly controlled by the authorities, there is awareness of a need to nurture and build up the capacity of communicators so that they are able to creatively explore innovative ways of collecting and disseminating information without violating the regulations of the Press Scrutiny Board of the authorities. Searching for viable media activities for engaging the public is being pursued through workshops on "Creative Thinking" and "Journalism Ethics" with the help of young and dynamic secular communication innovators who are leading figures of official secular journals and magazines. There are many other areas of activities that need networking. KDN is still in the planning and programme formulation stage in the areas of awareness-raising and capacity-building in the areas of conflict resolution and management and inter-religious dialogue. Preparation for working in this area is still at the stage of providing opportunities for expanding our experience through participation in relevant activities, both within the country and abroad.

Concluding Observations

Significant change has been occurring within the military regime over the past year, most significantly signalled by the removal in October 2004 of Prime Minister General Khin Nyunt and the purging of his followers from government. The full impact of this internal development is still to emerge. With regard to the substance of this survey of recent developments within the Karen community, it seems safe to conclude that, in spite of the limitations and constraints, the resurgence of civil society organizations continues. Clearly, the emergence of civil society organizations is a possibility. It is also self-evident that the effective functioning of civil society organizations is a vital issue.

Much has been said about the centrality of efforts to promote peace talks between the KNU and the military junta in stimulating many and varied initiatives to activate and strengthen the Karen community. While there remain great hopes in the community that the gentleman's agreement ceasefire made on 16 January 2004 will be consolidated, recent developments are not encouraging. Talks held in March, 2005, the first following the fall from power of Prime Minister General Khin Nyunt, appear to have led again to deadlock. While the two sides maintain lines of communication, and both sides declare themselves to be willing to talk, there has emerged again a sense of yet another lost opportunity for real dialogue.

Nevertheless, perhaps the greatest hope of the Karen people in Myanmar is that there can emerge an official consolidation of the ceasefire agreement followed up by a process of negotiated settlement of underlying political differences. The emerging Karen civil society organizations will then be in a better position to make a real contribution to post-conflict reconstruction and restoration of normality in the country.

10

Peace Initiatives among Ethnic Nationalities: The Kachin Case

Ja Nan Lahtaw

Introduction

Myanmar is a country inhabited by multi-ethnic nationalities with different customs, language and religion. This diversity can be an asset if the different ethnic nationalities appreciate each other's differences. Unfortunately though, most ethnic nationality groups adopted armed conflict as the means of protecting their cultural identity and seeking to meet their needs and interests as groups. Most of the ethnic armed conflicts have been dealt with peacefully after over forty years of armed struggle. Ceasefire agreements between the armed groups and the government were reached towards the end of the 1980s. However, there are three remaining groups — Chin, Kayin and one of the Kayah ethnic armed groups — that have not reached a similar agreement yet. Over forty years of armed struggle did not allow for the appreciation of diverse cultures and customs. Rather, it created serious divisions among ethnic nationality groups.

The country can at present be considered a deeply divided society and this divisiveness can be seen at various levels within the society — inter-personal, inter-communal, inter-group, and intra-group. Deep-rooted fears within individuals and groups lead to internal cohesion among like-minded groups. The stronger a group becomes, the stronger their view of other groups as their enemy. The relational gap between group and individual ethnic nationality is enormous.

Due to the lengthy armed conflicts, social-economic reconstruction and a reform of the system of governance have been ongoing. Since the beginning of the 1990s, religious organizations and a few NGOs have started community development programmes for the people at the grassroots level in some ethnic states. In a situation of protracted conflict, the transformation required can only take place through a comprehensive and integrated approach.

Peace initiatives described in this chapter indicate only the activities initiated by the Shalom Foundation, a local NGO working for peace and development among various ethnic nationality groups. The Shalom Foundation is not based on any ethnic group or religion. It is for all ethnic nationality groups. This chapter highlights the meaning of peace as understood by the Shalom Foundation, the need for peace initiatives by specifically examining a conflict situation in Kachin society as a case study. There are a number of conceptual frameworks behind the peace activities of the organization as there are challenges faced by it in order to bring about peace.

I. UNDERSTANDING OF PEACE

It is clear that understanding/accepting one idea is based on one's own passions, experience in life, threats to existence and human needs. The term "peace" has also been understood differently in accordance with the needs and desires of individuals. The meaning of peace as understood by the Shalom Foundation is described as follows:

> The word "peace" is understood as the absence of violence, war and overt physical harm to persons and property. The meaning of "peace" is looked at from a transformational approach of conflictual and destructive interaction to more constructive and cooperative relationships. It has been defined as a network of relationships full of energy and differences (Assefa 2000, Mennonite Conciliation Service, Lederach 1997).

The more comprehensive understanding of Peace is drawn from the Hebrew word for peace — *Shalom*. It simply means, "how things should be" in a normative way. This interpretation also has three fundamental meanings:

1. Material and physical well-being
2. Just and healthy relationships between people and nations
3. Moral or ethical sense which includes honesty, integrity, innocence and straightforwardness

(Yoder 1987, pp. 10–16)

The peace initiative activities of Shalom are designed in accordance with the normative guiding principle. Its general vision is that individuals or groups ought to live socially, economically and politically in certain positive ways.

In a setting like Myanmar where much destruction has taken place since the ethnic insurgent movements started forty-five years ago, a comprehensive understanding of peace is most appropriate and indeed necessary for the attainment of sustainable and enduring peace.

II. NEED FOR PEACE

In order to draw attention to the social fabric of the ethnic nationality groups in Myanmar, the "Present Landscape of Kachin society" is documented as a case study.

The Present Landscape of Kachin Society

At the 58th Anniversary of Kachin State Day on 10 January 2006, the northern commander and chairman of the Kachin State Peace and Development Council, General Ohn Myint, stated that people dwelling in Kachin state are Kachins comprised of six linguistic tribes, five Shan tribes, Bamar and other ethnic nationalities. Therefore, Kachin state symbolizes a small union within the larger Union of Myanmar. He emphasized unity among the ethnic nationalities as a nation and unity among the ethnic nationalities living in Kachin state.

The national leader emphasized unity so that cultural, religious, youth and armed group leaders will in turn express the need for unity among Kachin people and tribes. There are various means to bring unity among Kachin people by various groups within Kachin society. Why do the Kachin people want "Unity among themselves"? What is happening in the society at present? What are the issues that cause divisions among Kachin people?

Like some other ethnic groups in Myanmar, Kachin society is also divided due to different cultural needs, religious beliefs and values, and political approaches. This case study of Kachin society will highlight the present landscape of the society but will not thoroughly reflect the causes of division among Kachin people.

Linguistic Divisions of Kachin

Kachins are comprised of six different linguistic groups. The term "Kachin" is not a tribe name. There are different families and linguistic divisions.

While the group of families that speak the same dialect is called a tribe or a clan, the term "Kachins" is employed for the people as a whole. Following the linguistic divisions, they are the Jinghpaw, Lhaovo (Maru), Lachik (Lashi), Zaiwa (Azi) and Rawang tribes. Some groups in Kachin society say that there are seven tribes in Kachin rather than six tribes and that the seventh tribe is Nung. Those who support the Nung tribe as separate from Rawang say that Nung language is different from that of Rawang. Therefore, it should be recognized as one separate linguistic tribe. In the past, Rawang was always called Nung-Rawang, which shows that Nung and Rawang were treated collectively.

During the Burma Socialist Programme Party (BSPP) period, the Kachins were recognized as composing six linguistic tribes. It was at the Traditional Harvest Festival hosted by Shalom Foundation in November 2000, that Lieutenant General Khin Nyut, then Secretary of State Peace and Development Council (military government of Myanmar) affirmed that the Kachin ethnic group was comprised of six different tribes such as Jinghpaw, Maru, Lashi, Azi, Rawang and Lisu. The chairman of Kachin State Peace and Development Council and the Northern Commander, General Ohn Myint, stated that there were six linguistic tribes in Kachin on 10 January 2006 at the 58th Anniversary of Kachin State Day.

Among the Kachins, Jinghpaw is the biggest group within the six linguistic tribes and Jinghpaw language is the most common among the Kachins. Whatever dialect they speak, all Kachins felt comfortable calling themselves Jinghpaw until the mid-1970s. From the beginning of the 1980s however, the term "Jinghpaw" became controversial with the smaller linguistic tribes. They felt the term "Jinghpaw" does not reflect the identity of the other smaller linguistic tribes. At the present time, cultural groups and some religious organizations use the term "Jinghpaw Wunpawng" or "Wunpawng", which has a more inclusive meaning.

Since "Jinghpaw language" was the first written language developed by the American Baptist Missionary, Dr Ola Hanson in 1885, it has been most common and widely used in churches and on formal occasions in Kachin society. But in some parts of the Kachin region where not all speak Jinghpaw, the development of the written language of smaller linguistic tribes such as Lhaovo, Lachik, Zaiwa became a need and issue, particularly for religious worship. This development of the written language of smaller linguistic tribes became one of the dividing factors between Kachin tribes such as those between Jinghpaw and Lhaovo.

One of the Zaiwa (one of the tribes of Kachin) patrons of Kachin Culture Central Committee mentioned his unhappiness over the development of the written language for the smaller linguistic tribes. He said that if Kachins did not have one common language that every Kachin could understand, they might not be able to understand and communicate well with each other. He expressed his frustration that every linguistic tribe wants recognition of their language. By not encouraging each other to speak one common language, he noted that there would be lesser opportunity for the Kachins to be united. Many people in Kachin society share the same frustration and disappointment of this leader. While many see the need for smaller linguistic tribes, they also acknowledge it as an issue that creates disunity among the Kachin linguistic tribes.

Religious Groups in Kachin Society

The majority of Kachin people are Christian though there are Kachin animists as well. The Kachin Christians are composed of Baptist, Catholic, Anglican, Church of Christ, Assembly of God and other smaller denominations. The religious organizations are divided due to differences in ideologies, beliefs and values. One of the causes for church division between the Kachin Baptist Convention and Lhaovo Baptist Churches is over the language for worship. It was the Jinghpaw language (the most common language among Kachin) that united Kachin Christians for a little over a century while it was also the Jinghpaw language that caused the church split between the Kachin Baptist Convention and Lhaovo Baptist Churches.

Youth Programmes

As a consequence of poor education and rampant unemployment, many Kachin youth were disappointed with life and became drug addicts. A senior student leader once said that 70 per cent of Kachin youth are in one way or other related to drugs. They may not be addicts but they are associated with drugs as a means to reduce their anxiety, pessimism and to be recognized by their peers. Because of the need to uplift the Kachin youth, there are several groups in Kachin society that organize activities for young people. Some of the groups working for youth are the Kachin Baptist Convention Youth Department, Catholic Youth, Kachin Consultative Assembly Youth Committee, Kinlum Education Programme, KIO Youth Committee (Education, Economic and Development for Youth — EEDY programme), Jinghpaw Wunpawng Shan State Youth Organization, Myit Rum, Senior Friends, and those who are working for youth from outside the country such as All Kachin Youth Union (AKYU) and All Kachin Student Youth Union (AKSYU). The groups working inside initiate capacity-building programmes through awareness workshops and training on different topics such as Media, Health (HIV/AIDS), economics, management skills and developmental concepts. Some other activities include tuition classes after school hours and providing boarding schools, especially for poor youth unable to attend tuition class after school. Since the school education does not provide a good learning environment, the students have to take additional tuition classes after school hours to supplement the learning process.

It is encouraging to see that some people have deep concerns about young people's lives and initiate different programmes for Kachin youth. On the other hand, the programme activities initiated by different groups overlap and there is a lack of coordination among the leaders and groups/organizations/committees. As a result, a good programme initiated by one group may not gain support from the other groups or may even become a hindrance to the success of the work of another group. At this stage, the programmes run by those different youth groups/committee are difficult to sustain due to lack of financial resources, human capacity and cooperation. The leaders of youth groups see the need for coordination among themselves for better understanding about each other's work and stronger collaboration. Having the commitment to organize the programmes for youth is very good and honourable but how they organize the programmes is an issue. The intention is good but the process of organizing the programme is weak. That weak process creates conflict, misunderstanding and competition among the youth groups. Therefore, the leaders from those youth groups mentioned above got together on 7–8 March 2006 to build trust among each other and agreed to have unity and find ways to collaborate in implementing their programmes for youth.

Ceaesefire Groups in Kachin Society

This section briefly describes the ceasefire groups that exist in Kachin society. The ceasefire groups of Kachin are separated due to differences in ideology and approaches. Up till 2005, there were three separate armed groups in Kachin society. Kachin Independence Organization (KIO) was formed on 25 October 1960 and it is the leading organization of Kachin people and for Kachin people in promoting and protecting their rights and needs. KIO signed a ceasefire agreement on 24 February 1994.

The New Democratic Army — Kachin (NDA-K) left KIO in 1968 to join the Communist Party of Burma. In 1989 the group became NDA-K and made an agreement with the government and became the militia in the area where they had ground control. This group is mainly focused on business activities and believes in the building of Kachin society through economic development of the individual and people.

The Kachin Defence Army (KDA), the former KIO Fourth Brigade-Shan State decided to leave KIO due to increased military pressure from the Myanmar Army. The group made an agreement with the government in 1991 and became the militia in the area where they had ground control. Though KDA is not in a position to advocate for all Kachin people, they are respected by Kachin people living in Northern Shan state for their concern and protection of the Kachin community under their controlled area in the Northern Shan state.

The KIA-break away group, led by former Military Intelligence Chief of KIO came to exist as a separate group in 2005. The group named themselves as "KIA Ran Pru" (in Jinghpaw). The majority of the Kachin people do not recognize the existence of this group, but the group is trying to show its existence.On 4 January 2006 during the 58th Anniversary of Kachin State Day celebration, the second-line leader of "KIA Ran Pru" group announced that they had some differences with KIO and KIA. They therefore left KIO and KIA but agreed to be united with KIO and KIA. The group claimed that they are still KIA, according to the second-line leader of the "KIA Ran Pru" group. The first-line leader of this group was one of the key persons to lead a coup in KIO in 2004. The attempt failed and later the leader took refuge under NDA-K for a while. Now, the government has assigned the group to settle in "Gwihtu area" — in between Nmai Hka and Mali Hka, along the Washawng area. This area is situated east of Myitkyina and it is under KIO administration. The KIO officially opposed the group's settlement in the Guihtu area, which is less than an hour's drive from Myitkyina.

After the KIA Ran Pru group left NDA-K, a group of central committee members of NDA-K led by former Secretary of NDA-K, led the coup in July 2005 to take over power from the current NDA-K chairman. Unfortunately, the attempt failed and the current chairman retained control. The attempted coup was owing to dissatisfaction over the chairman's leadership strategies and economic partnership practices.

Attempts at Unity

1. Traditional Manau Festival and Kachin State Day

The Kachin Culture Central Committee has already hosted the "Traditional Manau Dance Festival" along with the celebration of Kachin State Day seven times every January since 2000. It is an attempt to bring different Kachin linguistic tribes, Shan tribes, Bamar, Chinese, Gorhka, and other ethnic nationalities living in Kachin state. It is understood that Singhpaw (Kachins are called Singhpaw in India) living on the Indian side and Kachins from Yunnan Province (China) also came to participate at the "Traditional Manau Dance Festival" and Kachin State Day. Regardless of the differences in language, ideologies or political goals, the participation of six or seven (depends on individual perception) linguistic tribes and armed groups have been gradually increasing every year. The Manau Dance is a big part of the identity of Kachin people that all different linguistic groups share in their history. The date 10 January 1948 is a historical marker for Kachin society for that day was officially announced by the government as Kachin State Day, according to General Ohn Myint.

The celebration of Kachin State Day is bringing back the spirit of unity that Kachin people had in 1948. With the desire to bring alive the spirit of unity in Kachin society, Kachin ceasefire groups (KIO, NDA-K, KDA), businessmen (Kachin and non-Kachin), professors and students of Culture and Literature Association from Myitkyina University, youth from different religious organizations, Shan Culture and Literature Committees, Chinese culture groups, Gorhka, Bamar culture dance group, high school students, and other civil organizations from the community came to participate with financial support, time and energy to make the "Dance Festival" and Kachin State Day of 2006 possible. The latest two separate armed groups — KIA Ran Pru and NDA-K breakaway also came to participate at the Kachin State Day festival of 2006. The support and collaboration from the chairman of Kachin State Peace and Development Council and the Northern Commander were also received. It was remarkable that he came to deliver the speech at the Kachin State Day ceremony in 2006 for the first time since 2000.

At the Kachin State Day celebration, the armed group leaders from various groups got a chance to meet again after the tension between them. The occasion is now the informal gathering for Kachin armed groups to rebuild relationships among themselves.

2. Kachin Consultative Assembly

The fist Kachin National Congress was held in 1947. From 21 to 25 October, 2002 Kachin nationals from all over Myanmar came together at Laiza, Momauk Township, Kachin State, to hold the second Kachin Nationals Consultative Meeting. Gathering under the leadership of the Kachin Independence Organization (KIO), New Democratic Army-Kachin (NDA-K) and Kachin Defence Army (KDA), the meeting was convened with the aim of creating goodwill through activities to support progress for the Union according to Kachin customs and traditions. A "Kachin Nationals Consultative Assembly" was formed at the meeting.

The meeting fully entrusted the responsibility for fulfilling and successfully implementing the following discussed issues to the Kachin National Consultative Assembly. An advisory group and a working committee were also set up as a result.

1. To exhort the Kachin National Peace Groups (KIO, NDA-K, KDA) to strive for sustainable peace in the Kachin state as well as for the whole Union.
2. The emergence of a strong Union based on justice and union solidarity.
3. The narcotics eradication policy, jointly initiated by the SPDC and the National Peace Groups, is a national cause. Therefore, all Myanmar nationals should participate earnestly in this endeavour.
4. The establishment of a genuine, democratic nation and the drawing up of a national constitution.
5. To help bring the national constitution to completion, and request the SPDC to call a national assembly soon, consisting of political parties, ethnic nationality delegates, Ethnic National Peace Groups and representatives from all levels of society.

It is now over three year since the setting up of a Kachin Consultative Assembly (KCA). The advisory group and the working committee felt the need to look back on what KCA had done so far for Kachin society. At the working committee meeting on 6 March 2006, the vice-chairman of KCA stated what had been accomplished by KCA in the past three years. He said that regardless of how much or little KCA has done for Kachin people, KCA had been fully supported by the Kachin people. Looking back at the over three-year journey of KCA, there had been no concrete or definite actions carried out by KCA for the Kachin people. KCA was mainly involved in preventing violence, building relationship and reconciliation work between the Kachin armed groups so that no bloodshed occurred during the conflict. The third Kachin Consultative Assembly is due to be held some time in April 2006 for the review of previous activities and restructuring/reorganizing of KCA so that it may become a stronger assembly and represent the whole Kachin society.

The Social Structure of Kachin Society

All Kachins trace descent patrilineally. Each individual male or female inherits a surname from the father, none from the mother. In any one community the individuals who share such a surname (*htinggaw mying* — "household name") are considered to be close patrilineal kin; they are of one "household" [*htinggaw*], though in practice this does not necessarily mean that they normally all live in one house.

In all social activities, a Kachin individual identifies himself/herself very closely with his or her *htinggaw* group. In the context of rights and obligations one seldom hears a Kachin claiming anything as exclusive to himself/herself; it is always a case of "we" [anhte]. This "we" normally refers to the individual's *htinggaw* group.

The most important set of relationships in any Kachin society is those which establish the mutual status relations between the various *htinggaw* groups that exist in the community. From the individual's point of view, every *htinggaw* group within the community falls into one of the following three categories:

1) *Kahpu-kanau* — literally it means "older brother — younger brother". "Older brother-younger brother are treated as being of the same clan as one's own and are related closely enough to form an exogamous group with one's own lineage.

2) *Mayu* (bride's side) are lineages from which males of one's lineage have married.

3) *Dama* (groom's side) are lineages into which females of one's lineage have married.

The social network among *kahpu-kanau, mayu and dama* is very strong and nowadays, one can say that the Kachin social network system functions as an "insurance" or "social security" system in Kachin society. For example, if a family is planning marriage for its son, *kahpu-kanau ni* (brothers from the same household) contribute money or material to be given to a bride's family as gifts or dowry. Similar relational ties are apparent at funerals. When there is a death in a family, *kahpu-kanau, mayu and dama* get together and contribute to the cost of the funeral by bringing cows, money, etc. It is also an expression of support and sympathy to the family. During this time, some families bond with the grieving family. Therefore, social bonding among different families is strengthened during times of family crisis, marriage and death.

While this three-pillar social system encourages the cohesion between or among the families, clans or groups, it also creates threats to the smaller identity groups or clans or families. For example, the Lamai clan and Nhkum clan are *kahpu-kanau* and through the line of *kahpu-kanau* (Older brother — younger brother relationship), the internal cohesion between Lamai and Nhkum becomes stronger in the sense of social relationship and economics (in some cases). This internal cohesion between clans makes other clans feel inferior.

The three-pillar (*kahpu-kanau, mayu, dama*) social system is a unique identity of Kachin people and it is a system for social tying, bonding and bridging among Kachin. Even in the case of a serious offence or murder, the three-pillar social system is applied as a conflict resolution mechanism. When Kachin people are in conflict with each other, the conflicting parties are one way or other related to each other by the three-pillar system. When the conflicting parties realize they are connected to one another, it then becomes much easier to discuss about the conflict. The British were aware of the strong social system of the Kachin and their traditional ways of dealing with conflict. Therefore, the British allowed Kachin customs to act as a mechanism for dealing with conflict among Kachin. The Kachin Hill Tribes Regulation was adopted in 1895. Kachin people and people living in Kachin state have a choice to bring a criminal or civil case to the court or to solve the conflict in Kachin Custom through the Kachin Hill Tribes Manual. Since the British colonial period, the Burma Socialist Programme Party period and up till the present, the Kachin custom has been widely used in dealing with conflict. The traditional way is good in the sense that it resolves the conflict and utilizes social ties to resolve conflict. But the weakness of the approach is that it does not help to transform the relationship of the individuals who are involved in the conflict.

As with Kachin society, the societies of other nationality groups are also divided. Unity among the ethnic nationalities is greatly needed. Myanmar is presently a deeply divided society. The setting of Myanmar society is "intranational" in nature, that is, there are conflicts or disputes between groups who come from within the boundaries of a region, an institution or organization or cultural or religious group. On the other hand, the conflict in Myanmar is "internationalized" in nature, that is, internal conflict is expanded to neighbouring countries in the form of displaced persons, refugees, illegal migration, and external employment (Lederach 1997, p. 11). As seen in the Kachin case, the conflict between religious groups, linguistic tribes and armed groups indicate the intranational nature of the conflict.

Another characteristic of deeply divided societies is that people seek security in smaller and narrower identity groups such as clan, ethnicity, religion or geographic/regional affiliation or a mix of these (Lederach 1997, p. 12). This type of behaviour is obvious in Myanmar society as well. Individual or group identity has been under threat and those whose identity has been under threat identify their security with something close to their experience and over which they have some control. The threat to their identity is the driving factor for strengthening internal group cohesion. The more a group strengthens its group cohesion, the more other groups see it as a threat to them. As a result, people of different groups label one another as enemies since they do not belong to the same group. This perception of enmity creates mistrust and deep-rooted fears in the minds of individuals and groups.

Since Myanmar has gone through ethnic armed conflict for over forty years, the social characteristics of daily life mentioned above is ingrained in the society. The families are divided, the religious organizations are separated, top-level leaders are divided over power or due to their fears or security over their existence, the ethnic armed groups are splintered and the ethnic nationality groups are divided into smaller groups over language, clan or customs.

There is no need to describe at length the need for peace in Myanmar since other chapters have discussed it from different perspectives. But the types of change and the levels of change required for peace are highlighted in a broad sense. The types of change which the people of Myanmar are most concerned with are primarily social, political and economic.

In brief, social change is described as "changes in the way that members of society — individual, families, clans, social classes, ethnic/cultural groups, religious groups, etc. — relate to each other, or in the ways that they organize themselves for the purposes of carrying out particular social activities, such as cultural celebrations, sports, education, etc." (Williams 2005, p. 9).

Williams again describes political change as "changes in the way that politics and governance is organized and the way that political actors and political parties relate to each other" while economic change is described as "changing the way that the economy is organized and possibly changing the economic system, and changes in the balance and distribution of wealth, resources, and job creation" (Williams 2005, pp. 9–10).

Like any other country which has gone through protracted conflict for over three or four decades and is going through a transitional phase, Myanmar is also going through these change processes in the different realms — social, political and economic. Whether a process of change is successful/ desirable or not depends on the values, attitudes and perceptions of individual or groups who are directly involved or who are affected by the process.

There is a need for change at different levels such as personal, interpersonal, communal and national in order to bring peace. Deep-rooted conflict among the ethnic nationalities causes emotional disorders such as fears, anxiety, anger, etc. in personal life while it creates relational gaps at the interpersonal level. At this level, the attendant symptoms like stereotyping, polarization, hatred and mistrust are obvious. The same types of symptom can be seen at the communal level and there are gaps between the different ethnic nationality groups. Their existence and identity as groups have been under threat. The desired change at the national level is a reform of the system of governance and a change of attitudes nationally to make people more conscious of the existence of various ethnic nationalities and inclusion in the participation of all ethnic nationalities at the national level.

There is a debate among scholars about which level of change should take place first — individual or societal. It is believed that both are equally necessary and important. If individuals are being reflective about their attitudes and behaviour at the societal level, they become "reflexive" individuals and can bring about change at the personal and societal levels. Reflexive individual are those who have developed the skills of self-awareness, able to pay attention to their own actions and their impact, and aware of their own inner feelings and motivation (Francis 2005, p. 13).

III. CONCEPTUAL FRAMEWORKS AND PEACE-BUILDING ACTIVITIES

Ethnic conflict in Myanmar is a protracted or intractable conflict and it can be transformed only by taking a comprehensive approach to the people who are involved in it and to the setting in which it is rooted.

Thus, the peace initiative activities of the Shalom Foundation are designed as a comprehensive approach to deal with both socio-political concerns and personal/individual issues (relationships) simultaneously rather than dealing with only one type of issue. The peace initiatives are also aimed at both the short term and the long term. The goal of working on the short term with key people is to support them while they are dealing with immediate crises involving socio-political change. The long-term strategies focus on capacity-building and relationship-building which will support the socio-political change in the future. The activities include peace-building training for both capacity- and relationship-building, facilitating dialogues on culture and religion for interactions between individuals, trauma healing for becoming healthy persons without fears and building moral integrity, and development projects for better livelihood and stronger relationship within the community.

In order to bring about social, political and economic change at different levels such as personal, interpersonal, communal and national, the peace initiatives of the Shalom Foundation are based on several peace-building concepts:

1. "Peace-building Pyramid" by John Paul Lederach, a founder of Conflict Transformation Programme at Eastern Mennonite University, USA
2. A four-cell peace-building matrix
3. Ceasefire agreements between SPDC and KIO

1. Peace-building Pyramid

When one starts to analyse conflicts, one will discover that there are many levels involved. This concept helps us to identify key actors or parties at each level who can make a difference to a conflict of which they are a part. Therefore working at only one level can make it difficult to bring about lasting change because of the impact of the other levels. This fact encourages the Shalom Foundation to design its work at many levels rather than aiming at only one level.

This theory also suggests the importance of locating critical resource people strategically for networking vertically within the setting and horizontally in the conflict. These types of key or strategic actors or parties have the ability to work with people or groups who are different from them at different levels and across the lines. These key actors can develop allies for working within the various levels as well as working simultaneously at all levels.

The following pyramid diagram shows the key actors and their involvement in peace-building activities initiated by Shalom Foundation.

FIGURE 10.1
Peace-building Pyramid of Nyein (Shalom) Foundation

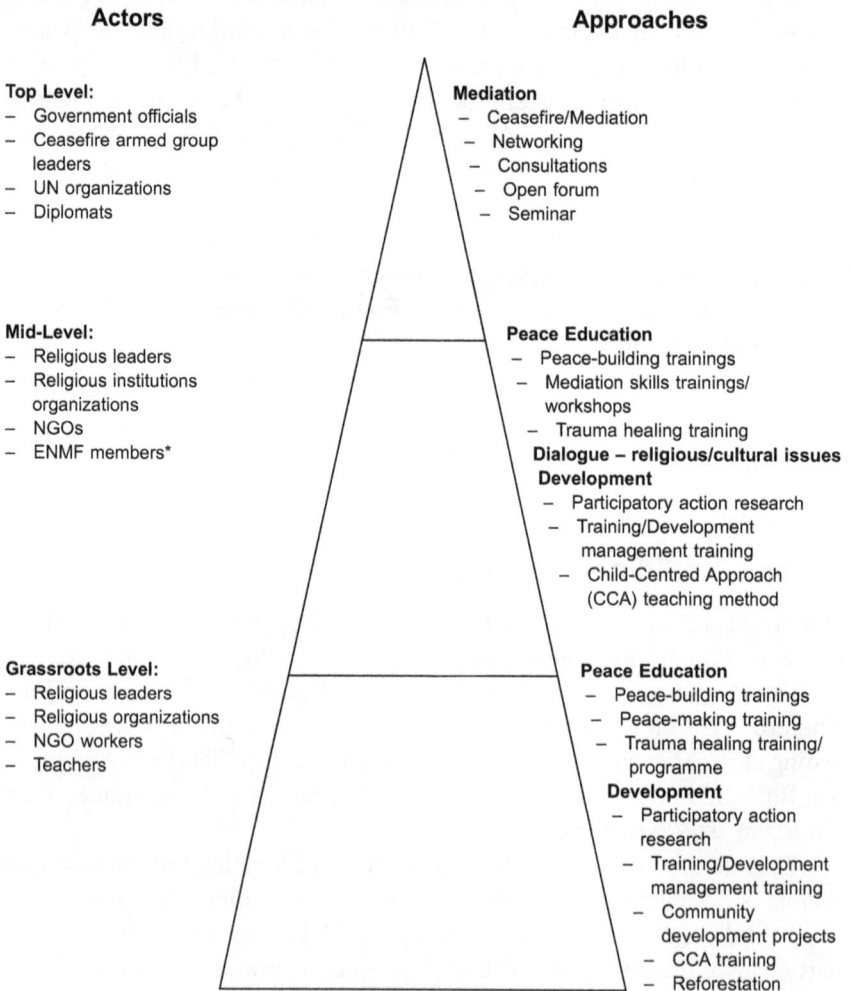

Actors   **Approaches**

Top Level: **Mediation**
- Government officials   - Ceasefire/Mediation
- Ceasefire armed group   - Networking
  leaders   - Consultations
- UN organizations   - Open forum
- Diplomats   - Seminar

Mid-Level: **Peace Education**
- Religious leaders   - Peace-building trainings
- Religious institutions   - Mediation skills trainings/
  organizations   workshops
- NGOs   - Trauma healing training
- ENMF members*   **Dialogue – religious/cultural issues**
                                              Development
                                               - Participatory action research
                                               - Training/Development
                                                 management training
                                               - Child-Centred Approach
                                                 (CCA) teaching method

Grassroots Level: **Peace Education**
- Religious leaders   - Peace-building trainings
- Religious organizations   - Peace-making training
- NGO workers   - Trauma healing training/
- Teachers   programme
                                              Development
                                               - Participatory action
                                                 research
                                               - Training/Development
                                                 management training
                                               - Community
                                                 development projects
                                               - CCA training
                                               - Reforestation

*ENMF — Ethnic Nationalities Mediators' Fellowship

The above pyramid indicates how the peace initiatives of Shalom Foundation are comprehensive and integrated according to the concept of peace as previously defined. It aims to achieve structural reform by working with top-level leadership through mediation, encouraging ceasefire, networking with UN organizations and diplomats, providing consultation on current political issues (for example, constitutional consultation) and creating open-fora for ethnic armed group leaders. It also focuses on relationship-building at the mid-level and grassroots level through capacity-building (for example, peace-building training, workshops and seminars) and community projects, which create space for people from different ethnic nationalities groups and different religious groups to be able to interact with each other.

While the immediate goal is restructuring relationships horizontally within and across the lines at top, mid and grassroots levels, the long-term goal is building a strong associational tie between groups who are different from each other, and to be able to influence from the ground up to mid-level to the top leaders vertically.

The urgent goal of working with top-level leaders from different groups is to deal with immediate crises, which are also rooted in the systemic level and that needs to be reformed, preferably within an immediate, intermediate or long-range time-frame.

2. A Four-cell Peace-building Matrix

This model was discovered as one of the results of Reflecting on the Peace Practice Project, 2004 (RPP). It is an experience-based learning process that involves varied peace agencies whose programmes attempt to prevent or mitigate violent conflict. Details about this concept is available at <www.cdainc.com/rpp>. There are four cells representing the matrix. Each cell can be a place to start activities for change.

Peace practitioners involved in the RPP project discovered that all peace activities or activities for change are based essentially on one or two approaches to those who are engaged for peace. The two ways include "More-people approaches" and "Key-people approaches". This model also describes all peace programmes as working at two basic levels: The individual/personal level and/or the socio-political level.

"More people approaches" focus on engaging large numbers of people in actions to promote peace while "key-people approaches" focus on involving particular people or groups of people who are influential or

FIGURE 10.2
A four-cell Peace-building Matrix of Shalom Foundation

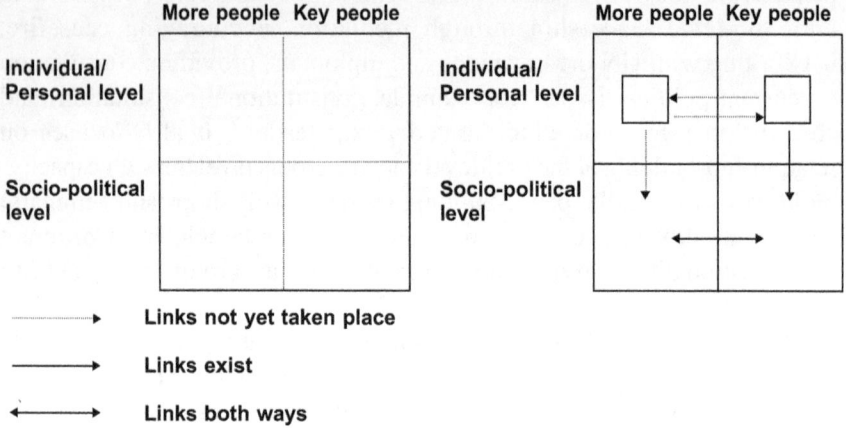

	More people	Key people			More people	Key people

Individual/Personal level

Socio-political level

Individual/Personal level

Socio-political level

- - - → **Links not yet taken place**

——→ **Links exist**

←——→ **Links both ways**

critical to the continuation or resolution of conflict because of their roles or positions of leverage. It is our belief that without the involvement of the key individuals or groups, no real progress can be made toward transforming the conflict.

"Individual/personal level engagement seeks to change the attitudes, values, perceptions or circumstances of individuals. It is believed that peace is possible only if the hearts, minds and behaviour of individuals as people are changed.

"Socio-political level is based on the belief that peace requires changes in socio-political or institutional structures. Those who focus on this level support creation or reform of institutions that address the causes of conflict and emphasize non-violent approaches of handling conflict within society.

The peace initiative activities of the Shalom Foundation cover primarily the two quadrants in a matrix — more people/individual level and key people/ individual level. The third quadrant in a matrix — key people/ socio-political level is the indirect outcome of the work at key people/ individual level. The last quadrant- more people/socio-political level remains as unavailable or risk conditions of the present situation.

More People-Approach at Individual Level

The inhabitants of Myanmar, who have experienced deep-rooted conflict, think narrowly about associating with people who are different from them due to mistrust and fears. It is necessary and crucial to take the "more-people approach" and work at the "individual/personal level". Therefore, the Shalom Foundation is taking this strategy in order to promote long-lasting peace in the country. With the belief that "peace begins within", the Shalom Foundation focuses its work at changing the attitudes, values and perceptions of individuals as the fundamental principle for peace. Individuals from all major ethnic nationalities (Kachin, Kayah, Karen, Chin, Mon, Bamar, Rakhine, Shan) and different religious groups (Buddhists and Christians) are involved in peace initiative activities of the Shalom Foundation. Changing the hearts of many people at the individual level is a time-consuming process.

At present, changing the hearts of many people at the individual level is Shalom's strategy and it is less threatening, at the same time moving from change at the individual level to socio-political level obtains more risk and is therefore a long-term strategy. It takes time to be able to move from one quadrant to the next — that is, to move from the individual level to the socio-political level. Since many people of the country have deep-rooted fears and insecurities, changing the hearts of the people cannot be rushed. At the same time, just working towards individual change and not moving to the socio-political systemic change will not create a sustainable peace either.

Key People-Approach at the Socio-political Level

The peace initiatives of the Shalom Foundation are also focused on the key-people approach. Most ethnic nationalities believe that only ethnic armed groups can represent them at the socio-political level. It is the hope that they in turn would articulate the voices of ethnic nationalities people at the grassroots on their needs, desires and interests. Because of their trust in ethnic armed groups, the Shalom Foundation is supporting them to be able to find peaceful alternatives in identifying needs and interests of the grassroots people.

Working with key people from the government and ethnic armed groups includes encouraging them to remain receptive to peace talks and ceasefire agreements for groups who have not signed them through an Ethnic Nationalities Mediators' Fellowship (ENMF) group. The members of ENMF includes mediators and members of cultural and literature committee from Kachin, Kayah, Karen, Chin and Mon nationalities. Other peace initiative programmes include coordinating the consultation for ethnic armed group leaders on immediate issues of socio-political concern (for example, constitutional consultation). Networking between ethnic armed groups and UN organizations is another type of support given to key people as part of the process of socio-political change at the national level.

By giving support to ethnic armed groups to seek alternative peaceful ways to reach their desired goals is indirectly supporting change at the socio-political level.

3. Ceasefire Agreement

The ceasefire agreement made between the government and Kachin Independence Organization (KIO) during the SLORC government in 1994 has been utilized as part of the strategies to implement peace and change involving ethnic conflict. The agreement was signed between the government and KIO with three representatives from each group with the three mediators in Myitkyina.

The agreements are not exclusively for the benefit of the Kachin ethnic group but also for other ethnic nationalities. As a result of ceasefire agreements, development activities have been implemented in Kachin state since 1994 and extended to other ethnic regions. Unfortunately, some agreements have not been implemented as agreed. Only after ten years of ceasefire agreements did political dialogue between the SPDC and ethnic armed groups eventually take place at the National Convention convened in May 2004 (Interview with lead mediator Dr Saboi Jum). Ceasefire agreements are meant to be the first entry point for political dialogue. In order to be able to implement the agreement, the Shalom Foundation is acting as an intermediary between the SPDC government and KIO, supporting the process of initiating an open forum among ethnic armed groups for strengthening unified perspectives on current socio-political issues and coordinating in networking with UN organizations and diplomats for undertaking development in the special region areas.

On the basis of the experience of the Shalom Foundation, the following challenges continue to obtain:

1. The creating of space to build links between key people and more people.
2. Lessened opportunities to build the capacity of individuals and to move from personal/individual level to the socio-political level.
3. Building trustful relationships between the key people from different groups.

4. Building a strong relationship/association between more people across different groups.

Conclusion

Building peace in a most sustainable way within a divided society requires changing the hearts of individuals or groups who are involved or affected by ethnic armed conflict at all levels — top, middle and grassroots — to be able to deal with multiple challenges at different levels. The strategies should be an integrated and comprehensive one that meets the social, economic and political needs of the people. Just working with "key people" without the involvement of "common people" or *vice-versa* may not be a suitable strategy. Therefore, strategies should be drawn from the point that both key and common people should be involved. It then becomes possible to move from the individual/personal level of change to socio-political change in order to have truly sustainable peace.

Ethnic armed conflict is internal in nature. Formal and governmental or international mechanisms for dealing with internal conflict are limited. Intervention in internal conflict is restricted not only by the charters of the major regional and international institutions but also by the lack of appropriate and adequate concepts, approaches and modalities for interventions. Therefore, in order to bring unity within a divided society, there should be collaborative effort to seek the most appropriate and culturally sensitive strategies of change and convert those into action.

References

Francis, Diana. *Action Research.* Birmingham: Responding to Conflict, 2005.

Lederach, John Paul. *Building Peace: Sustainable Reconciliation in Divided Societies.* Washington: United States Institutes of Peace Press, 1997.

Reflecting on Peace Practice Project, 2004. Cambridge: CDA Collaborative Learning Projects <www.cdainc.com>.

Schrock-Shenk, Carolyn, ed. *Mediation and Facilitation Training Manual.* Akron: Mennonite Conciliation Service, 2000.

Williams, Steve. *Conflict, Power and Change: Engaging with Actors, Systems, Structures and Policies.* Birmingham: Responding to Conflict, 2005.

Yoder, Perry. *SHALOM: The Bible's Word for Salvation, Justice, and Peace.* Nappanee: Evangel Publishing House, 1987.

11

The Shan in Myanmar

Sai Kham Mong

Introduction

The Shan *sawbwas* agreed in 1947 to join Ministerial Burma because of the provision provided for self-determination and the right of secession after ten years of independence. Aung San had correctly noted that it would be a failure on the part of the Myanmar leaders if the Shan still wanted to secede from the Union after the said period. Aung San's guarantee had moved the Shan *sawbwas* to join Myanmar forgetting what had happened to the Shan states during the past Burmese kings. Because of the decision of the Shan, the Kayah, whose state had been regarded to be in subordinate alliance by the British Government also came into the Myanmar Union. The sincere desire of the Shan and Kayah to live together with the Bamar could be seen at the outbreak of armed insurrections in 1949 by the Kayin, factions of the Burma Communist Party and army mutineers. Altogether thirty-one towns were reported to have been occupied by the rebels (Tinker 1957, p. 45). During that critical period it was the Shan, the Kayah, the Kachin and the Chin leaders who steadfastly stood with the Union government in suppressing the rebellions. Recruits for the Burmese Army were taken from hill people in forming the emergency battalions. In Shan state itself levies (volunteer forces) were formed in every sawbwaship state to repel the insurgents. These facts were provided as proof when the Shan denied the accusation of the Burmese leaders in the 1960s that the federal proposal of the hill people would only lead to the disintegration of the Union.

After the withdrawal of the KNDOs, the Pa-O insurgents remained in the Shan state primarily to disrupt the administration of the Shan state government run by the *sawbwas*. The Pa-O cause is interesting. The

Kuomintang (KMT) intrusion into the Shan state and the actions taken against them by the Union government was also a question that remained to be answered. The insurgents and the KMT intrusion had crippled the Shan state government administration providing a reason for the army to station its troops and to keep Shan state under military administration from 1952 to 1954. After nearly a century the Shan relived the experience of the rule under Burma. Encountering such issues the Shan *sawbwas* reconsidered the surrender of their hereditary rights and began to voice grievances of the Shan state in the Union. They also had witnessed the apparent defects of the Union constitution which finally led them to demand for amendments. In doing so, they might have been sincere in their desire for constitutional amendment but they failed to realize the concept was anathema to the Union leaders. For the latter, federation simply meant disintegration of the Union.

The demands for amendment of the constitution, followed by the military coup in 1962, were the causes of the emergence of armed rebellions against the Union government by various minority groups. Taking advantage of it, the Burma Communist Party (BCP) which had been in obscurity from the Myanmar political theatre, emerged in the 1970s by organizing the insurgent groups. Defeated in the fierce fightings with the government troops in the Shan state, their leaders took refuge in China. The defeat of the BCP resulted in bringing eighteen groups to peace agreement with the government. After achieving peace, the government initiated an attempt at national reconsolidation with an aim to drafting a new constitution for building a unified Myanmar.

The political events that occurred during the past fifty years has totally changed the situation in the Shan state. In the early years of independence, the then Shan state government would have been able to effectively handle the administration had it not been for the political confrontation opposing the rule of *sawbwas* led by *Yapala* and the Pa-O rebellion coupled with the intrusion of the KMT. In fact, these activities are assumed to have been externally engineered.

Regarding the administration of the Shan state government in Wa state, it is reported that the Was were generally friendly and agreeable to having the Shan state government. But the Shan state government administration in Kokang, however, was different from that of the Wa. The government officials posted in Kokang often reported the non-cooperative attitudes of the Kokang officials in government administration. Another issue with the Kokang was, being situated on the border with China and being populated mostly by the Chinese, border infiltration became a real danger. A ranking official of the Shan state government made a remark thus on the Kokang in 1954:

"Every Kokangese is a Chinese but every Chinese is not a Kokangese".

An equivalent saying to the above remark is: "Earth could not swallow a nation to extinction but another nation would". In addition to these issues encountered by the government there still are issues likely to arise with the demarcation of self-administered areas and zones. It is the responsibility of the officials framing the future Myanmar constitution to deal with such matters. Myanmar history, however, is a lesson in the need to establish a strong central government supported by genuine national unity.

The Shan State (1886–1948)

The British account on the Shan states noted:

It has an important geographical positions of a Buffer State; it is bounded on the North and North-East by China, on the East by French Indo-China, and on the South-East by Siam (Thailand). Its position therefore, in the defence of the North-East Frontier of Burma is strategically all important. It has an area of approximately 56,000 square miles, and a population of approximately 1,500,000. It is a rapidly developing country with vast natural resources in mineral wealth and in forests.

Memorandum of the Federated Shan States by
their Representatives, December 1930

The census in 1982 notes the Shan state as having 4.2 million inhabitants. The main block of the Shan live in Shan state but many of them are also found in Kachin and Kayah states. The Shan state that had formerly been divided into many independent principalities was ruled over by their respective hereditary chiefs called *sawbwa*. Since the establishment of the Konbaung dynasty (1752–1885), the Shan states unquestionably came under central control but as a tributary to the Burmese kingdom and not under direct Burma administration. When the British annexed Upper Burma in 1885 they treated the Shan states differently. The notification issued in 1886 under the Statute XXXIII Vic. Cap. 3, Upper Burma excluding the Shan states was constituted as a scheduled district.[1] The traditional Shan system of feudal administration was continued under the supervision and control of British officers.

The Shan states were first defined in 1887 under section 8 of the Upper Burma Laws Act. In November 1891 and again in July 1895, revised notifications defining the Shan states were issued. The Shan states, defined by the notification of July 1895, were divided into:

1. The Northern Shan states, with five states under their respective *sawbwas* and the territories east of Thanlwin river, were kept under the supervision of the superintendent, Northern Shan states.
2. The Southern Shan states were kept under the supervision of the superintendent and political officer, Southern Shan states. There were altogether ten *sawbwaship* and fourteen *Myosaship* states in the Shan states.
3. The Myelat division[2] in Southern Shan state under the supervision of the Superintendent and Political Officer, Southern Shan states comprised of one *Myosaship* state and fourteen Ngwehkunmu states (The 1947 Constitution I, pp. 21–22).

The British also had decided a separate administration for Kachin and Chin by enacting Kachin Hill Tribes Regulation in 1895 and Chin Hills Regulation in 1895 respectively. Myanmar scholars said the regulations for the Shan state, Kachin and Chin had implemented the "divide and rule" policy of the British (The 1947 Constitution 1, pp. 10–11). This policy was said to have been consistently followed up to the time of World War I (1914–18).

After the war the British had taken some measures towards the establishment of self-government in India and Myanmar (The 1947 Constitution I, pp. 18–19). The Government of India Act of 1919 that eventually put into effect in Myanmar in 1923 the dyarchy system of government was introduced. The Shan states, the Chin Hills and Kachin Hills Regions were, however, excluded from the sphere of the dyarchical system of government (Harvey pp. 82–83). The reason as given by Craddock[3] in his speech was:

> Herein the Shan States conditions are quite different. The leading Chiefs have urged upon me that the Shan States should not be subjected to the jurisdiction of a legislative body which will be mainly elected by Burmese (Bamar) electorates living in Burma proper. It is impossible to fit these States into a scheme for Burma proper. The people belong to a different race and live under a different system. Such communications with the people of your States have not yet advanced sufficiently in education or in material welfare to take part in a scheme such as that devised for Burma proper (Craddock 1920).

So much so that a scheme of administration for the Shan states based upon a study of the Federated Malay states was devised. With effect from 1 October 1922, the Shan states, grouped into the Northern and the Southern Shan states, was notified as a Federation (S.S. Manual 1933, p. 111). The newly formed Federated Shan States was declared to be a "backward tract". In December 1922 a new civil service named Burma Frontier Service was created for the administration of the Shan state, the Kachin Hills and the Chin Hills. This was criticized as to further set off the "backward tracts" from the rest of Myanmar (The 1947 Constitution I, pp. 19–21). The British Government, however, observed that the feudal system of administration was well suited to the Shan states and perceived that in it lay the only hope for the betterment of the Shan states (Nichols, H.L. 1931). Robert Taylor, however, argues that the creation of Shan states Federation was to protect the *sawbwas* from the effects of a more democratic government and of Burmese nationalism (Taylor 1987, pp. 96–97).

The main features of the federation was that the chiefs of all the states in the Northern and Southern Shan states, were constituted in the federation with an advisory council to discuss matters of general interest to the states. A commissioner was appointed as the local representative of the government of Burma. The proposed Federated Shan states came into effect on 1 October 1922 comprising the six states in Northern Shan states and thirty-four states in Southern Shan states under the charge of the governor (No. F-20A-11 Public, 15 August 1922). Throughout the period of British administration, the administrative reforms in Burma proper were never extended to the Shan states. When the dyarchy system introduced to Burma proper was replaced by a complete cabinet by the 1935 Government of India Act, the excluded areas comprising of the Shan states, Kayah, the Thanlwin District and the remaining hill areas were formed in excluded areas and set aside from Ministerial Burma and remained under separate forms of administration (Tinker 1957, pp. 4–5). During World War II, the Japanese Occupation forces also followed the British system of "divide and rule" by excluding the Shan state administration from Burma proper and allowed the Shan chiefs to administer their states according to their feudal tradition (The 1947 Constitution I, p. 40).

After the war the British re-entered Myanmar armed with the White Paper System providing self-government to Burma proper excluding the Scheduled Areas comprising the Shan states, the Chin, Naga and Kachin Hills regions. A special administration was applied to those areas by organizing the Frontier Administration Department to impose indirect rule over them through the respective chiefs and elders (The 1947 Constitution I, pp. 54-55). As noted, the constitutional advances in Myanmar had always been accompanied by the exclusion of the Shan state and the Hill Areas. The policy of the British Government on Shan states and Hill Regions had greatly affected the Shan chiefs into an obsession that the Shan state was not part of Myanmar. The Union government when it was formed in early 1948, inherited all those issues leading the country into civil war.

In the post-World War II years when Burma proper strove for complete independence, the Shan *sawbwas* also made efforts for future Shan states. Subsequently two successive conferences were held in March 1946 and February 1947 at Panglong. At the second Panglong conference, the Shan *sawbwas* finally agreed to join Burma proper in attaining independence on condition envisaged in the statement of the Executive Committee of the Shan States Sawbwa's Council on 14 November 1946. Paragraph 2 of the statement said:

> *Saohpas* (*Sawbwas*) of Shan States are willing to negotiate on question of federation with Burma on understanding and basis of full autonomy for Shan States and this condition to be duly provided for and guaranteed in future constitution for Burma whether as a Dominion in British Commonwealth of Nations or a complete Sovereign International State with right to secede from federation if so desired (The 1947 Constitution, p. 139)

Aung San, Chairman of the Anti-Fascist People's Freedom League (AFPFL), told Bottomley, the head of the British delegation that AFPFL was ready to grant internal autonomy to the Frontier Areas and the right of secession (The 1947 Constitution I, p. 190). The consent of the AFPFL had influenced the Shan *sawbwas* and the Kachin leaders. On Feburary 1947 an agreement was reached between them towards the early unification of the Frontier Areas and Ministerial Burma and to associate themselves with Burma proper for the attainment of independence and to participate in a "Confederation" on the basis of equality in status, rights and privileges and the right of secession (The 1947 Constittution I, pp. 192–93). Having acquired the consensus of the Shan and Kachin leaders, the draft constitution was approved by the 1947 convention of the AFPFL. The draft constitution provided that:

1. Burma should be Proclaimed as an Independent Sovereign Republic
2. The said Independent Sovereign Republic of Burma should be known as the Union of Burma (Maung Maung 1959, p. 231)

The Shan state thus became a constituent state in the Union of Burma. Chapter 1, paragraph 5 of the Constitution of the Union of Burma states:

> The territories that were heretofore known as the Federated Shan States and the Wa States shall form a constituent unit of the Union of Burma and be hereafter known as "The Shan State". (Maung Maung 1959, p. 258)

Insurgencies in the Shan State (1948–)

Following independence, the KNDO insurrection spread into the Shan state. Together with the KNDOs, the Kuomingtang troops from Yunnan also intruded into the Shan state after they were driven out by the People's Liberation Army of communist China. During the KNDO occupation of some areas in Shan state, the Pa-O people also took up arms against the Shan state government reportedly for democratic reform in the Shan state. They demanded the abolishment of *sawbwas* administration and the Shan State Council (The 1947 Constitution I, pp. 252–53; also *The Nation*, 29 August 1958*)*. In fact the Pa-O revolt was not against the central government but against the Shan rulers (*The Nation*, 20 August 1955) They surrendered to army authorities in 1958 (Tatmadaw Thamaing IV, pp. 36–37). Another issue with the Shan state government was the question of surrendering of hereditary rights of the Shan *sawbwas*. At the attainment of independence in 1948, the *sawbwas* planned to relinquish their hereditary rights but postponed it owing to the outbreak of insurgencies coupled with the intrusion of the KMT in the Shan state. The insurrections also paved the way for the army to station its troops in the Shan state leading to the military administration of Shan state from 1952 to 1954 (ASMI, 1955).

By 1953, the central government began to take a hand in the complex situation of the Shan state and suggested that the Shan chiefs surrender their feudal powers pointing to the popular unrest as a symptom of the necessity for change, and to the Union Constitution which was clearly framed for a socialist democracy (*The Nation*, 20 August 1955). The issue of the Pa-O insurgency and the KMT intrusion caused the Shan *sawbwas* to reconsider their position for the future of Shan state and their positions as hereditary chiefs as well. Two conferences of the *sawbwas* were held in Mongyai in 1954 and in 1957. The conference on 20 April 1957 resolved that the situation in the Shan state was not favourable yet for the *sawbwas* to relinquish their hereditary rights (Tatmadaw Thamaing V, pp. 62–63*)*. The decision of the *sawbwas* to reschedule the surrendering of their hereditary rights grew into a purely political situation in Myanmar with the central government aiming to establish socialist democracy, a highly centralized form of government in the entire country.

In the meantime the split in the AFPFL, the leading political party of Myanmar, resulted in the handing over of power to General Ne Win. Consequently, a caretaker government was formed in 1958 (Maung Maung 1959, p. 217). During its tenure in office the caretaker government had accomplished the following achievements:

On 29 April 1959, 25 Shan and Kayah *sawbwas* surrendered their power; on 28 January 1960 the Myanmar-China boundary agreement was signed (Tatmadaw Tamaing IV, p. 257) and military offensives were also taken against the ethnic insurgents and the KMT remnants (Tatmadaw Thamaing IV, p. 252).

The Federal Issue

When an election was held by the caretaker government in February 1960 the Stable AFPFL Party was defeated by AFPFL Union Party led by U Nu. (*The Nation*, 8 February 1960). During its tenure in office, a significant work done by the Union Party government was the promulgation of Buddhism as the state religion on 26 August 1961 (Tatmadaw Thamaing IV, pp. 260–61). The Christian and Muslim communities resented the promulgation of Buddhism as state religion. This was followed by the demand for the amendment of the state constitution led by Shan leaders.[4] It is said the proposal for constitutional amendment for a federal form of government was motivated by a desire to see a really strong and stable government of the Union of Burma (*The Nation*, 15 June 1961). The achievement of the caretaker government in making the *sawbwas* surrender their hereditary rights and the promulgation of Buddhism as state religion by the Union Party were the immediate causes of the insurrections against the government by the Shan and Kachin. Since the drafting of the constitution in 1947, there were differences in outlook between the leaders of the AFPFL and the ethnic races. Whereas the former looked to forming the Union state with a unitary system, the latter understood the constitution as being federal.

The form of the government of Myanmar as provided in the constitution is termed the Union of Burma without signifying a federal or a unitary system. The word "Union" in Myanmar language is *pyidawnsu*, that could mean both federal or unitary system. Chief Justice E. Maung relates that though it is conceived that unitary is the best system for the then Myanmar situation, a federal form of government was provided in the constitution. Chief Justice Chan Htoon in his speech at the session of parliament also said that since the situation between the Western democratic countries and Myanmar were different, the Western system of government could not be a model for the form of government in Myanmar. In the Myanmar system, he said the Shan, the Kachin and the Kayah states were provided autonomous status with governmental and legislative power whereas Myanmar proper and the remaining areas were kept under the administration of the central government (The 1947 Constitution II, pp. 515–23).

The 1947 Constitution was received as the root cause of problems that Myanmar encountered in the past fifty years and still remains a major issue to be solved. Referring to the defects in the constitution, the leaders of the hill peoples said that the Union Constitution is not a genuine federal system. In the set up of the Union, they said though the minorities are constituted as constituent states, Myanmar proper was incorporated within the central government and enjoyed the monopoly of Union power whereas the status of the remaining states are lowered to that of tributary states to Myanmar (Myanma Nainggnan Ye III, p. 376) Regarding the controversial issue of constitution Chan Htoon notes:

> "Burma's (Myanmar) Constitution, though in theory federal, is in practice unitary" (*The Guardian*, 11 March 1961).

The aim of the leaders of the hills people to amend the constitution was by no means to disintegrate the Union of Myanmar, said Sao Hkun Hkio, the then head of the Shan state. He was reported to have told U Nu that the proposal for a federation, made by all the political parties in the Shan state, was inspired by the laudable motive of making the Union of Burma stable for all time (*The Nation*, 2 July 1961). Nonetheless, giving the example of the United States of America, U Nu, the premier of the Union government, warned the Shan leaders that in the early history of the United States a long and bloody war was fought among its states on the issue of secession (Maung Maung 1959, p. 194). The Shan leaders, however, relying on chapter XI of the constitution,[5] expected to submit the constitutional amendment proposal to the Union Parliament in due course.

Such was the background history of the Myanmar Constitution that when it came to a call for amendment, the army promptly seized power on 2 March 1962.

The statement issued by the Army Chief of Staff, General Ne Win, announced that the army had taken over the government in order to save the Union from a difficult situation in which it had found itself (*The Nation*, 3 March 1962). Inviting the politicians to Dagon House in Yangon on 4 March 1962, he explained that the country was beset with numerous problems, but the gravest of them all was the problem of federalism whereby the Union itself was threatened with disintegration. In such circumstances, he said: "… we had no alternative but to take the drastic step we took in order to avert the impending danger…." General Ne Win also stressed the importance of drawing up of a new constitution, blaming the existing constitution as imperfect and full of loopholes (*The Nation*, 5 March 1962). He said a new state based on socialist democracy, socialist economy and a new administrative machinery setup would be built to replace the existing bureaucratic one (*The Nation*, 9 May 1962). Most of the Myanmar leaders regarded a federation simply as a means of disintegration and subsequent devastation of the country.

Ten years after acquiring independence, ethnic groups challenged the government with various armed insurrections. The factors responsible for them include the spilt in the ruling AFPFL political party,[6] and the surrendering of the hereditary rights of the Shan chiefs called *sawbwas*.[7] Another major factor was the promulgation of Buddhism as state religion in 1961.[8] This was followed by the demand for amendment of the state constitution by the leaders of the constituent states led by the former Shan chiefs and Shan state government.[9] This so-called federal issue became the cause for the army to seize power in 1962 on the pretext of safeguarding the Union of Burma. The military government named the Revolutionary Council of Burma also arrested all the thirty-three former Shan chiefs and prominent figures in the Shan state. The dissatisfaction of the ethnic minorities with the central government, the Shan and Kachin in particular, centred on the action taken on federal issue and the promulgation of Buddhism as state religion.

The Shan armed resistance movement began in 1958 and developed into the Shan State Army in 1965 with its headquarters in Northern Shan state (Tatmadaw Thamaing VII, pp. 98–99). It was the first Shan armed insurrection against the government in the modern history of Myanmar. It was also the period of the outbreak of insurgencies by various ethnic groups like the Kachins, the Mons, the Shans, the Rakhine, the Karen, the Kayah, etc. Taking advantage of the outbreak of the armed insurrections by the various ethnic groups, the Burma Communist Party, with its headquarters on the Myanmar-China border supported by the Chinese Communist Party, adopted the military strategy aimed at organizing the ethnic insurgent groups in order to raise the manpower strength of the BCP and to penetrate into Myanmar heartland.

Gaining support of some of the insurgent groups, the BCP extended its area of influence into the Northern Shan state. By 1969 Kokang, Wa and Kachin sub-states came under the administration of the Burma Communist Party. Kokang, Wa, Kachin and Shan were also recruited in the armed wing of the BCP. Most of the areas in the Northern Shan state were thus overrun by the armed insurgent groups like Shan State Army, Kachin Independence Army, and the Burma Communist Party (Tatmadaw Thamaing VII, pp. 170–77).

Together with the resurgence of insurgencies, Kokang and Wa began to take an important role in post-independence Myanmar politics. Thus in studying the modern political history of Myanmar, careful attention should be paid to the history of the Kokang and the Wa states about which very little is known to the outside world.

The Kokang State

Kokang is a Shan name meaning nine gates. It is situated on the strategic area of Myanmar-China border and is inhabited mostly by ethnic Chinese. Taking the name of the place, the Chinese inhabitants called themselves Kokangese though by race they are Yunnanese. With the area of roughly 800 square miles (210,000 hectares) and with a self reliant economy based on opium cultivation, Kokang was kept under its own administration since the British administration period. It was raised to a *sawbwaship* state in 1951 when the KMT intruded into the area. Being a wholly Chinese State in the Shan state and with a sound economy based on opium, the leaders of Kokang always strove for self administration and non-interference in their internal affairs. The 800-strong Kokang levy force was formed during the Japanese Occupation of Burma during World War II. After the war it was disbanded but was re-organized in early 1950 when the KMT came into the Shan state, resulting in the growth of the opium market and the Kokang levy force. The centralization of administration in 1962 following the military coup in Burma affected the self administration status of Kokang. The leaders of Kokang who were dissatisfied with the new administrative set-up prepared for armed resistance against the military government. Some prominent figures joined the resistance forces and went underground. One of the ruling families of Kokang, Yang Kyin Sein *alias* Jimmy Yang together with some Kokang levies joined the National Liberation Front (Tatmadaw Thamaing VI, pp. 66–73).

The leftover levy force in Kokang under Lo Hsin Han with some 1,400 men was reformed into *Kakweye*[10] and kept under the supervision of the area commander of the Myanmar Army. The *Kakweye* in Northern Shan state was formed to counter act the Shan insurgents and the growing influence of the BCP. Thus, in the 1960s, Kokang armed groups were divided into three factions: The first group under the BCP; the second group under Jimmy Yang which aligned itself with the Democracy Party of Burma; and the third group under Lo Hsing Han with 1,400 men which was organized into People's Volunteer Force or *Kakweye*. In the Northeast Military Region of Kokang, Wa and Kachin sub-state, there were altogether twenty-three groups of *Kakweye* formed with 4,211 men (Tatmadaw Kanna III, pp. 109–10).While some locals like Kachins, Shans, and Kokang were enlisted in the *Kakweye* groups and fought alongside with the government troops, some locals joined the BCP (Tatmadaw Kanna III, pp. 97–99). Since 1971, the Shan State Northeast Special District developed into a fighting zone between the BCP and government troops. Ironically, the Kokang and Wa *Kakweye* formed for the defence of their areas, were reported to have engaged in large scale opium trafficking and had established connection with the KMT remnants and Taiwanese intelligence. When the *Kakweye* in the Northern Shan state were disbanded in 1973, some groups failed to respond to the government order and surrender their arms. They became insurgents instead (Tatmadaw Kanna III, p. 111).

In the meantime the Shan state army in Northern Shan state approached the BCP for help. Military training and arms support was given to the SSA. The alliance of the SSA troops in Northern Shan state with the BCP resulted in the division of SSA into two groups — the northern and southern groups. The southern SSA group did not agree an alliance with the BCP (Tatmadaw Thamaing VII, pp. 200–01).

The BCP, having organized the Shan, Kachin, Kokang and Wa, drew up a five-year plan aimed at gaining control of the Cis-Salween area, to re-organize the local insurgent groups, to expand the activities to Shan and Kayah states and then to penetrate into Bago Yoma in Central Myanmar. The eighteen members of the Central Committee of BCP in China were also reformed and BCP troops were sent to the inner Northern and Southern Shan state (Tatmadaw Thamaing VI, pp. 2–4). Nevertheless their efforts at penetration into Central Myanmar failed after their defeat in fighting with government troops in the frontier area.

Following this defeat, the support for the Chinese Communist Party was greatly reduced. This caused the disagreement and cracks in BCP leadership and also among the local insurgent groups that aligned themselves with the BCP (Tatmadaw Thamaing VII, pp. 19–20).

Among the Kokang resistance leaders, one Hpon Kya Shin who joined the BCP in 1963 became a member of the BCP Central Military Commission. He quit the Central Committee as well as the Central Military Commission in 1984 because he felt that the BCP was controlled by Bamar members and the ethnic groups had no voice in it. The BCP Central Committee also disagreed with him because of his thriving opium business. He retired himself at Mong Yang in the eastern Shan state district. While residing at Mong Yang, the government contacted him in 1987 through agents[11] for peace talks. He quit the BCP in 1989 and formed the "Myanmar Nationalities Democracy Alliance" group. The manifesto of the Kokang Democracy Alliance states:

1. Equal rights and self determination for all nationalities
2. To establish trade centres in Mongko and Kokang
3. To observe ceasefire but to retaliate only when the government troops start fighting
4. Despite a dislike for communism, the political situation compelled the Kokang to make an alliance with the BCP. Kokang seceded from BCP because Myanmar is making headway in democracy
5. Kokang will not demand secession

Peace agreement with the government was obtained but Kokang still kept its 893rd, the 983rd and the 894th armed brigades at Cis-Salween and Trans-Salween areas (Tatmadaw Thamaing VII. pp. 42–43).

Kokang remains a major issue in Shan state politics since the attainment of Myanmar independence in 1948 because of its entire population being Chinese with a sound economy of opium cultivation and its location being situated on the Myanmar-China frontier. In addition to this, the small Kokang levy force formed during World War II grew into divisional armed strength and was posted to areas outside Kokang. Following Kokang, another issue confronting the government was the Wa state, also located on the Myanmar-China border.

The Wa State

The region inhabited by the Wa is named Wa state. Both Wa and Kokang states lie on the Myanmar-China border. Wa state, theoretically was ruled by a *sawbwa* recognized by the government since the British administration period in the Shan state. The *sawbwa* of Manglun was the only legitimate *sawbwa* of the Wa state. In 1891, the British Government absorbed West Manglun in the list of the Northern Shan state, putting the recognized area of the Wa into Shan state (Foreign Department Notification No. 14, 26 November 1891. Govt. Of Burma)

Except for Manglun, other Wa areas were regarded as untamed and the British Government had never tried to administer the area. This judgement was because of the wild nature of its inhabitants and the terrain. The British Government had not allowed its officials and troops to cross the River Thanlwin into the inner wild Wa area which became an unadministered area. (Hendershot 1952, p. 262).

Thus throughout the British administration period of the Shan state (1886–1948), except for Manglun, the Wa state was kept as no-man's land. The Shan state government had inherited the neglected land of the Wa which came under its administration (1948–62).

The whole Wa state with an area of some 5000 square miles (1.3 million hectares) had a population of 250,000 in 1959. The report of the Shan state government in 1950 notes:

> In practice Wa state was divided into many statelets each ruled over by its chief. These statelets were also divided into many circles and the circles were again divided into many villages. The real rulers of the Wa state were the chiefs of the circles and villages and these chiefs would never take any outside influence. The Wa chiefs like their subjects, the villagers were all illiterates and none of them could run the administration properly. The Was were distinguished between "tamed" and "untamed" Wa. The tamed Wa are Buddhist but retained their animistic beliefs and practices. For a Wa the village in which he lives in is his world. Everyone outside of his village is a stranger and strangers are never allowed into their village.

Scott[12] states that the Was were not enterprising nor an ambitious race. They did not trade but on every five-day bazaar, the Was would bring their opium weighing 16.3 to 8.33 kilogram. to sell and with the money obtained from the sale they bought rice and salt. Another official report of the Shan state government also notes:

> The Was were backward, superstitious having no mind for any change. All they desired is to have a good crop. The two most important items in the livelihood of the Was were rice and salt. They would be well contended (*sic*) if they had enough rice and salt. (Sai 2004)

The condition of life and the situation of the Wa state as mentioned remained until the 1960s. The development of the political situation in Burma like the AFPFL split, the surrendering of the hereditary rights of the Shan *sawbwas*, promulgation of Buddhism as state religion, and the military coup in 1962, had not bothered them at all. The intrusion of the KMT and the encroachment of communist Chinese troops into the Wa state in the 1950s, however, changed the Wa people. The backward, superstitious and illiterate Was were drawn into twentieth century politics and introduced to modern warfare and weapons. Some of the Was became KMT followers while some became pro-communist. After the withdrawal of the communist Chinese troops in 1954, the exiled BCP in China came into the Wa state and established their headquarters there. Since then, Wa state, one of the most backward areas in the world, became a fighting zone between the BCP and the government troops. Most enlisted men in the BCP were Was. The BCP as a matter of fact had dragged the Was, who never wanted any change, into the complicated political theatre of Myanmar. It is doubtful that the illiterate Was without any knowledge of the outside world and who never allowed strangers into their village, are united to demand for political change and the development of the Wa state.

The Wa group in April 1989 also declared secession from the BCP and formed the Myanmar Solidarity Party.

The manifesto of the party states:

1. Alliance with Kokang for defence if attacked by outside forces
2. Shared information between the two parties if approached by outside organization to strive for democracy or independence
3. To form a steering committee for Kokang and Wa
4   Economic cooperation and free trade between Kokang and Wa
5. Cooperation in administration and management for Kokang and Wa. In the meantime to work independently from each other (Tatmadaw Thamaing VII, pp. 42–43).

Ethnic Issues under Military Rule (1988–)

Ethnic dissension which had taken root since the British administration period led the country to the brink of disintegration on three occasions in 1949, 1958, and 1962. Scholars of Myanmar modern history in their bid to rewrite Myanmar political history argue that the British Government consistently followed a divide-and-rule policy between Myanmar proper, the Shan states and the hill regions resulting in dissension, distrust and the creation of suspicion among the indigenous races of Myanmar. It also brought many unwanted problems at a time when Myanmar needed to build national solidarity among its people. Besides it also created many problems in the drafting of a new constitution for Myanmar during the post-independence period (The 1947 Constitution I, pp. 19–21).

The year 1990 could be termed as the beginning of the establishment of peace and development era in Myanmar. By the efforts of the SLORC (State Law and Order Restoration Council), ceasefire agreements were reached with the seventeen insurgent groups that had fought the government for almost fifty years.

Having gained peace agreements with the insurgent groups the government attempted to solve the age-old unsettled political issues left behind by the British and the parliamentary government of Myanmar.

In order to amicably solve the issues and to sustain national unity, the SLORC on 2 October 1992 formed the Commission for National Convention to draft the fundamental principle of constitution underscoring six major points:

a. Solidarity of the Union of Myanmar
b. Solidarity of the national unity
c. Perpetuation of national sovereignty
d. Development of parliamentary democracy
e. Development of justice, freedom and equality in the political arena
f. The participation of *Tatmadaw* in the future state's national politics

Aimed at achieving the above points, the National Convention for Myanmar's new constitution was held in August 1993 (Commission for National Convention. Proposals: 9 August 1993 to 14 August 1993).

The guidelines for drafting the new constitution were also laid down as follows.

Nation of the State

The first part of the constitution envisaged:

−   Myanmar as an independent sovereign state
−   The said independent sovereign state shall be proclaimed Union of Myanmar
−   Sovereignty comes from the citizens of Myanmar and is affirmed throughout the country

–   The territorial limits of Myanmar is fixed on the day of the promulgation
    of the constitution

The Form of Government

–   Union system
–   Myanmar will be formed with self administered regions, states, and
    self-administered areas without the right of secession.

The existing seven divisions will be made into seven regions by raising
their status to that of the state. The seven states will remain as they were.
Equal rights and privileges for the seven divisions and seven states.

    The self-administered division would be formed with the right to
exercise legislative, judicial and administrative powers. Their status is,
however, not to be equal to that of the status of the region but higher than
the status of district or township.

–   The status of the self-administered zones is lower than the status of
    division and equal to that of district (Speech delivered by U Aung Toe,
    1 January 1994, Reports of National Convention 23 March 1993 to 31
    March 1994, pp. 6–13).

    Given the right to demand for self-administration, the ethnic groups
with a population of over 50,000 in the Shan state each seek Self-
Administered Areas. The Danu, claimed to comprise 220,000-population
spread in six townships in Southern Shan state and one in the township in
Northern Shan state, wanted the Danu-inhabited areas of seven townships
be fixed as Danu Self-Administered Division (National Convention:
Proposals 23 March 1993 to 31 April 1994, pp. 63–69).

    The Inntha population count in Nawngshwe and around Innle lake are
said to number over 100,000. They claimed the area around Innle lake to
be fixed as "Inntha Self-Administered Zone" and to keep the area under
the direct administration of central government (National Convention,
23 March 1993 to 31 April 1994).

    The Pa-O people with some 600,000 population in the Shan state are
spread in fifteen townships in Southern Shan states and claimed all the
fifteen townships as Pa-O Self-Administered Division (National
Convention, 23 March 1993 to 31 April 1994).

    The Ah Kha in ten townships in Eastern Shan state District claimed to
have over 100,000 people, also requested for Ah Kha Self-Administered

Zone comprising the ten townships (National Convention, 23 March 1993 to 31 April 1994).

The population count of Kokang by the Manpower and Immigration Department of Myanmar stated some 70,000 people but the Kokang delegates to the Convention claimed over 700,000. They said that unlike the other states and regions in Myanmar, the people with the same language and culture are grouped together in Kokang state. They also claimed that Kokang, being situated on the Myanmar-China border with different traditions and customs should manage their own affairs (National Convention, 23 March 1994).

The 1947 Constitution section 5 on Wa state envisaged that

> the territories that were heretofore known as the Federated Shan States and Wa State shall form a constituent unit of the Union of Burma and be hereafter known as the Shan State.

The Wa state which had been left as an un-administered area by the British Government during their administration in Myanmar also sent their representatives to the National Convention. They argued that in order to maintain economic and social development of the Wa region, they required

1. The right of self determination and
2. Government help for development and social consciousness of the Wa

They claimed the seventeen townships in the Shan state to be absorbed in Wa Self-Administered Division (Reports submitted to the National Convention for Constitution, 23 March 1993 to 31 March 1994, pp. 98–103).

The Kachin also have their self-administered state called Kachin sub-state of Northern Shan state created by the British Government. After the ceasefire agreement with the government, the former Kachin sub-state was fixed as No. 5 region. The name Kachin Independence Army (KIA), was also changed to (KDA). The Kachin delegates to the convention opted for self-administration in former Kachin sub-state in Northern Shan state and argued to keep it under the Shan state administration (Reports submitted to the National Convention for Constitution, 23 March 1993 to 31 March 1994, pp. 104–05).

Such were the situations and diverse views of the ethnic races in Myanmar. Embracing the complicated political and racial issues the National Convention for drafting the Constitution for Myanmar that began on 2 October 1992 has not yet drawn to a close. Hoping to wipe out all the suspicion, dissension and divisive views of the people and to achieve lasting peace, tranquility and fraternity among Myanmar citizens, the SLORC and later State Peace and Development Council (SPDC) gives the right to demand for self-administered areas to all ethnic races. As the Danu delegate put it, "a little bird also wants a little nest", almost all of the ethnic races laid claim to self-administration.

With Myanmar bordering Bangladesh and Pakistan on the west, India on the west and northwest, People's Republic of China on the east and northeast, Laos on the east, Thailand on the southeast and east, political stability is vital to the establishment of peace and development. Given the past and the present experience with seventeen of the armed ceasefire groups in the country, and the claims of the various ethnic races in the National Convention, it is imperative that a centralized strong government is necessary to uphold peace and unity of Myanmar at least for some years until all outstanding issues have been overcome and solved.

Notes

1. Early in 1886 a notification was issued under the Statute XXXIII Vic. Cap. 3, constituting Upper Burma, except the Shan states as a scheduled district. At the same time the whole of Upper Burma, including the Shan states, was declared to be part of British India. By section 8 of the Upper Burma Laws Act, 1886, the local government is empowered, with the sanction of the Governor-General in Council, to define the Shan states from time to time, and by the same section the Shan states are excluded from the operation of any Act not specially extended to them by the local government with the sanction of the Governor-General in Council (GUBSS Ii:313).
2. The majority of the population in this area is Danu, Pa-O and Palaung ethnic races.
3. Craddock, speech delivered by His Honour the Lieutenant Governor at the Durbar held at Taunggyi, Southern Shan states, on 20 March 1920.
4. Incredibly it was the leaders of Yapala who had advocated joining with Ministerial Burma and who had opposed the rule of *sawbwas* throughout the period from post-World War II to a decade of post- independence years. Finally they came to take a leading role with the Shan *sawbwas* in demanding for the amendment of the Constitution.
5. See Maung Maung, Burma's Constitution, p. 295.
6. The AFPFL (Anti-Fascist People's Freedom League) formed during World War II for an independence movement became the ruling party at the attainment of Burma's independence in 1948 (Myanma Naing Ngan Yei 1958–62,

I" 175). In 1958, U Ba Swe and U Kyaw Nyein quit the government and the AFPFL also spilt into two factions, *viz*. Clean AFPFL led by U Nu and U Tin and Stable AFPFL led by U Ba Swe and U Kyaw Nyein (Myanma Naingngan Yei III, 1958–62, p. 90).

7. The thirty-three Shan *sawbwas* surrendered their hereditary rights to the government in 1959 after receiving commuted pensions.

8. Myanmar independence movement under the British was religion — Buddhism played a significant role. In the early years of the movement an association like the YMBA (Young Men's Buddhist Association) was formed primarily to inspire the people towards independence. This was taken into account when the Myanmar Constitution was drafted in 1947. After the 6th Buddhist Synod in 1954, the *sangha* (Buddhist clerics) intensified their demand for the promulgation of Buddhism as the state religion. This issue was accommodated by U Nu's government in 1961. The Third Amendment of the state constitution states: "The majority of the Myanmar people being Buddhists, Buddhism must be a State Religion" (Myanma Naingngan Yei III, 1958–62, pp. 116–17).

9. The proposal for amendment of the state constitution was approved at the meeting of the Parliament on 10 November 1960. The Shan state government formed a committee named "Steering Committee (Shan state) for the Amendment of State Constitution of Myanmar". The Shan Committee drafted a paper entitled "A Paper Submitted by the Shan State for the Amendment of the Constitution Of Myanmar". The main theme of the paper was to transform Myanmar into a federal state (Myanma Ngaingngan Yei III, 1958–62, pp. 5–10).

10. The policy to form Kakweye (People's Defence Forces) was laid down at the Conference of the Commanding Officers (CO) of the Myanmar army held in 1964. There was the consensus that the question of defence should not be concerned with only the Tatmadaw (Myanmar Army) but also the people of the country. The defence forces were thus formed in the insurgents infested areas to help the army whenever military operations were launched against the insurgents. By 1968, defence forces numbering 67,736 men were formed in 212 townships and 1,831 villages (Tatmadaw Kanna III, p. 83).

11. Lo Hsin Han, a prominent figure of Kokang arrested by the Thai authorities in the 1960s, was handed over to the Myanmar Government. He was the leader of the Peace Mission. He was also a known opium warlord. He is reported to have said that for being a native of Kokang he would strive for peace, development and eradication of opium cultivation in Kokang (Tatmadaw Thamaing, VII, p. 180).

12. During my visit to the last *sawbwa* of Manglun at his residence in 1978 he told me that Sir George Scott while on his tour in the Wa state was killed by a bush fire set by the Wa.

References

A Supplement Proposal of the Pa-O Representatives. National Convention, 23 March 1993 to 31 April 1994. First Printing. Yangon: Baho Press.

ASMI, *"Spotlight on the Shan State"*. *The Guardian Magazine*, April 1955.

"Chief of Staff Announced Take-Over of the Union". *The Nation*, 3 March 1962.

Harvey, G.E. *British Rule in Burma (1824–1942)*. London: Faber and Faber.

Hendershot, Clarence. "The Conquest, Pacification, and Administration of the Shan States by the British 1896–1897". Unpublished manuscript, 1952.

Maung Maung. *Burma's Constitution*. The Hague: Martinus Nijhoff, 1959.

Memorandum of the Federated Shan States by their Representatives. The Sawbwa of Mongmit and the Sawbwa of Yawnghwe State. London, December, 1930. Rangoon: Superintendent, Government Printing and Stationary, 1931

Myanma Nainggnan Yei III [Politics in Myanmar]. Yangon: University Press, 1991.

"New Constitution Suggested Instead of Patchwork Amendment". *The Guardian*, 11 March 1961.

Nichols, H.L. ESQ., I.C.S., No. 142 B 31. *Shan Chiefs — Status of Government of Burma*, Political Department, 21 September 1931.

No. F-20A-11 Public, from the Secretary to the Government of India, Home Department, 15 August 1922.

Notification No. 14. Foreign Department.,Commission for National Convention. Proposals: 9 August 1993 to 14 August 1993, 26 November 1891.

"NUF Presidium Issues Gist of Talks With Gen. Ne Win", *The Nation*, 9 May 1962.

On Myint, "Will there be a Shan State in 1957?". *The Nation*, 20 August 1955.

Proposals submitted by Danu representatives. National Convention: Proposals, 23 March 1993 to 31 April 1994. First Printing. Yangon: Baho Press.

Proposal submitted by Inntha delegates. National Convention, 23 March 1993 to 31 April 1994. First Printing. Yangon: Baho Press.

Proposal for Akha Self Administered Zone. National Convention, 23 March 1993 to 31 April 1994. First Printing. Yangon: Baho Press.

Proposal submitted by the Kokang delegates from Northern Shan state. National Convention, 23 March 1993 to 31 March 1994. First Printing. Yangon: Baho Press.

Proposal submitted by the delegates of Wa in Northern Shan State. Reports submitted to the National Convention for Constitution, 23 March 1993 to 31 March 1994. First Printing. Yangon: Baho Press.

Proposal submitted by the Kachin delegates of Northern Shan state.

Reports submitted to the National Convention for Constitution, 23 March 1993 to 31 March 1994. First Printing. Yangon: Baho Press.

Reports of National Convention 23 March 1993 to 31 March 1994. First Printing. Yangon: Baho Press.

Scott, J.G. and Hardiman. *Gazetter of Uper Burma and the Shan States I.* Rangoon: Superintendent Govt. Printing, 1900.

Shan States Manual (SSM Corrected up to 31 January 1932). Rangoon: Superintendant, Govt. Printing and Stationary, 1933.

"Shan State Proposal Evolutionary Process. Dr E Mg Gave Green Light; U Nu Accepted Bona Fides of Taunggyi Conference"? *The Nation,* 2 July 1961.

"S.U.O. A Mere Political Front, Delegate Says". *The Nation,* 15 June 1961.

Tatmadaw Thamaing IV, 1948–62 [History of Myanmar Armed Forces]. First edition. Yangon: News and Periodcals, 1996.

Tatmadaw Thamaing V, 1962–74 [History of Myanmar Armed Forces]. Second edition. Yangon: News and Periodicals, 1999.

Tatmadaw Thamaing VI [History of Myanmar Armed Forces]. Yangon: News and Periodicals, n.d.

Tatmadaw Thamaing VII [History of Myanmar Armed Forces]. Yangon: News and Periodicals, n.d.

Tatmadaw Kanna III [Role of the Myanmar Armed Forces], n.d., n.p.

Taylor, Robert. *The State in Burma.* Honolulu: University of Hawaii Press, 1987.

The 1947 Constitution and the Nationalities I. Yangon: Universities Historical Research Centre and Innwa Publishing House, 1999.

The 1947 Constitution and the Nationalities II. Yangon: Universities Historical Research Centre and Innwa Publishing House, 1999.

Tinker, Hugh. *The Union of Burma.* London: Oxford University Press, 1957.

U Aung Toe. Speech by Chairman of the Working Committee of National Convention at Yangon, 1 January 1994.

U Ba Swe. "U K. Nyein Defeated in 'Clean' Sweep to Victory". *The Nation,* 8 February 1961.

12

Reality Check on the Sanctions Policy against Myanmar

Khin Zaw Win

Introduction

The political upheaval of 1988 and its aftermath occasioned violent excesses committed by both the military-backed one-party state and its direct-military rule successor, as well as by groups of angry citizens. As a result of actions of the government, while feelings ran high, a retaliatory international response was demanded. The United States, Japan and other donor countries either terminated or cut back their aid programmes, and an arms embargo was imposed.

At the same time foreign governments adopted a wait-and-see attitude with regard to the expected changeover to a democratic political system. General elections were held in May 1990, although without any previous provisions for a transfer of power. The outcome of those elections led to expectations, unrealistic in the end, of a swift end to military government.

Two intertwined issues need to be looked at — the transition to democracy and the international measures deployed to bring about this change. More specifically, the intention is to gauge how skilfully or unskilfully various actors have gone about achieving both outcomes. It should be noted that broad sanctions were not applied until much later, by which time things in the domestic political scene had deteriorated quite badly in terms of a quick handover of power. It is very much the case of a long, slow slide to failure and stalemate.

Against the backdrop of uncertainty, misery and hope that pervades this period, a closer analysis of events, actions and attitudes reveals a number of significant portents that presaged the present breakdown in relations between the military regime and the democratic opposition, particularly the National League for Democracy (NLD). In September 1988 then-president Dr Maung Maung had announced that all state employees were required to resign from the Burma Socialist Programme Party (BSPP), the only legal party at that time. This act meant that not only the carpet but the very floor beneath that party was removed — in fact, sounding the death knell to the organization. Dr Maung Maung also proposed general elections to be held in three months' time. Despite these drastic concessions that would quite probably have opened the door to a democratic system, the newly-emergent democracy movement turned him down flat. What ensued a few days later was the military coup of 18 September.

Following the demise of the authoritarian BSPP edifice, political parties were allowed to register and a veritable deluge of parties resulted. Another significant window of opportunity opened up again, when from January till about April 1989, General Saw Maung, Armed Forces chief and chairman of the ruling military council of that time, made conciliatory overtures to the leadership of the NLD, the major party that had come to enjoy overwhelming popular support. For example, in 1989 he invited Aung San Suu Kyi to work together with him to rebuild the country and its institutions, and again in a television speech, he stated that he had invited her to consult with him on any matter. However his words fell on deaf ears and the possibility and hope of an early rapprochement were extinguished. The NLD instead deliberately embarked on a course of confrontation, civil disobedience and agitation, culminating in the house arrest of its leader Aung San Suu Kyi on 20 July.

In the politically-heady days of 1988–89, it is perhaps understandable that wiser heads did not prevail and wise counsel was passed over, as a result of which a good deal of suffering was visited upon the country. But when an attitude of recalcitrance and intransigence — heedless of consequences — rises to the top time and again in the ensuing years, it becomes as unproductive as it is downright inexcusable. The stage was then set for punitive measures to be imposed upon a least-developed country, home to much travail.

One could say that sanctions have existed as long as states have, and there had been relations between states. They have been a weapon in the arsenal of statecraft, no less so in modern times. With the proliferation of nation-states in the twentieth century and the advent of international bodies like the United Nations, sanctions came to the forefront and have come to be enacted with increasing frequency. The frequency of sanctions after 1990 — coinciding with the end of the Cold War — has been noted by many observers and scholars. And a good deal has been written against both the concept and the tool from the viewpoints of morality and legality, but then this would hardly cause a dent in the hard-nosed world of *realpolitik* and national interests. The voice of moral suasion is more often than not drowned out or over-ridden.

It is unquestionable that sanctions do have their uses and can be regarded as an option of statecraft. But as with all instruments, there has to be a sound rationale as well as judgement and skill in the handling of them. They should not be a "one size fits all" vehicle, or as the Burmese saying goes, used like "thrashing about with a long bamboo pole".

Sanctions are justified if the target country had committed blatant aggression against another country, for example, Imperial Japan *vis-à-vis* China in the 1930s and Iraq with regard to Kuwait in 1990. These sanctions are employed with the rationale that diplomatic action has failed and yet, concerned powers were unwilling or unready to wage war against the aggressor nation. Even when sanctions were actually applied against Iraq, the collateral damage and the undesirable effects on Iraqi civilians had been of a severe enough nature to raise considerable international concern about their proportionality. It was found that, even with the undeniable reality of a brutal dictatorship and aggression on neighbouring Kuwait providing sufficient justification, if the "spillover" effect severely victimizes masses of innocent men, women and children, a backlash emerges, questioning the legality and morality of such measures. If such widespread negative consequences are taken as a yardstick — and Iraq is very much an international issue — the present actions against Myanmar, which has not committed aggression against another state and indeed has no intention of doing so, become even less conscionable.

The primacy of trade, trade-dependent economies, and globalization has made economic sanctions more effective on the one hand, and less so on the other. For important trading nations like China, the facilitation or crimping of trade has immense consequences. The granting of Most Favoured Nation (MFN) status prior to World Trade Organization (WTO) entry is such an example. The earlier status provided access to the immense U.S. market and had other implications as well. Concomitantly, it was implicit that a prolonged tussle over trade would only sour relations and hurt U.S. corporations seeking to enter China. The presence of alternative trading partners also meant that excessive measures would only push China towards other countries. So again, in the more globalized setting, sanctions are indeed a double-edged weapon.

The Consequences of Sanctions against Myanmar

Different types of sanctions have been enacted by various Western countries against Myanmar — comprising an arms embargo as well as financial, trade and travel-related sanctions. As to the arguments about their consequences, the most disingenuous happens to be the one that sanctions are meant to hurt the regime and not the people. No matter what arguments are used, it is undeniable that those advocating sanctions are willing to condone the ensuing hardships upon the people as a "necessary price for democracy".[1] The people have been subjected to all this for a decade or more. The proponents of sanctions have not only accepted this negative outcome, they have hardened themselves to the plight of the people. However, the effects of sanctions go much beyond that:

–   They have effected a pronounced polarization of political life. What used to be a gap has become a chasm.
–   The consequences are askew: To begin with, the near-absence of ODA and concessional loans has hit the social sector (health, education, social welfare etc.) particularly hard. Fuel imports are also affected. Very little FDI has meant that unemployment and under-employment are high. Trade sanctions impacts upon industrial growth, the prices that primary producers get, and on employment, as in the thousands laid off in the garment industry. For having multiplied the people's travails while having little effect upon the regime, both the democratic parties and the governments that have enacted sanctions have lost a great deal of credibility. This is something those actors should pause to consider.
–   They have underwritten and encouraged personalism. This is to be seen as the antithesis of institutionalism, which goes hand-in-hand with modernization and is something that Myanmar needs badly.
–   They have sapped the strength and impaired the future of democratization which will become more prolonged, and the military's (and the public's) regard and trust of political parties has been impaired. Besides the economic effects, the social fabric has frayed also on account of widespread poverty, high employment and lack of basic services coupled with a high disease prevalence, thereby jeopardizing the entire process of eventual democratization. Whatever is achieved in Myanmar's subsequent political development has to take this reality into account. It will

happen without or despite the agency of the West. In this matter of no little import, Western countries are marginalizing themselves.

Even if sanctions do succeed in their stated goals, the notion of a democratic system established and paid for in this way, is not going to go down well with many people. It is like an exorbitant down payment demanded from the country, on uncertain promises of a nebulous rosy future.

Among the many prominent voices that have articulated arguments against sanctions is that of Jeffrey Sachs, who has pointed out that:

> America's misguided sanctions against Myanmar, for example, have done nothing in the past year to resolve the country's political and economic crisis. In the process, they have systematically weakened the economy by limiting trade, investment and foreign aid. Yet weakening a country's economy does not necessarily weaken a regime relative to its political opposition. Often, the impasse is merely deepened. Civil society and the political opposition suffer from brain drain, a squeeze on financial resources and reduced contacts with the outside world, while the regime is able to blame foreign meddling for policy mistakes. Hardliners on both sides, meanwhile, gain the upper hand over moderates, obstructing changes that might otherwise be encouraged.

> For the past 14 years, US foreign policy has remained fixated on the clash between the military regime and the NLD. Yet there has been some internal progress. The government successfully negotiated an end to 17 of the 18 major armed insurrections. It has also skilfully negotiated with thousands of peasants to cut poppy cultivation and shift to alternative crops, cutting narcotics production by about 75 per cent over just a few years. Finally, the government has attempted to address poverty, in part through investments in infrastructure. Yet without access to international aid, these efforts have fuelled inflation and macroeconomic instability. Sanctions have also helped crush an incipient manufacturing export sector resulting in significant job losses.

> It is time for the West to look to Myanmar's next elections, not backward to 1990. Sanctions should be lifted because they do not work. All parties should be encouraged to look for step-by-step change. In Poland's smooth transition from communism, for example, the popular Solidarity movement judiciously agreed to several years of power-sharing with the Communist regime.

> The US and Europe should listen more closely to Myanmar's neighbours, which are keen for Yangon to consolidate the delicate peace processes and create a dynamic of political accommodation under a new

constitution. Lifting sanctions and giving aid to fight poverty and disease would not be a concession to power - but steps towards democracy and prosperity.[2]

The sanctions provided by the European Union's Common Position on Myanmar are more "targetted", but when we look closer at the effects, measures like the visa ban and freezing of assets of top Myanmar officials barely have an impact because those officials rarely travel to Europe in any case, and have little or no assets there. And when it comes to investment and import sanctions, the brunt is felt by the working people. With the multiplier effect, the impact is felt over the entire economy. Export industries like garment manufacturing were particularly hard hit when the United States imposed total trade sanctions in 2003.

Needless to say, the suspension of aid has also had deleterious consequences, most notably in basic social services and social development. A particularly grotesque situation has developed over humanitarian aid, with endless arguments and lobbying against the provision of even the most basic and minimal humanitarian assistance.[3] Witness the withdrawal from Myanmar of the Global Fund for AIDS, Tuberculosis and Malaria in August 2005, stating reasons of restrictions on the delivery and monitoring of aid. There had been pressure from quarters in the United States even before the Global Fund had entered Myanmar, and last August, strong elements in the U.S. Congress threatened to revoke the U.S.' contributions to the ongoing Myanmar programme. It is particularly hard to square all this with protestations of liberalism, benevolence and sympathy for the Myanmar people. With all the talk about human rights, perhaps it is time to call for a human rights audit of policies against Myanmar.

The limitations on the efficacy of sanctions as such should be quite apparent by now; continued sanctions are not going to produce more concessions from the State Peace and Development Council; indeed they have become extremely counter-productive, both for those who advocate them and those who impose them. On all counts sanctions have not succeeded and evidence accumulates as to how completely misguided they are.

Myanmar's many problems are simply not helped by what Western powers have been doing — and this goes a long, long way, much earlier than 1988. Diagnoses and solutions have to come from within. The trouble with most of the developing world is that people look to the West — and are dependent on it — not only for the wherewithal but also for ideas. It amounts to a multi-layered dependency. And Western governments connive in this outsourcing and encourage it. In addition, the United States has very little sense of time-depth. U.S. administrations do what they think is required for the moment, and are oblivious to the consequences thereafter.

Myanmar can be characterized as an unfortunate country. It has had a long run of bad luck, since the outbreak of World War II at least. But this negative development has had more to do with poor leadership choices than with anything innate in society and culture. Of course, the propensity to "run with the herd" and follow prophets and messiahs has to be mentioned, but this inclination is only secondary. The problem is primarily not about weaknesses in political development; rather it is about leadership attitudes. Amongst the failings is the lack of skill in judging just how far a political "weapon" or course of action is to be employed. It is in the recognition of a point beyond which it becomes an act of wanton destructiveness, of callousness, of outright war. Beyond that point it becomes a drive for power riding upon the wave of a country's pain. Eerily enough, there are echoes from an event that took place almost exactly 700 years ago.

In 1285 the armies of the Mongol Empire of Kublai Khan invaded the kingdom of Bagan and routed the Myanmar forces at the decisive battle of Ngasaunggyan. The king fled to the south, the Mongols occupied Bagan and the kingdom fell into decline. A period of lawlessness and disarray set in.

Against this backdrop, a bastion of stability and resistance grew up around the walled town of Myinsaing, ruled by three brothers. It is situated beside the Shan escarpment, at the edge of the Ledwin paddy-growing region, a granary then and now. From this realm the three brothers kept the kingdom from falling apart and going under. Contemporary stone inscriptions speak adoringly of "Athinkhaya, Raza and Theingathu the three rulers who without perturbation administered the country, allaying the fear of the people".[4] By means of effective administration, the area provided the fertile, well-watered land in the vicinity and most importantly, by its being the centre of indigenous resistance to the invader, Myinsaing became the *de facto* capital and the population gravitated towards it.

The king of the Bagan kingdom, Kyawswa, was dethroned in 1298 by the three brothers, who took his ineffectuality and appeasement of the Mongols against him.

When he was executed in 1299, the Mongols supported one of his heirs to take the throne. To back this up, they prepared and sent an expeditionary force in the open season of 1300–01.[5]

They reached central Myanmar in 1301 and laid siege to Myinsaing but the citadel did not fall. At that time the Mongol hordes were the masters of Eurasia and the world's military super power of those times, but they could not bring Myinsaing to its knees. Finally, astute diplomacy plus a hefty "inducement" carried the day. However it did not save the generals from being executed for their failure. In 1303 the Mongols abolished the province they had set up and withdrew entirely from Myanmar. It may be debated whether the Mongol campaign was a success or a failure, but the important thing was that they withdrew without further blood-letting or destruction to the country.

This achievement too is inscribed and recorded in stone. Theingathu who "With determination and wisdom and courage overcame the twelve hundred thousand warriors sent by the Great Khan to destroy the lotus pond of the Faith that had arrived in Tamradip (Bagan)."[6] The account of that siege — and the lifting of it — reverberates in Myanmar to this day. If such attachment exists with something that took place 700 years ago, what of the present siege? One can perhaps imagine that which may unfold in the future. Since independence, the super power — the United States, has interfered in Myanmar affairs a number of times, with disastrous and long-term consequences. In the current episode the United States has lost a great deal of leverage, without gaining even a tiny fraction of its intended results. As Myanmar hunkers down and braces for a long investiture, one sees not only a national response but also a larger global one of which it forms a part, in the building of a world which is not U.S.-centred nor posited upon U.S. dominance. During the Cold War period, Myanmar stayed neutral but tilted towards the West. Not many people may be aware of this, but a long proxy war was fought in Myanmar against the Communist Party of Burma, which was backed by the PRC until 1978, when Deng Xiaoping came to power. Now in the post-Cold War configuration, Myanmar is again thrust to the forefront in the shaping of a new order that refuses to accept the imperiousness, the wilfulness and the destructiveness of an unbridled super power.

Conclusion

A question was posed earlier in the chapter about what it means to be a Burmese or what Myanmarness denotes. All would agree that it includes delighting in the *pwes*, the music-and-dance performances ranging from roadside shows to grand gilt-and-velvet affairs. And then one must have been to Bagan — Tampadipa of hallowed memory. There are quite a few other ways, to be sure, of seeing if the metal rings true, so to speak. If another "tell-tale sign" is to be added, it would be this:

The Eleven Districts of the Ledwin region mentioned above (around present-day Kyaukse, south of Mandalay) have been an important granary for the nation since at least the Bagan period. Wet rice cultivation in the country dates from the eighth century B.C., and Bronze Age finds in the Samon valley in the Ledwin attest to early settlement and culture. One school of history believes that the first Bamar settlements were those districts (but there had been people cultivating rice there much earlier than the Bamars). In a number of ways they are comparable to the early settlements associated with the coming of the Saxons to the south of England. The names of the districts are early Bamar: Myittha, Pinle, Myinkhondaing, Tapyetha, Tamokso and so on. If one recites these names and feels a deep indescribable thrill, it does point to another authentic hallmark.

Myinsaing, the Ledwin, the Irrawaddy and the Shan Yoma ranges — if one is a Burmese and these places and their significance do not resonate in one; if they are not part of one's growing up and one does not value them enough, one has to realize how much the poorer one is. It is hard to conceive of someone who is part of this ardently advocating for its strangulation in the name of a political construct or concept. With all the talk about legitimacy, the legitimacy of this act is called into question. But as Macbeth has said, the deed is done. The siege engines are before the city walls and the populace is in dire straits. This deed is now placed in the balance against the deep, unwritten and timeless conventions that underlie Myanmar life, the Myanmar state and civilization itself.

When historians of the future look back to the Myanmar of the early twenty-first century and analyse the root cause for the failure of reconciliation, a degree of perceptiveness and impartiality should be able to lead them to the single, overarching issue: Sanctions. By some of the rules of the political game and of foreign relations, it may be argued that those who advocate for and those who impose sanctions are in the right and are justified. But according to the civilizational ethos that reaches to the bedrock, there can be no greater sacrilege or transgression than to actively advocate for punitive measures against one's own land and people. For this there can be no rationale whatsoever. This continuous, persistent act passes judgement and decides the fate of the people. It is quite amazing how few political people have come to realize this.

Notes

1. Referring to sanctions, Aung San Suu Kyi has said, "We should aim at the long-term interests of the people rather than the short-term benefits", meaning that "short-term" pain is to be endured. This sentiment is echoed at various levels of her organization.
2. Jeffrey Sachs, "Sanctions Won't Work", *The Financial Times*, 27 July 2004.
3. In 2004 aid per capita was only US$2.40, when that for Cambodia was US$35.30 and for Laos, US$50.30.
4. My translation of inscription from Nyein Maung, U., *Ancient Myanmar Stone Inscriptions* vol. iii. Yangon: Department of Archaeology, 1983. A.D. 1310, p. 245 (in Burmese).
5. Htin Aung, Maung, *A History of Burma*. New York and London: Columbia University Press, 1967, pp. 71–75.
6. My translation of Nyein Maung, U., Ancient Stone Inscriptions A.D. 1334 vol. iii. Yangon: Department of Archaeology, pp. 348–50 (in Burmese).

References

Badgley, John, ed. *Reconciling Burma/Myanmar: Essays on U.S. Relations with Burma*. The National Bureau of Asian Research, NBR Analysis, 2004.

Bossuyt, Marc. *The Bossuyt Report: The Adverse Consequences of Economic Sanctions on the Enjoyment of Human Rights*. New York: United Nations Economic and Social Council, 2004.

Elliott, Kimberley and Hufbauer, Gary. "Sanctions". *The Concise Encyclopaedia of Economics*. New York: Warner Books, 1993.

Gordon, Joy. "Economic Sanctions, Just War Doctrine, and the 'Fearful Spectacle of the Civilian Dead' ". *Crosscurrents* 49, No. 3 (Fall 1999).

Gordon, Joy. "Cool War". *Harper's Magazine* — Features, 2002.

Haass, Richard N. *Sanctions: Too Much of a Bad Thing*. Stanford: The Brookings Institution, Global Economics Policy Brief no. 34, 1998.

Karole. *Myanmar: Time for a Rethink?* Freedom Institute, 2005.

Paulson, Michael. "History of US Sanctions Show Most Haven't Worked". *Seattle Post — Intelligence Reporter*, 11 May 1999.

Index